E V A L
MEDIA
BIAS

Adam J. Schiffer

Texas Christian University

ROWMAN & LITTLEFIELD

Lanham · Boulder · New York · London

Executive Editor: Traci Crowell
Assistant Editor: Mary Malley
Senior Marketing Manager: Deborah Hudson
Interior Designer: Ilze Lemesis
Cover Designer: Chloe Batch
Cover Image: Richard Levine / Alamy Stock Photo

Published by Rowman & Littlefield
A wholly owned subsidiary of The Rowman & Littlefield Publishing Group, Inc.
4501 Forbes Boulevard, Suite 200, Lanham, Maryland 20706
www.rowman.com

Unit A, Whitacre Mews, 26-34 Stannary Street, London SE11 4AB, United Kingdom

British Library Cataloguing in Publication Information Available

Library of Congress Cataloging-in-Publication Data Available
ISBN 978-1-4422-6565-3 (cloth : alk. paper)
ISBN 978-1-4422-6566-0 (pbk. : alk. paper)
ISBN 978-1-4422-6567-7 (electronic)

∞™ The paper used in this publication meets the minimum requirements of American National
Standard for Information Sciences—Permanence of Paper for Printed Library Materials,
ANSI/NISO Z39.48-1992.

Printed in the United States of America

Dedication

In memory of Dustin Ells Howes—with gratitude, love, and a mandate to "make it work"

Contents

Preface

Media bias has been a hot-button issue for several decades, and it features prominently in the post-2016 political conversation. Yet it receives only spotty treatment in existing materials aimed at political communication or introductory American politics courses. It can also be a perilous topic for media-savvy citizens who want to understand and discuss it without getting caught in the crossfire of angry rants.

This book was conceived out of an ever-growing frustration with the lack of suitable reading materials on media bias. Most textbooks hastily summarize scholarly findings while sidestepping aspects of the issue that provide its enduring popular salience and controversy. For supplemental readings, instructors must choose between popular polemic screeds by ideologically motivated critics or scholarly research that is often too advanced for undergraduates. A middle ground was sorely needed. After all, if most of your students know about media-bias charges, have strong opinions on them, and expect to discuss them in class, then surely the topic deserves an in-depth but nontechnical primer.

My aim is to provide an academically informed but broadly accessible overview of the major concepts and controversies involving media bias. I designed it to be engaging and informative both for students of American politics and for politically aware citizens who worry about the state of the American news media. It reviews what we know about the topic, contains timely case studies, and introduces an original framework for unifying diverse conversations about media bias. My students have enjoyed applying the framework to in-class exercises and written assignments.

In short, I argue that the public conversation about news tends to look for bias in the wrong places. The argument's dual thesis has long been an organizing principle of my Media and Politics class: (1) partisan-bias charges tend to be flawed, and (2) citizens should be more concerned with other types of media bias. I call the latter "real biases" because the evidence supporting their existence is strong and they are more consequential than the occasional tilt to the left or right.

The first three chapters explore the contours of the partisan-bias controversy. Chapter 1 provides a history of the liberal-bias charge, chapter 2 reviews the best evidence for whether the media really do lean to the left, and chapter 3 creates a framework for understanding and evaluating individual charges of bias.

Chapter 4 pivots to the real biases, describing many of the most important shortcomings in political news content. Chapter 5 applies insights from the previous two chapters to evaluate news coverage of the 2009–10 effort to pass the Affordable Care Act.

The enduring questions covered in this volume became less abstract and more urgent during the 2016 presidential election, the aftermath of which launched a flurry of media criticism from a diverse array of scholars,

commentators, and thoughtful news professionals. In fact, in light of the intensity of the criticism and its relevance to the book's themes, the publisher and
I agreed to delay production by several months so that the election could be
fully incorporated. Chapter 6 explores the press's role in presidential nomination contests, with a focus on how media biases helped Donald Trump win the
Republican nomination. Chapter 7 evaluates the abundant media criticism that
followed the general election and concludes with an argument about the enduring importance of holding the press to high standards.

This topic has been of foremost interest to me for more than twenty-five
years. It was my master's thesis, the most common subject of my college newspaper column, and even the topic of a letter I wrote in high school to the editor
of a local paper (they didn't print it). Now that I have finally written the book
I always wanted to write, I need to acknowledge the many people who helped
bring it to fruition.

I benefited greatly from TCU's pool of high-achieving political-science
majors. My first three research assistants—Neeley Lawrence, Jake Bartel, and
Justine Grace—helped with the formative stage as I created the framework.
Jake also provided crucial assistance with early research. Allegra Hernandez
and Alayna Sublette stepped in on short notice to perform a difficult task with
great acuity. Finally, I owe a tremendous thanks to Kristy Cole for her masterful
coding work and creative input. She has unlimited potential, and I am lucky to
have crossed paths with her while she was still available for assistantship work.

Several scholars provided helpful comments on various drafts of the chapters, including Alec Ewald, Martin Johnson, Matthew Eshbaugh-Soha, Heather
Evans, Seth Bradshaw, Tibor Purger, Kajsa Falasca, Darren G. Lilleker, student
and faculty participants in the TCU Political Science Distinction Program, and
participants on various conference panels. I also owe gratitude to friends and
family who provided love and support during the writing process, including
Dustin Howes, Greg Petrow, Annette Schiffer, Becky Schiffer, and Michael
Schiffer, who supplemented his usual wisdom and encouragement with detailed
feedback on the manuscript. I also want to acknowledge my former colleague
Molly Scudder who helped me break out of a long slump with encouragement
and advice. I also thank TCU's AddRan College of Liberal Arts for providing a
summer grant to help with the late stages of the first draft.

As I tried to make this book both academically grounded and readable, I
need to thank those responsible for each of those attributes. First, I am grateful
to the professors who allowed me to pursue this topic early in my graduate
studies: Pat Kenney, Kim Fridkin, and Ken Goldstein. Equally important, I owe
much to the many teachers who taught me how to write, including Christine
Wald-Hopkins, Dixie Durham, and Susan Paterno. I am also grateful to Susan
for her keen mentorship and nurturing of my interest in journalism. Finally,
I am deeply indebted to Richard Kluck. My success as a teacher and scholar
would be unthinkable without his rigorous but patient instruction and the
example he set in his lively classroom.

CHAPTER 1

The Enduring "Liberal Media" Charge

Asking whether there is a liberal or conservative bias to the mainstream media is a little like asking whether al Qaeda uses too much oil in their hummus. The problem with al Qaeda is that they're trying to kill us.

—Al Franken, 2003[1]

Every Saturday morning during the fall academic semester, ESPN previews the week's college football games on a popular show called *Gameday*. It airs live from a different campus each week, with enthusiastic students gathered behind the anchors holding signs that typically boost their team or taunt the opponent. On the morning of October 3, 2015, *Gameday* broadcast from the campus of Clemson University prior to its showdown with Notre Dame.

Amid a flurry of vicious football taunts such as "Notre Dame players drink pumpkin spice lattes," a large sign could be seen clearly from near the front of the student crowd: "Don't Believe the Liberal Media."

Why would some Clemson student, staff member, or neighbor—in what is likely his/her only national television exposure ever—choose to accuse the mainstream news media of favoring one side of the political spectrum? To those who prefer their team sports to be actual sports, this might have seemed peculiar. But anyone immersed in the game of American politics understands why this *Gameday* interloper spent his/her fifteen minutes of fame accusing the news media of political bias. People feel *really strongly* about this issue.

Accusations of media bias are everywhere. When comedian and future senator Al Franken ridiculed them in 2003 with the above quip, bias charges had just begun to resurge in popular discourse, thanks to former CBS reporter Bernard Goldberg's 2001 book *Bias* and to the newly dominant Fox News Channel providing a steady platform from which to air the charges.[2]

Since then, the intensity and apparent influence of the partisan-bias charge has not wavered, despite a fast-changing media landscape.[3] It is likely the most commonly held opinion about the news media. It is often the most strongly held, or even the only, attitude toward the press that a politically aware student brings to class or that an uncle brings to the Thanksgiving table or your social-media feed. Talk-radio hosts, bloggers, and Fox News obsess over it, and several interest groups are devoted entirely to exposing it, including the highly influential Media Research Center (MRC), which produced the sign seen on *Gameday*. It also made a prominent appearance in the 2016 presidential race, as Republican nominee Donald Trump and his supporters cast frequent aspersions on the press for allegedly favoring his opponent Hillary Clinton.

Its purveyors typically display confidence that is brash even by the standards of political rhetoric. Goldberg's remark that the media's liberal slant "is so blatantly true that it's hardly worth discussing anymore" aptly summarizes the view of many attentive conservatives—and, switching "liberal slant" to "conservative slant," an increasing number of attentive liberals.[4]

But is it really so true that it isn't worth discussing? For that matter, is it true at all? For all the bluster in popular discourse, the question has proven difficult to answer. Those who insist that the press is liberal do so without compelling logic or evidence, while scholars who attempt to measure and characterize partisan bias paint an inconclusive, caveat-laden picture.

Meanwhile, Franken has a point: the obsession with partisan bias distracts critics and citizens from the more serious failures of political news. While the media aren't literally trying to kill us, they sometimes inflict serious injury on informed citizenship through a litany of routines, biases, and shortcomings that leave news consumers ill equipped to navigate contemporary politics. To name only a few, news coverage of politics focuses on the strategic game and the personalities at the center of political conflicts rather than the underlying policy issues, it presents events as isolated episodes rather than in any meaningful socio-economic-political context, it fails to adjudicate the veracity of politically loaded factual questions, and it privileges events that are dramatic, scandalous, simple, novel, timely, and emotional over more important events that do not meet those criteria. In short, the press is a mess, and not because of partisan slant.

Although partisan-bias charges may be merely hummus, they are as common as ketchup and have as loyal a fan base as Sriracha sauce. They also have a strong effect on public perception of the press. Thus, no matter how much one agrees with Franken's quip, conscientious citizens and critics must take bias charges seriously and address them on their own terms.

This book argues that too many citizens and critics are looking for bias in the wrong places. Specifically, the argument unfolds in two parts: (1) partisan-bias charges tend to be flawed, and (2) citizens should be more concerned with other types of media bias.

The story begins with partisan bias. The remainder of chapter 1 explores the history of the liberal-bias charge and identifies its most common varieties. Chapter 2 begins the two-part process of casting doubt on partisan-bias charges by reviewing the findings from forty years of scholarly attempts to measure bias in the mainstream media. Though their conclusions vary, researchers have mostly found no consistent, long-term, cross-issue bias. Next, chapter 3 introduces a systematic framework for evaluating the validity of partisan-bias accusations, showing the high hurdles they must clear in order to be deemed credible. It also identifies the most common logical and evidentiary shortcomings that plague popular bias charges from either side of the political spectrum.

Chapter 4 pivots from the hummus to the killing, documenting the vast array of news-media shortcomings—the "real biases" in political news—that hamper their ability to give citizens the information necessary to navigate the political world and make informed choices about it.

The next two chapters apply the insights from chapters 3 and 4 to analyze media biases, and charges thereof, regarding two hot topics. Chapter 5 scrutinizes news coverage of the 2009–10 debate over passage of the Affordable Care Act. It finds little support for the partisan-bias charges surrounding the issue while identifying more pressing informational shortcomings in the coverage, such as a limited range of sources, excessive personalization, and a lack of policy substance.

Chapter 6 explores media biases in presidential nomination contests, a realm in which the news media are both terribly powerful and powerfully terrible. The media's long-running tendency to treat nominations as substance-free, reality-show spectacles came home to roost in 2015–16 when an actual reality-show star used the media to his full advantage.

Finally, chapter 7 concludes the inquiry with a discussion of the future of news and news criticism. Two crucial concepts from the book's theoretical framework are revisited in light of the myriad media controversies from the 2016 general election: the tenuous role of "balance" in news coverage and the importance of holding news to high standards.

The Enduring Charge

The liberal-bias charge appears to be as widely believed as ever. The Pew Research Center has asked survey respondents about media bias intermittently since 1985, and the numbers have risen steadily. The percentage agreeing that news organizations "tend to favor one side" was 53 in 1985, 67 in 1997, and a record-high 77 in the most recent survey (2011). They also asked whether news organizations are "politically biased," with the results broken down by party. Among Republicans, 49 percent agreed in 1985, 69 percent in 2002, and 76 percent in 2011—just off the record 78 percent in 2009. Presumably they mostly perceive liberal bias. Interestingly, Democratic perceptions of bias are increasing as well, but not as steeply: 43 percent in 1985 and 54 percent in 2011. Independents have increased from 44 percent to 63 percent over that time frame.[5]

Given the increasing prominence of openly partisan news outlets, some might argue that the increase in bias perception actually reflects a change in what Americans perceive to be "the news media." But this in fact is not true. Political scientist Jonathan Ladd asked survey respondents to describe their mental images of the news media, finding that the term overwhelmingly evokes the traditional mainstream organizations "that adhere more to the professional norms that dominated in the mid-twentieth century."[6] Thus, citizens do increasingly see bias in ostensibly neutral outlets.

The persistence of the charge has taken a toll on public perception of the news media. Surveys show unequivocally that public trust has plummeted over the past forty years.[7] While this has a variety of causes, Ladd's study shows that elite criticism of the press—which most often takes the form of partisan-bias charges—is one of the leading contributing factors.[8]

The Puzzle of Persistence

At first glance, the increasing prevalence of the liberal-bias charge is puzzling. After all, irrespective of whether the press currently carries a liberal bias—a question to be broached in detail later—its bias surely has not increased in recent years. *Evening News* anchor Dan Rather, who found himself at the center of many bias controversies over the years, is long gone from CBS; liberal media mogul Ted Turner no longer owns CNN; and the *New York Times*—which once battled the Nixon administration all the way to the Supreme Court over the right to reveal embarrassing government documents concerning the Vietnam War—received so much flack for its uncritical cheerleading of the run-up to the Iraq War in 2003 that it ended up apologizing in an editor's note a year later.

Also, even if the traditional press's liberal bias was increasing or holding steady, its role in the media landscape has changed drastically. When Dan Rather took over the *CBS Evening News* in 1981, news was limited and homogenous. The elite media still acted as gatekeepers of political information, exercising profound control of the public agenda by deciding which tiny proportion of potential stories made it into their limited news holes, as well as how they would be covered and whose voices would be heard. To the degree that conservative citizens perceived the media's output to lean systematically in the wrong direction, their complaints carried a special urgency because of the small number of powerful, agenda-setting outlets.

Today, however, the media landscape is vastly altered from a generation ago. Not only are there more outlets providing political information from an increasing variety of platforms, but the content is far more varied as well. If the old-guard media fail to cover an event or statement that is potentially damaging to one side, someone else with different judgment will surely pick it up. This should, theoretically, dull the urgency of the liberal-bias charge. Yet it hasn't.

Thus, to solve this puzzle and begin to grasp why the charge is louder than ever, its origins and role in contemporary politics must be understood. The charge's prominence and persistence are a function of several disparate factors. Woven through all of them is a crucial insight: above all, the liberal-bias charge is a *strategic talking point*.

"The mainstream media tilt to the left" sits alongside other Republican Party or conservative-movement beliefs—such as "tax cuts create growth," "life begins at conception," or "heavy regulation is bad for business"—in the arsenal of talking points employed by partisan communicators in campaigns, books, and commentary.

Accusing the press of systematically favoring the other side is a particularly attractive and effective talking point. For one, it allows candidates and officeholders to defuse the impact of shortcomings or controversies—just blame the biased messenger for misreporting them. It becomes a vicious cycle—or maybe virtuous, depending on your vantage point—as persistent use of this tactic contributes to the erosion of public trust in the media, which in turn makes the press more vulnerable to such attacks. As perception of bias becomes a core belief of partisans, the talking point also serves as a reliable applause line to rally the troops during a speech or debate. As detailed in chapter 6, one of the candidate debates during the 2015–16 Republican nomination contest featured several bias charges that reverberated in the national political conversation for weeks.

The talking point serves an additional function, what writer Eric Alterman called "working the refs."[9] Every basketball fan knows that coaches levy frequent bias accusations against the referees, often delivered in profanity-laced shouts that can last for minutes at a time, when they perceive a call (or its lack) to have favored the other team. Some prominent coaches, like Duke University men's coach Mike Krzyzewski, do this incessantly as a key component of their coaching strategy. While it may appear on the surface as understandable venting in response to a perceived injustice, the deeper purpose is to convince the referees to watch for the other team's wrongdoing more diligently, as well as to think twice about blowing the whistle against the bias charger's team. Working the refs not only undermines their credibility to team partisans, but it may also move the refs—even if subtly or subconsciously—in the team's direction. Indeed, opponents have complained for years that Duke receives a disproportionate share of favorable calls.[10]

Likewise, the strategy of working the political refs is intended to get in journalists' heads and make them self-conscious about potential favoritism. While it would be nearly impossible to document the degree to which it actually succeeds in changing media behavior, there is no question that every working journalist is conscious of the ubiquitous liberal-bias charge.

While its status as a strategic talking point is indispensable to understanding the charge, the talking point wasn't created out of whole cloth and disseminated by luck or fluke. It (1) arose from an ideological movement, (2) gained plausibility through particular incidents, and (3) is amplified through commentary channels. Only in tandem with those three factors does the talking-point insight shed light on the charge's rise and persistence.

The Conservative Movement

Though criticism of the political tenor of news is as old as the printing press, the concept of partisan bias against a news outlet only makes sense if the outlet aspires to be neutral between the two sides of the American political divide. As such, the liberal-bias charge could, theoretically, only date back as far as the early twentieth century, when newspapers imported the mantle of "objectivity" from the sciences and adopted routines and practices meant to communicate neutrality to their audiences.[11] In fact, the contemporary liberal-bias charge arose out of a disconnect between news output and a changing political landscape during the tumultuous 1960s.

When the Great Depression ravaged the economy beginning in 1929, it also ravaged the Republican Party's electoral fortunes for a generation. After President Herbert Hoover's reelection bid was crushed by Franklin Roosevelt's landslide victory in 1932, Democrats began a thirty-six-year period in which they held commanding majorities in Congress for all but four years and a near monopoly on the presidency. During his four terms, Roosevelt and his Congresses left a lasting mark on public policy, greatly expanding the size and scope of federal government power. The only Republican president from 1933 to 1968 was war hero and political moderate Dwight Eisenhower, for whom challenging the New Deal and the liberal philosophy that guided it was never a priority. On the surface, conservatism appeared dormant during what many historians call the era of "liberal consensus."

However, the seeds of a conservative movement that would eventually elect Ronald Reagan and take back Congress were planted in the early 1950s. Venues such as William F. Buckley's *National Review* magazine fomented a backlash against the perceived excesses of New Deal liberalism, and scholars, activists, and politicians began to lay the groundwork for a movement to bring conservative ideas and governance into ascendancy.

The nomination of Arizona senator Barry Goldwater as the 1964 Republican presidential candidate was a crucial moment in the mainstreaming of conservative ideology. Four years earlier he had published the book *The Conscience of a Conservative*, an accessible expression of the most important ideas and goals of intellectual conservatism that became a how-to manual for budding activists and candidates. By defeating moderate New Yorker Nelson Rockefeller for the nomination, Goldwater offered solid conservative doctrine to the general electorate as a clear contrast to New Deal liberalism.

Though his self-described "extremism" was a poor fit for the times, leading to a landslide defeat at the hands of President Lyndon Johnson, history now recognizes him as the father of the contemporary Republican Party—the party that forcefully reversed its presidential drought by winning five of the next six elections. These victories, along with intermittent majorities in Congress and dominance at the state level, enabled the ideas incubated in the conservative movement to shape the direction of government in the Reagan/Bush era.

Of course, the insurgent ideology had to fight its way into the national conversation at all points. As the effort to be taken seriously even within the Republican Party was a long, often bitter struggle, the establishment news media naturally did not immediately recalibrate the range of ideologies it took seriously in the American conversation. This disconnect opened the door to charges of bias against conservative ideas.

According to Ladd, "antipathy toward the media was one of the basic characteristics of Goldwaterism," foreshadowing the liberal-bias charge's prominent role in the conservative movement.[12] In fact, the connection to Goldwater persists today. While *The Conscience of a Conservative* helped make him the figurative father of the conservative movement, the book's ghostwriter—thinker and activist L. Brent Bozell Jr.—was the literal father of the most prominent contemporary purveyor of the liberal-bias charge: Media Research Center founder and president L. Brent Bozell III.

Richard Nixon, whose career was defined by tension with the press long before Watergate, brought conservative-movement press criticism into the presidency. This confrontational stance was continued, to varying degrees, by all subsequent Republican presidents, as increasing party polarization gave government officials and party activists incentives to attack independent sources of information.[13] Donald Trump—who frequently lambasted the establishment press with caustic epithets such as "fake news" and "enemy of the people" during the first months of his presidency—has taken this animosity to new levels.

Dissemination

Although a president has a unique ability among Americans to command an audience for nearly any purpose, sporadic presidential criticism of the press did not, by itself, disseminate the liberal-bias charge. It also needed to be amplified by those with the ability to reach mass audiences through printing presses, microphones, cameras, and now keyboards. Fortunately for bias chargers, there are more ways than ever to air the accusation directly to receptive audiences.

In the old era of restricted news choice and even more restricted availability of commentary, a bias charge against elite gatekeepers, no matter how compelling, was extremely difficult to disseminate to the mass public. If the only source of political information for most citizens is the same press being accused of bias, then that crucial avenue of publicity is cut off for bias chargers. This is why the most prominent early bias charges had to come from presidents and other officials.

Books were another way to bypass the media filter, especially if press-loathing presidents aided their circulation. In 1971, Edith Efron wrote a scathing, content analysis–based critique of the mainstream press titled *The News Twisters* in which she argued that the establishment media were biased in favor of the "Democratic-liberal-left axis" of American politics. The book caught the attention of President Nixon, who reached into his bag of tricks to help spread its message. Former White House special counsel Charles Colson explained in a 1994 *Newsweek* remembrance of Nixon,

> He called me into his office . . . and asked me if I had read Edith Efron's book about biased network news coverage [*The News Twisters*]. I had. I had also concluded that it was a book destined for obscurity. Nixon then ordered me to get it on the best-seller list. . . . After finding the particular stores that The New York Times and others regularly checked to determine which books were selling, I enlisted the assistance of some Nixon supporters in New York. We literally bought out bookstores. We left the White House with perhaps 2,500 copies gathering dust in the basement.[14]

Needless to say, the targets of her criticism were not as cooperative in publicizing it. Case in point: her follow-up book was titled *How CBS Tried to Kill a Book*.

By the time another bias book shook up the political world in 2001—we'll get to that shortly—the media landscape had changed dramatically. The first big change was the advent of cable news in 1980, when Atlanta-based media and sports mogul Ted Turner founded the Cable News Network. Though CNN was hardly a key player in bias-charge amplification, it did air a weekly program called *Reliable Sources*, beginning in 1992, that featured frequent liberal-bias charges as it "turn[ed] a critical eye on the media."

Without a doubt, the most consequential change was the rise of talk radio. By the early 1980s, radio's political influence had largely petered out. One of the barriers to effective talk radio was the federal regulation known as the Fairness Doctrine, which required broadcasters to present controversial political issues in a balanced manner. This was a high bar to clear, as they had an affirmative duty to find a "fair cross-section of opinion on the issue" and air any opposing viewpoints—at their own expense if necessary—that were not heard in their sponsored content.[15]

In 1987, the Federal Communications Commission repealed the Fairness Doctrine, citing its tenuous constitutional status and obsolescence in an era of increasing media choice. This opened the door for radio shows of any length to cover political issues from only one ideological vantage point.

One Sacramento-based political talker—the staunchly conservative and undeniably entertaining Rush Limbaugh—was well situated to take advantage of this opportunity. He moved to New York in 1988 to bring his show to national syndication, and it soon spread across the AM dial, gaining a massive following during the Bush and Clinton years. By 1990 he was heard on more than three hundred stations by more than five million listeners, making him the top-rated radio talker. By 1996 he was on more than six hundred stations with an estimated twenty million listeners.[16] In the wake of his dominance, the radio dial exploded with political talk. The news/talk format grew from seventy-five US stations in 1980 to more than 1,400 in the early 2000s.[17] Every market had at least one Limbaugh clone.

Peculiarly, the format quickly became almost entirely conservative. Though some stations initially aired a variety of perspectives, they soon found that the Limbaugh-driven audience was not interested in having its viewpoints challenged during other time slots. Communication scholar William Mayer studied talk-radio audiences, finding that "conservatives dominate talk radio to an overwhelming, remarkable degree. Of the top twenty-eight talk-radio programs in spring 2003, eleven—including four of the top five—were hosted by outspoken, undisguised conservatives. By contrast, not one was hosted by someone who could be described as clearly and unambiguously liberal."[18]

For the first time, conservatives had an unfiltered venue from which to air liberal-bias charges to a mass audience. And air them they did, at an astounding rate. Limbaugh in particular mercilessly pounded the mainstream press for its alleged partisan tilt. A content analysis of his shows from 1993 to 1995 found 617 discussions of the news media, the most of any policy topic besides government spending, and only one hundred fewer mentions of the media than of President Clinton.[19]

This sustained attack clearly accomplished its mission. A study by political scientist Mark Watts and colleagues showed that increases in the volume of media criticism by political elites in the 1980s and 1990s led directly to increased public perception of bias, whereas variation in the actual levels of bias in news content had no effect on perception.[20]

Television soon got its own talk radio in the form of the Fox News Channel. Founded by conservative media mogul Rupert Murdoch—who appointed long-time Republican operative Roger Ailes to run it—its prime-time lineup brought conservative opinion to the airwaves. Though it began in 1996, it hit its stride after the terrorist attacks of September 11, 2001, becoming the top-rated cable-news network—a title it has never relinquished—just months later. Perennial prime-time stars Bill O'Reilly and Sean Hannity make frequent liberal-bias charges.

Aided by television and radio commentary, along with the burgeoning Internet, an antibias book exploded onto the scene in 2001, becoming perhaps the highest-profile bias charge ever. Longtime, Emmy-winning CBS reporter Bernard Goldberg had grown increasingly disenchanted with what he viewed as the mainstream media's persistent liberal slant. This concern culminated in February 1996 when he wrote a scathing antibias opinion column in the *Wall Street Journal*. He quit CBS in 2000 and wrote *Bias: A CBS Insider Exposes How the Media Distort the News*, which quickly rose to the top of the best-seller list. With adoring fans ranging from President Bush to every right-of-center personality with access to a microphone or modem, the book was a national phenomenon. The momentum it generated made bias charges a permanent fixture on Fox News, and Goldberg continues to appear frequently as a guest on various shows.

The contemporary media environment features several symbiotic entities working to keep the liberal-bias charge in heavy circulation. Bias-watchdog groups, once reliant on periodic newsletters, now use the Internet to amplify daily charges. In addition to spreading through radio and TV, the charges go viral through social media and particularly on conservative blogs and web-only news sites. Rather than making the charge against older news outlets less relevant, the diversifying media landscape has given it a louder echo chamber. The volume of the echo, combined with the immediacy and increased access points of the Internet, keeps traditional political journalists in the crosshairs of the charge. See the sidebar for an account of one unlikely target.

Incidents and Alamo Moments

During its crucial years of rapid growth, the liberal-bias charge was aided by high-profile incidents that lent themselves to being labeled as bias. Specifically, conservatives widely believed that the mainstream media treated President George H. W. Bush unfairly, a belief for which the evidence began accumulating even before he took office. In one of Dan Rather's more controversial moments—and that's saying a lot—he invited candidate and sitting vice president George Bush to do a rare live interview on the January 25, 1988, episode of the *CBS Evening News*. Contrary to Bush's understanding that the interview would cover a wide range of topics, Rather grilled him relentlessly for ten minutes over his role in the Iran-Contra scandal. The tone grew increasingly combative, with Rather frequently interrupting Bush and the two raising their voices at each other. Viewing the footage—easily found on various bias-watchdog websites—is

Caught in the Crosshairs

The *Fort Worth Star-Telegram* would seem to be an odd target for liberal-bias charges. Several studies show that newspapers tend to match the ideological tenor of their markets (see chapter 2), and the *Star-Telegram* is no exception. Serving Tarrant County, Texas—the most Republican-leaning urban county in America—it endorses mostly Republicans and tends toward just-the-facts, middle-of-the-road political news stories. Yet it was not immune from the increasing frequency and vitriol of bias charges as they gained channels of dissemination in the early 2000s. Veteran journalist David House, the paper's reader advocate (ombudsman) from 2001 to 2008, described the bias charges filling his voice mail and inbox as going from "annoyed" to "nasty" to "vicious" during the decade. As he tells it:

Every year there was a steady increase, as efforts in the Limbaugh/Hannity universe and politicians, from the Bush White House on down, seemed to work harder to discredit the news media. They were on a roll. I thought it was shameful on their parts—Third World tactics—to incite such hatred against the free press as though it was patriotic duty. They would blame all sorts of problems on the media. It was becoming absurd and very dangerous and still is.

One time the paper carried a mugshot of President George Bush on Page One, and somehow a press registration symbol—a circle with a cross through it, used to register press plates for 4-part color—wound up overprinted on Bush's face. It looked like a rifle scope zeroed in on Bush's head. I think it was the worst incident of reader fury on my watch. Many readers thought we were deliberately encouraging someone to shoot Bush.

Every year during the holidays, usually the Sunday before Christmas, I'd try to write a light-hearted column that looked only at some of the funny things that readers had said and funny issues they'd raised. I'd usually be able to select from at least a dozen or more such items. That was an easy task and a lot of fun, but by Christmas 2006, I could barely find three or four with enough humor for a column. By Christmas 2007, I couldn't find any, because of the sea of anti-media vitriol that just kept pouring in over the phone and in email. It was with great sadness that I wrote nothing light-hearted for that year's holiday season.

unsettling even today.[21] But it was downright shocking in an era before cable shout shows were common.

The main grievance against the Bush-era press, though, concerned its role in his unsuccessful reelection bid in 1992. As the Gulf War passed beyond the media's short attention span, campaign coverage focused mostly on the state of the economy. This played right into the hands of Bush's general-election opponents, Arkansas governor Bill Clinton and billionaire independent Ross Perot, who sought to shift attention from the popular war to Bush's handling of the troubled economy. In fact, the now-common phrase "it's the economy, stupid," originated from Clinton's top strategist, James Carville, as a reminder to campaign staff to keep attention on the economy. According to conservative critics, the media eagerly complied.

If the accusation were merely that the press saddled a sitting president with blame for a weak economy, then that would be shaky grounds for a partisan-bias charge. After all, Democrat Jimmy Carter took a pounding for the terrible economy of the late 1970s on the way to his 1980 reelection defeat. However, media coverage of the 1992 campaign featured a peculiar quirk that lent more credence to the bias charges: the tone of the coverage did not match the state of the economy. The country had indeed fallen into a recession in 1990—but it ended by March 1991, before the news even turned its attention from Iraq to the economy. By the time the general election heated up in mid-1992, the economy was in full recovery mode, while the tone of coverage continued to get worse. As political scientist Thomas Patterson explained,

> during the general election, more than 90 percent of references to the economy on network news were negative, as opposed to 75 percent in the immediately preceding period—a remarkable statistic. *The networks' portrayal of the economy got worse as the economy improved.* Bush was forced to run not only against a bad economy but against negative coverage of an economy that was in fact getting better.[22]

And the disconnect mattered. Political scientist Marc Hetherington analyzed public opinion data to show that higher levels of media consumption had a strong negative effect on citizens' economic perceptions in 1992. These negative perceptions in turn made voters less likely to choose the incumbent Bush.[23]

Though Patterson attributed much of Bush's bad coverage to factors other than partisan bias, he concluded, "The charge of bias cannot be dismissed entirely."[24] Conservative commentators lacked his scholarly equivocation and charged full speed against the media's purported role in Bush's defeat. The complaints began during the campaign—a popular bumper sticker said, "Annoy the Media: Re-Elect Bush"—and they continue to this day as part of the canon of evidence for a systematically slanted "liberal media."

Types of Bias Charges

According to bias chargers and scholars, the media can slant stories to favor one side in several different ways. Sometimes a charge references both sides of the political spectrum—"the Democratic candidate received better coverage than the Republican candidate." Many charges, however, reference only one side—"the Democratic scandal received less coverage than it deserved." This is an important distinction that chapter 3 will broach in detail. For now, partisan-bias charges against mainstream news content typically fit one of four types: gatekeeping, coverage, tone, and quality.[25]

First, a *gatekeeping* charge is an accusation that one side's issue received more coverage than the other side's equally newsworthy issue, or that one side's issue received more/less coverage than it deserved.

To understand what "one side's issue" means, note that contested political issues typically fall into one of two categories. For some, both sides of the political spectrum want to discuss the issue. For instance, both Democrats and Republicans have prioritized immigration reform recently, though their preferred solutions obviously differ. By contrast, there are issues that only one side wants discussed in public discourse, while the other would rather they disappear unnoticed. One notable example is the Democratic focus on America's growing income and wealth inequality, a topic that Republicans have mostly avoided for the more than fifteen years it has been on the policy radar.

A gatekeeping charge arises when a critic accuses the press of giving too little coverage to an issue favored by the critic's side and/or too much coverage to an issue favored by the other side. Thus, the longtime complaint on the left that income inequality fails to receive sufficient coverage is a gatekeeping charge.

Scandals are among the most common topics of gatekeeping charges, as it is nearly always the case that only one side—the side that didn't take a bribe or text lewd pictures to random women—wants them in the news. Week after week, MRC and other media critics lob accusations such as "ABC Continues to Ignore Planned Parenthood Scandal," "Blackout! Big Three [broadcast networks] Ignore Major New Findings in Fast & Furious Scandal," and "'Big Three' Networks Ignore White House Reversing Lobbyist Ban."

Next, a *coverage* charge accuses one or more news outlets of giving one side of an issue more/less coverage than it deserves—which usually, but not always, means more/less coverage than the other side. Unlike the gatekeeping charge, this applies to issues of which both sides desire public discussion, and accordingly they both make active attempts to communicate their side of it.

Giving coverage to "one side of an issue" means including any type of persuasive consideration—arguments, talking points, facts, or frames—that fit the preferred narrative of that side. They consist most commonly of direct quotes or paraphrases, wherein the complaint is something like "more Democrats were quoted than Republicans." They may also include unattributed statements by the newswriter or anchor that are deemed by the bias charger to support the narrative of one side.

The two most prominent left-leaning media-watchdog groups—Media Matters for America (MMfA) and Fairness and Accuracy in Reporting (FAIR)—frequently conduct studies showing that Republicans appear as guests or panelists on the Sunday-morning political talk shows more often than Democrats.[26] This constitutes a broad-based coverage charge against the aggregate content of these shows, as more Republican voices are heard than Democratic.

Next, a *tone* charge asserts that one side is receiving more positive or negative coverage than the other side, either within a single news story or across many stories. These include accusations that a person or idea from the other side is being "praised" or that one from the charger's side is being "attacked," "criticized," or "mocked." Tone charges are rampant during elections but can appear in any political context.

Finally, a *quality* charge arises when a news story is accused of including factual or logical errors that have the effect of favoring one side. The mere accusation that a news story got the facts wrong is not, by itself, a partisan-bias charge unless it states or implies that the error occurred because of the outlet's partisan inclinations.

In early 2014, MRC ran a story titled "AP, Dallas News, WashPo, etc., Lie about Ted Cruz' Abortion Statement," in which they document an AP-originating claim that Cruz called abortion-rights activists "Satanists." In fact, Cruz said no such thing, and thus the charge of a factual error against AP and its client outlets was correct. And of course the error was no coincidence to MRC: "You'd think conservatives Ted Cruz and Mike Lee are outspoken enough without liberal media sources having to lie about their words. But you'd be underestimating the unscrupulous partisanship of 'political journalists.'"[27] Hence, a partisan-bias charge.

Quality charges are among the most common made by MMfA. However, most of theirs are against openly conservative outlets like Fox and talk radio, so they don't qualify as partisan-bias accusations.

A Note on Charge Sources

The bias charges analyzed in this book come from a wide array of critics and commentators on both sides of the political spectrum. After all, neither side has a monopoly on any of the most common evidentiary and logical shortcomings that afflict popular bias charges. However, as liberal-bias charges are far more prevalent than conservative-bias charges, it follows that a majority of the examples come from conservative critics of the purported "liberal media."

A high proportion of the charges analyzed originate with MRC, the country's preeminent organization devoted to documenting examples of liberal bias in the mainstream press. There are two reasons for this.

First, although the readership of its website is small compared to the audience of Fox News and talk radio, it wields tremendous influence over the national conversation about media bias. It cranks out a large number of accusations—sometimes several per day—and they are often amplified across the conservative Internet. When Fox News programs such as *Hannity* air bias charges, they are likely to have originated with MRC. The organization's founder and president, Brent Bozell, is a frequent guest on Fox and, along with Bernard Goldberg, is probably America's most influential bias cop. Even if you do not know the name Media Research Center, you have undoubtedly been exposed to its work.

Equally important, MRC deserves a prominent place in a book that shines a critical light on bias charges not because it is an easy target, but just the opposite: because it is good at what it does. As any consumer of political rants knows, one of the annoying habits of ineffective commentators is to scour the far corners of the Internet to find something that some no-name person blogged or tweeted and then criticize or debunk it. And indeed, if the goal were to expose the fallacies of the worst bias charges out there, one could effortlessly fill a book with them. The Internet is riddled with bias charges that range from irredeemably nonspecific—"everybody knows the mainstream media love Hillary Clinton"—to utterly ridiculous. As an example of the latter, a conservative blogger wrote a post in late 2015 titled "Media Double Standard: Ben Carson Is a Liar but Barack Obama Isn't a Kenyan."[28] While that surreal mash-up of non sequitur and debunked smear provided amusement for liberal bloggers, a book-length collection of such charges would be intellectually unsatisfying.

By contrast, all of MRC's charges look reasonable to knowledgeable observers at first glance. Far from being throwaway comments by pseudonymous bloggers, they are crafted by experts who do this for a living. They are typically precise in specifying both the nature of the charge and the exact content being charged. Whenever possible, they include the full text of the accused story so that readers can reverse engineer the charge and evaluate it themselves. Sometimes they even do larger-scale studies of media content, and, though they typically don't meet social-science standards of transparency, chapter 6 successfully replicated one of their studies and found it to be accurate. Thus, MRC represents the gold standard in nonacademic engagement with media bias and is a worthy source for careful analysis.

What about Conservative Bias?

While an increasing number of liberals believe the mainstream press is too conservative, there is no liberal equivalent to the widespread, multiplatform, coordinated attack on the media from the right. The left-leaning critics who most loudly criticize the media from an ideological perspective vacillate between refuting the liberal-bias charge, calling out openly conservative outlets, and making conservative-bias accusations against the ostensibly neutral press. For example, MMfA—the most high-profile media-watchdog group from the left—spends most of its bandwidth exposing the falsehoods and inflammatory rhetoric of openly conservative outlets like Fox and talk radio. Also, the blowback to Goldberg's *Bias* book brought several retorts from the left, including Alterman's *What Liberal Media?* and Franken's *Lies and the Lying Liars Who Tell Them*. But both spend more time refuting the liberal-bias myth than affirmatively asserting bias in the other direction.

It is easy to find bloggers and other commentators who believe the media's corporate ownership pushes their content to the right. But this charge has not been institutionalized in the liberal political/communication infrastructure the way the "liberal media" accusation has in the conservative movement. As such, this book focuses on the latter.

Conclusion

The idea that mainstream outlets carry a consistent leftward tilt is one of the most commonly held opinions about the American media. Partisan commentators, losing presidential candidates, and even *Gameday* attendees amplify it until no working journalist can escape its reach. Born of an ideological movement and given space to grow in an increasingly diverse and opinion-saturated media landscape, the charge holds a preeminent place in the canon of conservative talking points.

The intensity of a talking point, however, says nothing about its truthfulness. The next two chapters turn a critical lens on charges of partisan bias. Chapter 2 summarizes, and draws lessons from, forty years of scholarship on the subject, while chapter 3 presents a framework for scrutinizing individual charges of bias from any source.

Notes

[1] Al Franken, *Lies and the Lying Liars Who Tell Them: A Fair and Balanced Look at the Right* (New York: Dutton, 2003), 1.

[2] Bernard Goldberg, *Bias: A CBS Insider Exposes How the Media Distort the News* (New York: Perennial, 2002).

[3] Though partisanship and ideology are distinct concepts, most bias charges use them interchangeably to mean "favoring the Democratic/Republican or liberal/conservative side." Accordingly, this book uses "partisan bias" as shorthand for "partisan or ideological bias."

[4] Goldberg, *Bias*, 19.

[5] "Press Widely Criticized, but Trusted More than Other Information Sources," Pew Research Center, accessed December 18, 2015, http://www.people-press.org/2011/09/22/press-widely-criticized-but-trusted-more-than-other-institutions.

[6] Jonathan Ladd, *Why Americans Hate the Media and How It Matters* (Princeton, NJ: Princeton University Press, 2012), 65.

[7] See Ladd, *Why Americans Hate the Media*, for a review.

[8] Ladd, *Why Americans Hate the Media*, ch. 5.

[9] From a quote from RNC chair Rich Bond in 1992. See Eric Alterman, "Think Again: 'Working the Refs,'" Center for American Progress, accessed December 18, 2015, https://www.americanprogress.org/issues/general/news/2005/05/26/1476/think-again-working-the-refs.

[10] See, for example, Dan Steinberg, "Even Christian Laettner Thinks Refs Are Sometimes Biased in Favor of Duke," *Washington Post*, March 10, 2015, accessed January 5, 2016, https://www.washingtonpost.com/news/dc-sports-bog/wp/2015/03/10/even-christian-laettner-thinks-refs-are-sometimes-biased-in-favor-of-duke; Chris Dufresne, "In the Interest of Fairness, Duke Needs to Take a Foul," *Los Angeles Times*, April 9, 2001, accessed January 5, 2016, http://articles.latimes.com/2001/apr/09/sports/sp-48870.

[11] Bill Kovach and Tom Rosenstiel, *The Elements of Journalism: What Newspeople Should Know and the Public Should Expect*, 3rd ed. (New York: Three Rivers Press, 2014).

[12] Ladd, *Why Americans Hate the Media*, 74.

[13] Ladd, *Why Americans Hate the Media*, ch. 4.

[14] "Remembrances," *Newsweek*, May 2, 1994, LexisNexis Academic.

[15] Kathleen Ann Ruane, "Fairness Doctrine: History and Constitutional Issues," Congressional Research Service: CRS Report for Congress, July 13, 2011, accessed January 7, 2016, http://www.fas.org/sgp/crs/misc/R40009.pdf.

[16] "Call-In Political Talk Radio: Background, Content, Audiences, Portrayal in Mainstream Media," Annenberg Public Policy Center, August 7, 1996, accessed January 7, 2016, http://www.annenbergpublicpolicycenter.org/Downloads/Political_Communication/Political_Talk_Radio/1996_03_political_talk_radio_rpt.PDF.

[17] William G. Mayer, "Why Talk Radio Is Conservative," *The Public Interest* 154 (2004): 86–103.

[18] Mayer, "Why Talk Radio," 90.

[19] David Barker and Kathleen Knight, "Political Talk Radio and Public Opinion," *Public Opinion Quarterly* 64 (2000): 149–70.

[20] Mark D. Watts, David Domke, Dhavan V. Shah, and David P. Fan, "Elite Cues and Media Bias in Presidential Campaigns: Explaining Public Perceptions of a Liberal Press," *Communication Research* 26 (1999): 144–75. See also Glen R. Smith, "Politicians and the News Media: How Elite Attacks Influence Perceptions of Media Bias," *International Journal of Press/Politics* 15 (2010): 319–43.

21 "Dan Rather's Liberal Bias," Media Research Center, accessed January 15, 2016, http://archive. mrc.org/projects/rather20th/welcome.asp.

22 Thomas E. Patterson, *Out of Order* (New York: Vintage, 1994), 113.

23 Marc J. Hetherington, "The Media's Role in Forming Voters' National Economic Evaluations in 1992," *American Journal of Political Science* 40 (1996): 372–95.

24 Patterson, *Out of Order*, 111.

25 As this is a typology of bias *charges* rather than of bias types, it differs slightly from other scholarly typologies. The terms "gatekeeping" and "coverage," though re-rendered here to apply to charges, come from Dave D'Alessio and Mike Allen, "Media Bias in Presidential Elections: A Meta-Analysis," *Journal of Communication* 50 (2000): 133–56.

26 See, for example, "Right and Early: Sunday Morning Shows Are GOP TV," FAIR, accessed December 19, 2015, http://fair.org/extra/right-and-early; Rob Savillo, "Report: Once Again, Sunday Morning Talk Shows Are White, Male, and Conservative," Media Matters for America, accessed December 19, 2015, http://mediamatters.org/research/2013/10/11/report-once-again-sunday-morning-talk-shows-are/196404.

27 Katie Yoder, "AP, Dallas News, WashPo, etc., Lie about Ted Cruz' Abortion Statement," MRC NewsBusters, March 13, 2014, accessed February 2, 2016, http://www.newsbusters.org/blogs/katie-yoder/2014/03/13/ap-dallas-news-washpo-etc-lie-about-ted-cruz-abortion-statement.

28 Jim Hoft, "Media Double Standard: Ben Carson Is a Liar but Barack Obama Isn't a Kenyan," Gateway Pundit, November 6, 2015, accessed February 2, 2016, http://www.thegatewaypundit.com/2015/11/media-double-standard-ben-carson-is-a-liar-but-barack-obama-isnt-a-kenyan. And that's actually one of the most popular conservative blogs, with millions of annual hits and mentions by many of the most popular talk-radio and cable hosts.

CHAPTER 2

The Scholarly View
of Partisan Bias

A re the mainstream news media liberal or not? This chapter tackles the question directly by summarizing the social-science findings on the subject. Unfortunately, these studies paint a muddy picture that evades simple summary descriptors such as "yes" or "no." Also, they are not without significant theoretical and empirical limitations. Welcome to social science.

Nonetheless, the preponderance of evidence finds no overall, systematic bias in the mainstream press toward one side of the political spectrum. Important exceptions will be given due attention—but the generalization is fair.

Educators charged with making such an assessment—for example, textbook writers—tend to converge on this point. Among the leading introduction to American politics textbooks, treatment of partisan bias tends to be extremely brief, with some avoiding the issue altogether. Most, though, give pithy summaries such as, "Research has failed to find empirical evidence that news reporting is biased in favor of either party," or "Studies [show] no discernible partisan bias in the media."[1]

Meanwhile, the leading media and politics textbooks tell it like this: "Notwithstanding the hue and cry over allegations of conservative or liberal bias in the news, the fact remains that political motives are less important determinants of news content than are commercial and organizational pressures. The evidence indicates that the American media have performed quite well according to the criterion of balanced political coverage."[2] And, "Public discussions about pervasive ideological or partisan bias in the media are not supported by evidence. Prominent examples of the ideologically branded major cable networks aside, most claims about surreptitious media bias from an ostensibly objective press are based on little supporting evidence."[3]

That sounds about right. Now let's explore how they came to those conclusions.

The Advantages and Challenges of Social Science

The attempt to impose social science on a fiercely debated question is fraught with peril. It is easy to dismiss or even ridicule those who lay claim to the elevated prestige of science as they delve into a hot-button, ideologically polarizing topic. And, indeed, popular bias cops often dismiss academic scholarship—or at least the subset with which they disagree—as having the same biases as the news sources being analyzed.

Imperfect as it is, however, social science deserves its position of privilege. For one, it operates on a much larger scale than journalistic or interest-group analysis of news content, with the number of stories analyzed often running into the thousands or tens of thousands. Also, contemporary political scientists— particularly some of those who have tackled media-bias questions recently— tend to be trained in the most sophisticated, state-of-the-art statistical and computer-aided content-analysis techniques. Additionally, while social scientists obviously have political opinions that could subconsciously color their work, they have safeguards against such contamination that popular news critics lack.

Social scientists generally have no material stake in the outcomes of their studies. Their incentives for employment, promotion, and compensation are unrelated to the type of slant, if any, they find in news coverage. In contrast, an employee of an organization whose entire mission is to expose liberal bias has a compelling incentive to work backward from a conclusion rather than to conduct a fair analysis.

Also, transparency serves as a formidable safeguard against letting ideology taint analysis. All studies published in recognized scholarly outlets must describe their methods in excruciating detail, to the point that another scholar could replicate the study if desired. In contrast, even the most respected nonacademic bias analysts tend to be opaque about their methods. See, for example, chapter 6's replication of an MRC study.

Most important, all published journal articles have survived rigorous, double-blind peer review, meaning the reviewers are anonymous to the author and vice versa. Academic-press books also require review. A typical journal uses between three and five reviewers, all or at least most of whom study the same question. Skeptics might argue that peer review could break down if a cabal of like-minded scholars ruthlessly enforces an orthodoxy by giving findings they like a free pass and vetoing high-quality dissenting work. However, that theory fails here in light of the wide diversity of published findings highlighted in this chapter.

If social science is the best way to learn about the political world, it can also be the most frustrating. Unlike the work of ideologically motivated critics—who have full license to let their brash assertions, and the data molded to fit them, race ahead at full speed—academic prose, by design, oozes caveat, equivocation, and the humility inherent in the chaotic task of trying to quantify abstract concepts such as "bias." That's not to say that scholars themselves are humble, but peer review is a reliably effective mechanism for chiseling arrogance and certainty off a research report.

The scholarly study of bias typifies this. The best recent compendium of the field was an essay by political scientist Tim Groeling—himself a prolific generator of original media-content studies—for the *Annual Review of Political Science*.[4] Rather than celebrating the canon of accumulated wisdom, much of the focus is on the "vexing problems" facing scholars who attempt to ascertain news slant.[5]

He begins by defining partisan bias as "a significantly distorted portrayal of reality that systematically and disproportionately favors one party over the other."[6] By his read of the literature, two problems stand out in scholarly attempts to measure it. The first, afflicting studies that require assessment of tone, is "subjectivity." Scholars must take care to create replicable, defensible measures of subjective categories such as good/bad or positive/negative news.

The second issue is what he calls the "problem of the unobserved population." If bias is a "distorted portrayal of reality," then "reality" must be measured concretely so that media coverage can be compared to it. Unfortunately, while coverage is relatively easy to measure, the full universe of events from which the coverage was selected is often impossible to characterize with any specificity. In short, we cannot say with confidence whether the media's choice of stories (gatekeeping) or sources within those stories (coverage) is a biased sample from the whole population of potential stories or sources, because we cannot see the population.

The most common solution is for the researcher to bypass the question of "reality" and simply argue that coverage is unbiased when it is balanced between the two sides. This assumption—discussed extensively in chapter 3—will be known hereafter as a "balance baseline." However, this assumption is often inappropriate. If reality is slanted but the bias charger/researcher uses a balance baseline, then slanted coverage would be called biased even though it adheres to the ideal of faithfully conveying reality.

The broader the study, the more the balance baseline is defensible. For the newer, large-scale studies that look at multiple issues over a long time frame, the assumption that both sides should be treated equally over time and across issues comports nicely with agreed-upon ideals of good journalism. However, although academic studies never focus on only one news story, as many popular charges do, they often focus on a single issue during a single snapshot in time. As such, a failure to establish that the sides actually deserved equal coverage, or that the coverage imbalance could not be explained by nonpartisan news-selection criteria, would undermine the validity of the balance baseline and thus the implications of the study's findings for the question of partisan bias. This issue, among others, was identified in a seminal academic study of media bias.

Baselines and Structure

Edith Efron's 1971 book *The News Twisters* was the showpiece of the Nixon-era bias-charge bonanza. Although appearing scientific to a casual reader, it violated some of the basic principles of sound social science, such as independent coding of subjective categories. After ripping it to shreds for its shoddy research methods, political-science and mass communication scholars soon stepped into the fray to tackle the broader question of bias.[7]

Richard Hofstetter quickly set a high bar with his study of the 1972 presidential election.[8] His book, *Bias in the News: Network Television Coverage of the 1972 Election Campaign*, remains atop the canon of classic bias studies in part because of its thorough analysis of the election, but mainly for its theoretical contributions, which have informed countless subsequent bias studies.

His analysis of the election was on an impressively large scale, particularly for the era. Using videotapes of every ABC, CBS, and NBC evening news program from July 10 until the day before the election, he and his assistants coded a wide array of content attributes, including the amount and tone of coverage for each candidate and party—overall, over time, and across various issues.

His main finding was clear: "based on the evidence in this study, the objective reader would be forced to conclude that partisan bias was not a significant factor in news coverage."[9] While some of the findings pointed to a slight favoritism of Democrats by CBS, the magnitude was always insubstantial.

An important theoretical contribution was his distinction between "political bias" and "structural bias." Political bias is "caused by the political views held by individual news personnel or executives," whereas structural bias is "caused by factors associated with the medium itself," such as "the need to maintain an audience by dramatization of stories" and "the excessively brief time period that even the most important story can be given."[10] As either type of bias could cause an observed slant—but only political bias has any conceptual relation to partisan bias—structural bias must be accounted for before a slant can be interpreted as partisan bias. And indeed, he found a considerable amount of structural bias in the election coverage.

To separate the two biases, he interpreted coverage patterns that were common to all three networks as structural biases, while slants that were unique to one network were political biases. This method has an obvious limitation, which Hofstetter acknowledged, in its inability to distinguish between structural bias and political bias if all three networks carried an identical political slant. This is important, of course, because that was exactly the popular charge that motivated the scholarly analysis. Subsequent studies have used multivariate statistics to parse the different types of bias in a more convincing fashion.

In another prescient discussion, he wrote of the need "to discern a baseline for comparisons of news coverage."[11] The apparent difficulty in doing so led him to conclude that assessments of bias should be "relative" rather than "absolute," foreshadowing the recent movement, discussed below, toward characterizing the slant of news outlets in relation to each other rather than to a balance (or reality) baseline. This view, however, is not shared by the preponderance of scholars who continue to measure coverage against a baseline.

Political scientist David Niven clarified and expanded the concept of a baseline in several studies of partisan bias. In his 2002 book, he criticized the tendency of most prior studies to employ a balance baseline—what he calls the "50–50 fairness standard"—without adequate justification:[12]

> [A] popular means of demonstrating fairness or bias in the media is to compare the coverage of Democratic and Republican candidates. But, is fair coverage treating two candidates or the two parties similarly? What if one of the candidates is more qualified? Should both candidates still get equal coverage? Is fair coverage presenting the range of the parties' opinions regarding a situation?

What if one side is the position of most of our leaders and has the support of renowned experts?[13]

His solution was to test for bias through a "comparable performance" research design, in which he evaluated coverage of Democratic and Republican officeholders who have "produced comparable results or engaged in comparable behavior."[14] For example, he compared newspaper coverage of unemployment under Democratic and Republican presidents during months in which the unemployment rate was the same, finding the volume and tone of their coverage to be strikingly similar. The findings were replicated for a comparison of Democratic and Republican governors with similar "performance" on unemployment and the state murder rate.

In another study, he employed a particularly convincing strategy of holding everything else constant by studying Democrats and Republicans when they are the *same person*. That is, he studied coverage of high-profile party switchers, from each side, before and after their switch. Consistent with the "no bias" finding of his prior studies, he found a "startling similarity in treatment of former Democrats and former Republicans."[15]

Bias in Election Coverage

The limitations of the balance baseline, as well as the advantages and challenges of the social-science approach to ascertaining bias, are on full display in the much-studied electoral arena. In particular, presidential elections—a vital process with two clearly demarked sides fighting for the same prize—have been the subject of more bias studies than any other topic by an enormous margin. Reviewing all of the studies here would be tedious and unnecessary. Fortunately, someone already did that, and the findings will be discussed later. For now, a couple of countervailing exemplars illustrate one of the challenges.[16]

In 1983, political scientist Michael Robinson and analyst Margaret Sheehan conducted a thorough, multifaceted study of how the 1980 presidential election was covered on CBS and the UPI wire service, with an eye toward evaluating the degree to which they lived up to the press values of objectivity, fairness, seriousness, and comprehensiveness. Among their many findings was an absence of partisan bias.[17]

By contrast, the Center for Media and Public Affairs (CMPA) at George Mason University—which combines the public orientation of a media-watchdog group with the practices of good social science—employs many prolific scholars of media bias, including founder and president Robert Lichter. Their voluminous output includes numerous studies of presidential elections during the 1980s, 1990s, and 2000s, and most find a liberal slant to national news coverage.[18]

So who is right? Unfortunately, the very attributes that make presidential elections such a tempting topic for study also present some of the most difficult conceptual obstacles. As is often the case, the sticking point is the baseline. To unpack this, let's begin with a much-touted case of alleged liberal bias.

2008—A Slam-Dunk Case Hits the Rim

Did Barack Obama receive more favorable mainstream news coverage than his opponent John McCain in the 2008 presidential election?

Professional bias cops obviously would have made this allegation, regardless of its veracity, by utilizing cherry-picked anecdotes to portray a pack of hope/change-smitten reporters helping to sway the presidency back to the Democratic Party. That's their job. This time, though, they were probably right, at least about the raw, aggregate slant during the crucial last few weeks of the campaign.

The Pew Research Center's Journalism and Media division (formerly called the Project for Excellence in Journalism, or PEJ) frequently conducts high-quality news-content analyses on hot topics. Their extensive study of the 2008 presidential election included an assessment of the overall tone of mainstream news coverage from September 8 to October 16, conducted by experienced coders under the direction of some of the leading nonpartisan news scholars outside of academia.

While the candidates received nearly identical amounts of coverage—and it would have been shocking to find otherwise during the latter stages of a general election, at least prior to 2016—tone was a different story. Coverage of Obama was fairly balanced between positive (36 percent), negative (29 percent), and neutral (35 percent) stories. By contrast, McCain's coverage was highly negative, at 57 percent, while only 14 percent of stories were positive.[19]

In a more nuanced analysis, political scientist Robert Entman found a strong pro-Republican tilt in the days following the selection of Sarah Palin as McCain's running mate. However, the tone took a dramatic leftward shift late in the cycle, moving to the same pro-Democratic slant found by Pew.[20] Also, CMPA—whose presidential-election findings usually run in the "liberal bias" direction—found that Obama "got the best press CMPA has ever measured for a presidential nominee," while McCain's press was "2 to 1 negative."[21]

Not surprisingly, the election generated more bias charges than Obama and Palin Halloween masks. One day before the general election, the bias-watchdog group Accuracy in Media (AIM) captured the sentiment on the right in a long article that declared, "The verdict is in: the mainstream media were overwhelmingly in the tank for Barack Obama, and did their part to make sure he will be elected."[22] From sweeping claims like that to the amplification of allegedly telling anecdotes, bias cops had a rich palette from which to paint their color-by-numbers picture. On the anecdotal front, a Google search for the words "Chris Matthews," "thrill," "up," and "leg" returns 108,000 results.

On March 27, 2008, MSNBC host Matthews turned uncharacteristically sensual while discussing an Obama speech with colleague Keith Olbermann. "I have to tell you, you know, it's part of reporting this case, this election, the feeling most people get when they hear a Barack Obama speech, my, I felt this thrill going up my leg. I mean, I don't have that too often." It was a bit peculiar that this came to personify the alleged bias of the ostensibly neutral press, given that Matthews works for MSNBC. But apparently it was too vivid an image to forgo making hay of it.

Bias cops scarcely needed such anecdotes, though. Between Obama's historic run as the first minority nominee of either party, McCain's controversial pick of first-term Alaska governor Palin as his running mate, and the autumn economic crash under already-unpopular Republican president Bush's watch, any reasonably observant news consumer could see that the postconvention campaign's dominant narratives fell to the advantage of the Democratic candidate as he steamrolled his opponent on the way to a comfortable popular-vote win and an electoral-vote landslide.

At first glance, this could be a slam-dunk case of pro-Democratic bias, destined for a spot in chapter 1 of anti-liberal-bias polemics for years to come. The evidence of imbalance presented by Pew and other credible analysts was clear. Further, balance is a normatively defensible baseline for a presidential election, in which the country's two major parties each put their best face forward—along with every financial, human, and rhetorical resource they can muster—to fight for the nation's highest elected office. Surely if there is any venue that calls for balance, it would be this.

However, a balance baseline must clear an additional hurdle besides being normatively justified. To make the leap from an observed coverage slant to a plausible charge of media bias, the charger must rule out other potential causes of the slant besides favoritism of one political party or ideology. If nonpartisan "reality" factors were biased, then coverage that hews faithfully to them would appear slanted. And if a given news outlet would have given similarly slanted coverage in the other direction if the parties' fortunes were reversed, then the finding says nothing about the outlet's broader ideological tilt.

So, what is the "reality" of a presidential election? This type of question can get unwieldy in a hurry, but it seems appropriate to start with the factors that are known to swing general-election outcomes.

Above all, the state of the economy and approval of the current president set the stage for the fall contest. A small but high-profile cadre of political scientists uses statistical models of past elections to predict the outcome of a presidential race months in advance. While their models vary, most use measures of the macroeconomy and presidential approval. For example, longtime forecaster Alan Abramowitz uses only three variables to predict the incumbent-party candidate's share of the popular vote: GDP growth, presidential approval, and how many terms the incumbent party has held the White House.[23] His track record is impressive. He correctly predicted the popular-vote winner, before the conventions were even held, in every cycle between 1992 and 2012, with an average error of fewer than two percentage points—roughly the same as the final polls before the election.[24]

The lesson here is not that political scientists are brilliant sages, but rather that the "reality" of presidential elections is largely set by a handful of underlying conditions that are comparable across time. These conditions include the economy and whatever factors are baked into presidential approval—war and peace, scandals, legislative success, and so forth. The fall campaign itself, with all of its twists and turns, does matter at the margins, but not nearly as much as most casual observers assume.[25] In fact, as long as both candidates run competent campaigns, the fall events serve less as persuasion than as a way to bring voters to where we already knew they would be.[26]

This was true in 2008 despite the historic nature of Obama's candidacy and the extraordinary economic events of the fall. Using only data that was available in July—long before the conventions, Palin, or the crash—Abramowitz's model predicted that Obama would receive 54.3 percent of the two-party popular vote. In fact, he received 53.7 percent.

In addition, news-relevant reality slanted even further against Republicans than the summer forecasting models could measure. President Bush's Gallup approval rating was, by historical standards, atrocious. He bottomed out at 25 percent during three of the four polls taken in October 2008. His high for the whole year was 34 percent in January, and he mostly wallowed in the high 20s during the crucial campaign months.[27] And then, of course, the economy crashed. The Great Recession began with a string of bank failures and ended up tanking the stock market and dragging GDP growth deep into negative territory by the election quarter.

The campaign-related factors in the election only exacerbated the imbalance. Obama was the first major-party nominee of a minority ethnicity, a fact that surely would have garnered attention regardless of party. He also parlayed his youth, charisma, and a tech-savvy staff into generating enthusiasm, particularly among young voters, that was unprecedented in recent campaigns. It is tough to cover those factors, particularly in the horse-race style that dominates election news, without the measurable tone slanting in his favor. Further, McCain's choice of Palin as a running mate, though good for a short-term poll bounce, is widely seen in retrospect as a strategic mistake, a fact that became apparent in the fall as she struggled through a series of interviews.

With this backdrop, it is difficult even to imagine how "balanced" coverage could have come about, short of herculean efforts at leveling the tone—"McCain is way behind in the polls due to the terrible conditions, but did we mention that he's a war hero?"—that would have run afoul of the basic duty to paint an accurate picture. Just think about the stories each candidate had to tell. Obama: "The economy is horrible, the president is horrible, vote for change." McCain: "OK, conditions are bad, and I voted with the president nearly 100 percent of the time. However . . ." Even the well-respected political maverick—long a favorite of the DC press—was unable to follow the "however" with a convincing story.

Problems with Baselines

The implications for assessing bias in coverage of the 2008 election are clear: reality was slanted. Thus the mere observation of news slant at the end of the campaign, when the same outlets had showered Republicans with positive coverage just weeks prior, is insufficient to declare a pro-Democratic bias. As Entman noted,

Unless one assumes the media restrained or forgot their liberal bias for the initial campaign phase then suddenly rediscovered it, the explanation for the radical shift in slant must lie in the interactions of the other decision biases with skill and real-world events. It does not seem much of a stretch to identify the onset on 15 September of the gravest financial crisis to hit the USA since the Great Depression as a key event. This unhappy coincidence for McCain understandably dominated the news.[28]

However, the presence of a slanted reality does not, by itself, let the media off the hook. After all, their coverage might have been *more* slanted than is justifiable by reality.

A measurable standard is obviously required to answer this question. If "faithful adherence to reality" is the goal, then to what degree *should* the coverage have been slanted in Obama's favor? Unfortunately, this is where the "problem of the unobserved population" rears its ugly head for anyone—scholars, bias cops, or otherwise—with an ambition to evaluate media bias in any one presidential election. How could we possibly quantify the entire election—the underlying conditions and all relevant campaign phenomena—into a single measure that somehow can be converted into the "proper" proportion of coverage slant for a given election? The philosophical and measurement challenges are daunting, probably to the point of impossibility.

One solution is to leverage variation in the underlying conditions from more than one election to create a reality baseline. Though this has never been done formally at the presidential level, I did this for newspaper coverage of Senate races.[29] Utilizing a large-scale content analysis generously provided by political scientists Kim Fridkin (Kahn) and Patrick Kenney in the 1990s, I assessed coverage and statement bias (I called them "amount" and "tone") in local newspaper coverage of ninety-five Senate races during the Senate cycle of 1988–92.[30]

The slant in the amount of coverage received by each candidate varied dramatically. The Democrats got as high as 80.5 percent of the coverage—Texas senator Lloyd Bentsen in 1988—and as low as 16.9 percent—South Carolina senator Strom Thurmond's Democratic opponent. Other dominant Democrats included Al Gore of Tennessee, David Boren of Oklahoma, and Robert Byrd of West Virginia. The other top Republicans were Ted Stevens of Alaska, Alan Simpson of Wyoming, and Orrin Hatch of Utah.

A naive analysis of any given race might find bias: Wow, the Democrat-loving *Houston Chronicle* was totally in the tank for Bentsen! The *Salt Lake Tribune* is obviously a Republican mouthpiece to favor Hatch to that degree! But such claims fall apart when the different races are viewed together. The lopsided coverage advantages all went to long-serving, popular senators—usually in states favorable to their party—who faced only token opposition from unknown and underfunded challengers. Oh, and Bentsen was also Democratic presidential nominee Mike Dukakis's running mate. While one could muster a normative argument that Senate candidates always deserve equal coverage—no doubt a tougher argument to make than in a presidential election, given the spending and experience imbalances common in congressional races—the deviation from that ideal that favored Bentsen, Hatch, et al., surely has an explanation other than partisan bias. And in fact, across the 95 races, Democratic incumbents received an average of 58.4 percent of the coverage in their races and Republican incumbents received 57.8 percent—a statistically insignificant difference.

Tone showed similarly wide variation across the ninety-five contests—except this time, Democratic candidates fared a bit better than Republicans on average. The proportion of positive to negative mentions was about 13 percent higher for Democrats than Republicans. While that is not the sort of "overwhelming" or "lopsided" slant that bias cops claim exists in the national media, it was statistically significant and certainly notable across so many different newspapers.

However, even though individual quirks are canceled out by averaging ninety-five races together, it is still a balance baseline and thus is not adequate for assessing the true level of bias. To control for "reality"—or the nonpartisan factors that might affect slant within a given paper's coverage of a given race—I used measures of several such factors as control variables: incumbent and challenger spending, incumbent seniority, poll standing (prior to the measured newspaper coverage), the total amount of coverage of the race, and the ideology/partisanship of the state, among others.

The analysis was rerun with this new "reality baseline." While Democrats still enjoyed a statistically significant tone advantage, it shrunk to an even less consequential 8 percent. In fact, the 8 percent might still be exaggerated because an important attribute of reality—the fact that Democrats held the majority in the Senate during the entire period of analysis—could not be factored in. As Groeling pointed out in critiquing this study, "one obvious limitation to this approach is the difficulty of controlling for all possible structural factors."[31] Regardless, while the average reduction in slant was modest, the reality baseline fundamentally changes the interpretation of the most lopsided races, just as it did with coverage volume. When popular incumbents face a sacrificial warm body on the other side, they garner a coverage advantage mostly because of those underlying conditions, not because the newspaper favors their party.

Mega Meta-Analysis

In 2000, two communication scholars utilized a different approach to transcending the limitations of analyzing a single election, and in the process contributed one of the most important overall assessments of partisan bias in the American press. Dave D'Alessio and Mike Allen conducted a meta-analysis of presidential-election bias studies, meaning a systematic statistical analysis of the findings of previous peer-reviewed studies. The analysis covers fifty-nine studies of elections from 1948 to 1996, some analyzing multiple elections or multiple types of bias, for a total of 132 unique bias assessments.[32]

A meta-analysis has considerable advantages over any given individual study. In addition to concisely summarizing the cumulative wisdom from a tremendous amount of scholarly effort, it also tames the idiosyncrasies of any given scholar's decisions on how to sample and code the content, which statistical techniques to use, and so on.

They examined gatekeeping, coverage, and statement (tone) bias separately. Only five studies measured gatekeeping bias, and overall there was no significant lean in either direction. For the much-studied coverage bias, they also found no significant slant toward either party, both overall and for any of the specific media types (newspapers, television, and magazines). For statement bias, no overall slant was found across the studies of newspapers. They did find a slight pro-Democratic lean on television and a pro-Republican lean in newsmagazines. Both were so small that they would be extremely difficult for even an attentive audience to pick up.

Their grand assessment across all studies was "zero overall bias." The conclusion was unequivocal: there is no "liberal media," in the sense of a systematic, cross-platform, over-time imbalance in presidential-election coverage during the second half of the twentieth century. Recently, the lead author extended the study through the 2008 election, with essentially the same results.[33]

Looking at the individual elections separately further shows the folly of using a balance baseline to evaluate coverage of a single election. Notably, Ronald Reagan enjoyed favorable coverage in both of his elections. Of the ten unique scholarly bias assessments of the 1980 election featured in the meta-analysis, Reagan received more favorable coverage than his opponent, President Jimmy Carter, in eight of them. Of the fifteen bias assessments in 1984, Reagan held the advantage in ten. By contrast, Democrat Bill Clinton benefited from the majority of demonstrated slant in the academic assessments of his two elections: eight of fifteen in 1992 and seven of eight in 1996.

It is important to note that this cross-president comparison is merely impressionistic and that the slant was sometimes statistically insignificant within a given study. Nonetheless, it corroborates the Senate study's finding that balance baselines do not work for individual elections. Otherwise, are we to infer that the news media showed a consistent pro-Republican bias in the 1980s—right before the pro-Democratic charges against them went mainstream—only to fall into a deep pro-Democratic bias by the mid-1990s, just in time to prove the critics right? That simply makes no sense.

Unfortunately, neither the Senate study nor the presidential-election meta-analysis provides a realistic baseline from which to make confident evaluations of any one presidential election. Thus, returning to the question of whether a pro-Obama slant in 2008 would be evidence of a broader favoritism of Democrats, (1) it is difficult to know for sure, but (2) the combination of no over-time bias in presidential elections and the hazards of using a balance baseline when underlying conditions are unbalanced raises significant doubt about a critic's ability to infer bias from coverage of the 2008 election—or any election for that matter. Despite the tremendous attention showered upon them by scholars and critics alike, elections turn out to be a tough nut to crack.

Measuring Nonelectoral Reality

Beyond elections, recent studies have taken a variety of clever approaches to measuring biases, including partisan ones, as deviation from a reality baseline.

Groeling used changes in presidential approval as the underlying reality, testing whether the three broadcast networks and Fox News were more likely to report positive or negative changes in approval for Democratic or Republican presidents from 1997 to 2008.[34] He finds evidence of a pro-Democratic bias on the broadcast networks—a greater likelihood of reporting bad polls for Bush and good polls for Clinton—and pro-Republican bias on Fox. Given the quirks of those two presidencies—for example, Clinton's baffling approval rise during the Lewinsky scandal and Bush's whiplash rise and fall after 9/11—it would be interesting to see if these findings hold up over a longer time span.

Economist Valentino Larcinese and colleagues used economic indicators as the reality baseline to test for variation in the degree to which newspapers were more likely to report good or bad news for Democratic or Republican presidents.[35] They "find that newspapers with a pro-Democratic endorsement pattern systematically publish fewer pieces about unemployment when the national unemployment rate is high and the president is Democratic than when the national unemployment is equally high and the president is a Republican." They find no such bias, however, for coverage of inflation, the budget deficit, or the trade deficit.

Similarly, political scientist Stuart Soroka compared objective measures of unemployment and inflation to the volume and tone of thirty years of *New York Times* coverage of those topics.[36] He found no partisan bias in the deviation of the coverage from reality.

Finally, Daniel Butler and Emily Schofield used the methodology of field experiments to create their own reality baseline. They sampled one hundred US newspapers and sent letters to the editor during the 2008 election. The newspapers were randomly assigned either a pro-Obama or pro-McCain letter, which were carefully designed to be nearly identical except for their candidate choice.[37] Interestingly, newspapers (1) were much more interested in the pro-McCain letters and (2) were more likely to accept the letters if the paper did *not* endorse the candidate.

Breakthroughs in Methods and Controversy

Recently, bias studies have undergone a renaissance in scope and statistical sophistication, though not without controversy. While the best of them have avoided controversy by modeling the slant of news outlets *relative to each other* rather than relative to a balance baseline, the one that alleges imbalance has gained the most attention.

If a nonacademic reader is familiar with only one scholarly study of partisan bias, it is almost certainly the large-scale analysis published in 2005 by political scientist Tim Groseclose and economist Jeffrey Milyo. Examining twenty of the top national media outlets in the 1990s and early 2000s, they found a liberal slant to the straight-news content in all but two of them.[38] Needless to say, it was manna from heaven for professional bias cops, and the project's early drafts received more attention from activists and commentators *before it was even published* than most studies garner in a lifetime. Groseclose also wrote a popularly targeted book in 2011 based on the original study's findings, which earned him a wave of national media attention.[39]

Sidestepping nearly every insight and finding from the political-science and mass communication literature on bias, the authors expanded the then-tiny niche for bias studies in economics by creating an intricate measure of media slant. In short, they estimated the ideology of a given news outlet by placing it along the congressional ideological spectrum. To bridge the two entities, they took advantage of the fact that both Congress and the media regularly cite advocacy groups and think tanks. Using a common political-science metric of congressional ideology—which ranges from 0 (most conservative) to 100 (most liberal), with 50.1 as the estimated "average American voter"—they first gave the most influential groups an ideology score based on the ideologies of the members of Congress who cited them. Then they calculated the scores for each news outlet based on the ideologies of the groups they cited.

Nearly all of the outlets fell to the left of 50. *CBS Evening News*, then anchored by bias-charge magnet Dan Rather, scored 73.7; the ABC and NBC evening shows scored 61.0 and 61.6, respectively. The *New York Times* was 73.7, and the *Washington Post* was 66.6. The only right-leaning outlets were the *Washington Times* (35.4)—well known as DC's conservative alternative to the *Post*—and Fox News's *Special Report with Brit Hume* (39.7). By comparison, the average congressional Democrat of this slightly less polarized era was 84, and the average Republican was 16. In a bizarre twist that the authors were unable to explain convincingly, the *Wall Street Journal* was rated the single most liberal outlet, at 85.1.[40]

The alleged bias may be consistent across outlets, but how big is it? Many fans of the study tout it as a demonstration of "overwhelming" or "profound" liberal bias in the news—but this is a faulty conclusion because the metric is less intuitive than something like "Democrats received *X* percent of all positive/negative mentions." The *Los Angeles Times*'s 70, for example, does not mean they are 70 percent liberal. This misunderstanding likely drove some of the hype in popular discourse about the magnitude of the findings, as nearly all other quantitative bias measures interpret 0–100 scales as percentages.

Taking the findings at face value for the moment, if members of Congress had written the news in the 1990s and early 2000s, most outlets would have employed the services of the most conservative Democrats. All but six of the outlets fell between Democratic senators Joe Lieberman and John Breaux. Lieberman is a notable reference point because his non-party-line views on many key issues caused him to be loathed among the burgeoning liberal blogosphere in the early 2000s, and to this day the now-independent former senator, who endorsed John McCain in 2008, is cursed frequently in Left Blogistan as the archetype of a bad Democrat. Breaux, who was first elected to Congress in 1972, was a pro-life, pro-gun, pro-tax-cut, old-school Southern Democrat. In short, the study found the group-citation habits of news outlets to be left of the US ideological center, but not Nancy Pelosi or Ted Kennedy left.

Just as the study drew more praise from conservatives than any study since Edith Efron's, it predictably became a lightning rod for liberal criticism. Bias scholars within the political-science and communication fields also raised a litany of methodological and interpretation concerns. Setting aside the authors' intentional oversight of the scholarly media-bias canon, where does this study fit within it?

The study matter-of-factly shows that the news media's pattern of interest-group and think-tank citations maps onto the ideological spectrum to the left of the typical American voter, roughly in line with the right flank of the Democratic congressional contingent (back when there was one). But it takes a tremendous leap of inference to read this as evidence of an overall, systematic slant toward the Democratic Party or the liberal side, and there are several important barriers to doing so.

First, though of impressive scope and complexity, the findings have important limitations as to their generalizability. In a reanalysis of the data, political scientist John Gasper found the estimates of media ideology to be (1) unstable, (2) highly sensitive to which think tanks are included, and (3) moving in a conservative direction over the period of analysis.[41]

Also, as political scientist Brandon Nyhan argues, the measure assumes that "the processes generating journalistic and Congressional citations to the think tanks and interest groups in their sample are identical."[42] He provides several alternative explanations for the media citation patterns other than liberal bias. For example, conservative groups like the Heritage Foundation attempt to influence Congress more than the media. Thus, if they succeed in placing their work more prominently in the congressional record than in the news, that would appear as liberal news bias in the study.

More fundamentally, expert citations are just one component of the news product—a relatively small component, given the media's tendency to cite mostly government officials in political stories (see chapters 4 and 5). When a study partitions the news and examines only part of each story—in this case, a small subset of the cited sources—it carries a heavy burden to prove that the sampled content is representative of the whole and that the highly indirect nature of the measure nonetheless taps the underlying concept of systematic favoritism of one side. This burden was simply not met.

As one example of a countervailing pattern when sources are partitioned differently, studies of government officials quoted in the influential Sunday-morning political shows demonstrate a consistent pro-Republican slant to the guest lineups.[43] Although these studies are typically conducted by left-leaning groups, their methodology of counting sources is straightforward and objective. One obvious criticism is that they fail to account for the ideology of the host—but that just reinforces the point about the danger of partitioning content.

The bottom line is that, despite the unprecedented hype, the Groseclose-Milyo study is ultimately just one piece of evidence—with considerable shortcomings—to be weighed alongside the other findings highlighted in this chapter, most of which find no overall leftward tilt to the news product.

Recent Innovations

As computing power has enabled larger-scale studies, new approaches have advanced our understanding of news slant. One recent study in particular has already been cited nearly as many times as Groseclose-Milyo, with none of the controversy.

In 2010, economists Matthew Gentzkow and Jesse Shapiro published the results of a massive data-gathering effort that quantified the slant of 433 US newspapers.[44] It also utilized Congress for ideological calibration, but in a more intuitive fashion. They first isolated the short phrases in the *Congressional Record* spoken disproportionately by one party in 2005. For example, Republicans were much more likely to reference "illegal aliens," "adult stem cells," and the "oil for food" scandal, while Democrats preferred to speak of "Rosa Parks," "minimum wage," and "victims of gun violence." They then calculated a score for each newspaper based on the degree to which its stories used phrases preferred by Democrats or Republicans. The result was a ranking of the relative partisan slant across all of the newspapers in the study.

Importantly, they explicitly disavowed the idea that they had measured absolute bias in a newspaper: "The resulting index allows us to compare newspapers to one another, though not to a benchmark of 'true' or 'unbiased' reporting."[45] Instead, they employed the index to answer the question: What explains variation in newspaper slant? Their statistical analysis showed a strong relationship between a newspaper's slant and the ideological bent of its consumer market, but no relationship between characteristics of the newspaper's owner (including ideology) and slant.

Despite the authors' intentions, might the findings inform us about the degree of deviation from a balance baseline in American newspapers? Probably not.

If "balance" were to be defined as using preferred Democratic and Republican phrases with equal frequency, then that overlooks the fact that many of the Republican phrases of that era were newly coined, focus-group-tested alterations of existing phrases, employed strategically to influence public opinion. Democrats on the other hand, lacking a counterpart to renowned Republican wordsmith Frank Luntz, typically stuck with long-established terms that were already standard in news stories because they had previously been used by both sides. For example, the Republican list included "tax relief," which replaced "tax cuts," and "death tax," which replaced "estate tax." Also, in the middle of the 2005 debate over Social Security reform, Republicans changed their own moniker for one of the planks in Bush's plan from "private accounts" to "personal accounts." Further, the Republican slogan "global war on terror" appeared on their list, while the matter-of-fact descriptors "Iraq War" and "War in Iraq"—which are consistent with how the media have described other post–World War II wars such as Korea, Vietnam, and the Gulf War—apparently came disproportionately from the mouths of Democrats.[46]

If journalists either consciously chose to stick with the more neutral-sounding Democratic terms, or even if they were merely slow to catch up to the new framing battles, their content would appear slanted to the left vis-à-vis a balance baseline. Thus the authors were wise not to go down this rabbit hole, sticking instead with their measure of *relative* slant, which is not at all damaged by the asymmetry in mid-2000s partisan strategic framing. This article is sometimes cited as evidence of "no liberal bias," however, on account of one section in which they found no significant deviation from consumer preference in either ideological direction.

Another recent study expanded the boundaries of this topic by measuring newspapers' overt slant—that is, their editorial pages. Calibrating the content to Supreme Court cases rather than Congress, legal scholar Daniel Ho and political scientist Kevin Quinn studied twenty-five newspapers from 1994 to 2004.[47] They found a large and intuitively pleasing spread of editorial ideologies. *Investor's Business Daily*, the *New York Post*, the *Washington Times*, and the *Wall Street Journal* all cluster on the right between the ideology of Justices Scalia and Rehnquist; while the *Detroit Free Press*, the *Minneapolis Star-Tribune*, the *San Francisco Chronicle*, and the *Boston Globe* sit between Justices Ginsburg and Stevens. The *New York Times* is to the left of Stevens. Meanwhile, nine papers, including the *Dallas Morning News* and the *Atlanta Journal-Constitution*, sit between the liberal and conservative blocs on the court.

To explore the relationship between explicit editorial positions and the tone of news content, they compared their measure to three existing metrics of news-page slant, including Groseclose-Milyo, finding strong correlations between it and all three news measures. This is consistent with several prior studies that found substantial leaks in the "wall of separation" between news and editorial content.[48]

A different take on editorial slant comes from political scientists Riccardo Puglisi and James Snyder, who collected more than thirty thousand editorials on ballot propositions nationwide.[49] They employed a more nuanced baseline than most other studies, measuring the paper's slant against the median voter in a given state.

In the aggregate, they found no bias. Newspaper editorial slants are well matched to the electoral majorities in their states, at least for the topic of ballot propositions. However, when they separated the analysis by issue, they found a liberal slant to coverage of social issues and a conservative slant on economic issues. They also replicated two measures of relative news slant, including Gentzkow-Shapiro, and found a strong correlation between news and editorial slant. From this they concluded, "On average both the news sections and the editorial sections of the newspapers in each state are balanced around the state median voter."

The same scholars also took a cut at modeling relative slant across newspapers by studying coverage of thirty-two scandals involving either prominent

Democrats (thirteen) or Republicans (nineteen), assessing whether the editorial partisanship of a newspaper made it more likely to cover scandals from the opposite party.[50] Indeed, they found a large effect. They also showed slant to be correlated with audience ideology, but only if the scandalized official came from the local market.

The authors made no effort to assess absolute bias vis-à-vis a balance (or any other) baseline, which was a smart move. The magnitude of the scandals studied were asymmetric with respect to partisanship, as the Republican scandals involved officials in higher offices than the Democratic scandals—including the majority leaders of both chambers of Congress—plus an important matter of national security involving the vice president's chief of staff.

Conclusion

Political-science and mass communication scholars have spent forty years characterizing the degree of tilt in the mainstream US news media, with varying levels of quantitative sophistication and attention to crucial theoretical and definitional quandaries. The most defensible read of the literature is that the popular claim of an overall, systematic leftward tilt is unsupported.

Recent innovations in content gathering, data structuring, and computation have expanded the scope of bias studies far beyond what was possible when scholars first tackled the question. Still, contemporary scholars should be mindful of the foundational insights necessary to tell a convincing story about partisan bias. In particular, it is vital to theorize adequately about how bias is defined in a given context. This task includes defending—and, if necessary, moving away from—the default assumption that any deviation from "balance" constitutes partisan bias.

The next chapter introduces a systematic framework for scrutinizing individual bias charges. Although it is primarily an evaluative tool rather than a testable theory for descriptive or explanatory social science inquiries into bias, it nonetheless may provide guidance for scholars who endeavor to tell a theoretically satisfying tale about bias within their empirical models.

Notes

[1] Daniel M. Shea, Joanne Connor Green, and Christopher E. Smith, *Living Democracy*, 4th ed. (Boston: Pearson, 2014), 395; Christine Barbour and Gerald C. Wright, *Keeping the Republic*, 7th ed. (Los Angeles: SAGE CQ Press, 2015), 573.

[2] Shanto Iyengar, *Media Politics: A Citizen's Guide*, 3rd ed. (New York: Norton, 2016), 88.

[3] Doris A. Graber and Johanna Dunaway, *Mass Media and American Politics*, 9th ed. (Los Angeles: SAGE CQ Press, 2015), 344.

[4] Tim Groeling, "Media Bias by the Numbers: Challenges and Opportunities in the Empirical Study of Partisan News," *Annual Review of Political Science* 16 (2013): 129–51.

[5] Groeling, "Media Bias by the Numbers," 132.

[6] Groeling, "Media Bias by the Numbers," 133.

[7] For "ripping it to shreds," see Robert L. Stevenson, Richard A. Eisinger, Barry M. Feinberg, and Alan B. Kotok, "Untwisting *The News Twisters*: A Replication of Efron's Study," *Journalism Quarterly* 50 (1973): 211–19.

[8] C. Richard Hofstetter, *Bias in the News: Network Television News Coverage of the 1972 Election Campaign* (Columbus: Ohio State University Press, 1976).

[9] Hofstetter, *Bias in the News*, 187.

[10] Hofstetter, *Bias in the News*, 33.

[11] Hofstetter, *Bias in the News*, 189.

[12] As far as I can tell, I coined the terms "balance baseline" and "reality baseline" in my 1998 master's thesis, which became Adam J. Schiffer, "Assessing Partisan Bias in Political News: The Case(s) of Local Senate Election Coverage," *Political Communication* 23 (2006): 23–39.

[13] David Niven, *Tilt? The Search for Media Bias* (Westport, CT: Praeger, 2002), 73–74.

[14] Niven, *Tilt?*, 74.

[15] David Niven, "Objective Evidence on Media Bias: Newspaper Coverage of Congressional Party Switchers," *Journalism and Mass Communication Quarterly* 80 (2003): 319.

[16] Beyond the examples here, some of the most cited studies include the prolific work of Guido Stempel, who was among the first to study candidate coverage volume. See, for example, Guido H. Stempel III, "The Prestige Press Covers the 1960 Presidential Campaign," *Journalism Quarterly* 38 (1961): 157–63. Dennis Lowry also studied several elections. See, for example, Dennis T. Lowry and Jon A. Shidler, "The Sound Bites, the Biters, and the Bitten: An Analysis of Network TV News Bias in Campaign '92," *Journalism and Mass Communication Quarterly* 72 (1995): 33–44.

[17] Michael J. Robinson and Margaret A. Sheehan, *Over the Wire and on TV: CBS and UPI in Campaign '80* (New York: Russell Sage Foundation, 1983).

[18] See, for example, Center for Media and Public Affairs, "Campaign 2004 Final: How TV News Covered the General Election Campaign," *Media Monitor* 18 (2004), accessed April 24, 2016, http://cmpa.gmu.edu/wp-content/uploads/2014/02/2004-1.pdf.

[19] "Winning the Media Campaign: How the Press Reported the 2008 General Election," Pew Research Center: Journalism & Media Staff, October 22, 2008, accessed December 18, 2016, http://www.journalism.org/2008/10/22/winning-media-campaign.

[20] Robert M. Entman, "Media Framing Biases and Political Power: Explaining Slant in News of Campaign 2008," *Journalism* 11 (2010): 389–408.

[21] Center for Media and Public Affairs, "Election Watch: Campaign 2008 Final; How TV News Covered the General Election Campaign," *Media Monitor* 23 (2009), accessed April 24, 2016, http://cmpa.gmu.edu/wp-content/uploads/2013/10/media_monitor_jan_2009.pdf.

[22] Roger Aronoff, "Media Are Big Losers in Election 2008," Accuracy in Media, November 3, 2008, accessed April 25, 2016, http://www.aim.org/aim-column/media-are-big-losers-in-election-2008.

[23] He added a fourth variable in 2012, "polarization," to correct for previous overestimation of the winner's margin.

[24] "Time for Change Model," PollyVote, accessed April 29, 2016, http://pollyvote.com/en/components/econometric-models/time-for-change-model.

[25] Lynn Vavreck, *The Message Matters: The Economy and Presidential Campaigns* (Princeton, NJ: Princeton University Press, 2009).

[26] Andrew Gelman and Gary King, "Why Are American Presidential Election Campaign Polls So Variable When Votes Are So Predictable?," *British Journal of Political Science* 23 (1993): 409–51.

[27] "Presidential Approval Ratings—George W. Bush," Gallup, accessed April 29, 2016, http://www.gallup.com/poll/116500/presidential-approval-ratings-george-bush.aspx.

[28] Entman, "Media Framing Biases," 399.

[29] Schiffer, "Assessing Partisan Bias."

[30] The data were gathered for their comprehensive study of Senate campaigns, featured in Kim Fridkin Kahn and Patrick J. Kenney, *The Spectacle of U.S. Senate Campaigns* (Princeton, NJ: Princeton University Press, 1999).

[31] Groeling, "Media Bias by the Numbers," 143.

[32] D'Alessio and Allen, "Media Bias in Presidential Elections."

[33] Dave D'Alessio, *Media Bias in Presidential Election Coverage, 1948–2008* (Lanham, MD: Lexington Books, 2012).

[34] Tim Groeling, "Who's the Fairest of Them All? An Empirical Test for Partisan Bias on ABC, CBS, NBC, and Fox News," *Presidential Studies Quarterly* 38 (2008): 631–57.

[35] Valentino Larcinese, Riccardo Puglisi, and James M. Snyder Jr., "Partisan Bias in Economic News: Evidence on the Agenda-Setting Behavior of U.S. Newspapers," *Journal of Public Economics* 95 (2011): 1178–89.

[36] Stuart N. Soroka, "The Gatekeeping Function: Distributions of Information in Media and the Real World," *Journal of Politics* 74 (2012): 514–28.

[37] Daniel M. Butler and Emily Schofield, "Were Newspapers More Interested in Pro-Obama Letters to the Editor in 2008? Evidence from a Field Experiment," *American Politics Research* 38 (2010): 356–71.

[38] Tim Groseclose and Jeffrey Milyo, "A Measure of Media Bias," *Quarterly Journal of Economics* 120 (2005): 1191–237.

[39] Tim Groseclose, *Left Turn: How Liberal Media Bias Distorts the American Mind* (New York: St. Martin's, 2011).

[40] The authors point out that they only studied news content and that the *Journal* maintains a strict separation of news from their overwhelmingly conservative editorial pages. Still, this doesn't explain why it would be the *single most* liberal. They also cite one other study from economics alleging a liberal slant to the *Journal*'s news content, and they cite a poll showing that more Democrats trust the *Journal* than Republicans. However, not only is that an extremely indirect measure of slant, but it could also be explained by the fact that Democrats generally trust the press more than Republicans.

[41] John T. Gasper, "Shifting Ideologies? Reexamining Media Bias," *Quarterly Journal of Political Science* 6 (2011): 85–102.

[42] Brendan Nyhan, "Does the US Media Have a Liberal Bias? A Discussion of Tim Groseclose's *Left Turn: How Liberal Media Bias Distorts the American Mind*," *Perspectives on Politics* 10 (2012): 767–71.

[43] See ch. 1.

[44] Matthew Gentzkow and Jesse M. Shapiro, "What Drives Media Slant? Evidence from U.S. Daily Newspapers," *Econometrica* 78 (2010): 35–71.

[45] Gentzkow and Shapiro, "What Drives Media Slant?," 36–37.

[46] Gentzkow and Shapiro, "What Drives Media Slant?," 45. The authors discuss the Republican strategic framing in making the case that their measure effectively differentiates preferred party phrases.

[47] Daniel E. Ho and Kevin M. Quinn, "Measuring Explicit Political Positions of Media," *Quarterly Journal of Political Science* 3 (2008): 353–77.

[48] See, for example, Kim Fridkin Kahn and Patrick J. Kenney, "The Slant of the News: How Editorial Endorsements Influence Campaign Coverage and Citizens' Views of Candidates," *American Political Science Review* 96 (2002): 381–94. Jeffrey S. Peake, "Presidents and Front-Page News: How America's Newspapers Cover the Bush Administration," *Harvard International Journal of Press/Politics* 12 (2007): 52–70.

[49] Riccardo Puglisi and James M. Snyder Jr., "The Balanced US Press," *Journal of the European Economic Association* 13 (2015): 240–64.

[50] Riccardo Puglisi and James M. Snyder Jr., "Newspaper Coverage of Political Scandals," *Journal of Politics* 73 (2011): 931–50.

CHAPTER 3

How to Evaluate
a Bias Charge

This chapter introduces a comprehensive framework for characterizing and evaluating individual bias accusations. The framework demonstrates the high hurdle that charges must clear before being deemed convincing and shows the most common logical and evidentiary flaws in popular bias charges. By extension, it could also serve as a guide for how to level more intellectually cogent bias charges, to whatever degree bias cops are interested in doing so.

Chapter 2 examined the "universal charge" that the ostensibly neutral, mainstream news organizations favor one side of the political spectrum—over time, across outlets, and irrespective of the subject. The evidence, though varied, generally does not support this claim.

However, the scholarly findings will not end this debate, nor should they. The diverse nature of the findings surely leaves room for reasonable critics to allege bias in specific outlets, during particular time frames, and/or for individual issues. Further, even if every credible study found absolutely no bias anywhere, professional bias cops such as MRC, and the partisan commentators who amplify their assertions, would not simply admit defeat and go home. The talking point is broadly disseminated, widely believed, and effective at dominating popular discussion of the press. Informed consumers of media criticism must therefore be armed with the tools to respond to the talking point in all its varieties.

Also, though most discussions in popular commentary are tacitly linked to the universal charge, they operate on a smaller scale. A typical accusation airing on Fox News or originating from a watchdog group criticizes one news outlet like the *New York Times* or CNN for showing a liberal bias in its coverage of a single person, issue, or event. At most, a charge will cover a whole election or the duration of a scandal.

These individual charges must be held to a high standard. Too often they are spread by sympathetic commentary channels with no regard to their coherence or plausibility. And, though answering every charge with, "But scholars have generally shown no overall bias," would be neither intellectually satisfying nor practically effective, the scholarly findings do demand that individual charges face tough scrutiny.

Bias Charges: Easy to Make but Hard to Get Right

During the summer of 2015, while Republicans engaged in an unprecedented seventeen-candidate melee for their presidential nomination, the national press paid little attention to the Democratic contest. That was convenient for frontrunner Hillary Clinton, who held a commanding lead in all national polls over four relatively unknown challengers.

Despite her desirable position, supporters saw some cause for concern. Democratic senator Bernie Sanders was drawing the largest crowds by far of any candidate, reflecting dissatisfaction among the Democrats' progressive base with Clinton's relatively moderate economic and foreign-policy stances. She was also dogged by several alleged scandals stemming from her tenure as secretary of state, including her handling of the attack on a US consulate in Benghazi, Libya, and her use of a private e-mail server.

On July 16, these concerns came to life in an Associated Press–GfK opinion poll showing a steep drop in her favorability rating. AP's write-up of it, which was reprinted widely in national and local news outlets, was overwhelmingly negative, with the lead paragraphs setting the tone:

> Hillary Rodham Clinton's standing is falling among Democrats, and voters view her as less decisive and inspiring than when she launched her presidential campaign just three months ago, according to a new Associated Press–GfK poll.
>
> The survey offers a series of warning signs for the leading Democratic candidate. Most troubling, perhaps, for her prospects are questions about her compassion for average Americans, a quality that fueled President Barack Obama's two White House victories.
>
> Just 39 percent of all Americans have a favorable view of Clinton, compared to nearly half who say they have a negative opinion of her. That's an eight-point increase in her unfavorable rating from an AP-GfK poll conducted at the end of April.[1]

MMfA decried the negative tone of the AP story.[2] Their biggest complaint was an apparent "double standard," wherein Clinton's bad favorability ratings dominated the story, while the similarly bad ratings of some Republican candidates were "buried in the 18th and final paragraph of the AP's report."

> Bush's favorable ratings, which have been underwater all year, lag behind Clinton's in the latest AP poll (31 percent Bush, 39 percent Clinton) and his unfavorable ratings are on the rise? Correct. But at the AP, there were no warnings about what those "troubling" numbers mean for Bush's campaign, and there were no AP interviews with Republican voters voicing their disappointment in the candidate.
>
> For the AP, Jeb Bush and his soft poll numbers were clearly *not* the story. They barely even garnered a footnote.
>
> Welcome to the often-baffling world of polling reporting for the 2016 campaign, where perceived dips by Clinton are obsessed over by the press while Bush stumbles rarely draw interest.[3]

Meanwhile, MRC had an entirely different take on news coverage of the poll. First, they took no issue with the tone of the AP story. In fact, they quoted it approvingly in setting up their main argument, which is that the three broadcast networks—ABC, CBS, and NBC—showed their liberal bias by not covering the poll.

> On Thursday, all three network morning shows skipped a new poll showing that Hillary Clinton's favorability rating had fallen to 39 percent. . . . Despite such negative ratings for the Democratic frontrunner, NBC's *Today*, ABC's *Good Morning America*, and *CBS This Morning* all ignored the story.
>
> However, both ABC and CBS did find time to tout Clinton's fundraising numbers. On *GMA*, fill-in news anchor Paula Faris gushed: "Hillary Clinton's campaign raised more than $47 million between April and June. That is more than the top six Republican candidates combined."[4]

The competing charges are enough to make a news consumer's head spin. Were the networks guilty of liberal bias by omitting a newsworthy story that made a Democrat look bad? Was the AP guilty of a double standard in criticizing only the Democrat's negative ratings but not the Republicans'? Could both be true simultaneously?

Each argument might look convincing at first glance. And, given that similar bias charges are made every day, it is easy to see how consumers of the commentators that amplify these charges would come to believe that the mainstream press carries a consistent partisan slant. The task here, though, is to move beyond the ideological back-and-forth of cable, radio, and blogs and try to assess whether these charges have merit as genuine media criticism rather than just as partisan talking points.

Start with the most obvious question: How do the watchdogs define "bias" in this case? And, relatedly, what should the media have done to avoid the bias charge? MMfA appeared to want a more balanced story, meaning one that gave equal, or at least less lopsided, coverage to the bad favorability ratings of each party's leading candidates. However, while the article is patently imbalanced, the "double-standard" charge lacks sufficient evidence. It is impossible to determine from only this story whether the AP has a consistent pattern of treating Republicans more favorably or whether the reporters' honest, objective appraisal in this case was that a dominant frontrunner's low favorability rating—as well as low marks on other poll questions regarding honesty, compassion, and decisiveness—amounted to a worthy news hook for a single story.

In contrast, MRC clearly wanted the three broadcast networks to cover this poll. To make a convincing claim that the omission was due to liberal bias, however, they would need to explain why, by objective standards of news selection, it was worthy of a spot in the networks' limited news allotment. The networks cover only a small proportion of commercial polls released during a given campaign, so why was this one so newsworthy that its omission could only be interpreted as favoritism toward Clinton? And why wasn't Bush's equally bad rating newsworthy? By not answering these questions, MRC risks giving the impression that they only wanted Clinton's numbers covered because they make her look bad, which is not exactly a defensible standard for nonpartisan news.

Many more questions can be raised about these—or any—bias charges. Did they analyze the news content in a systematic fashion? Or did they cherry-pick content that best makes their case? Is their subjective perception of bias tainted by their own biases? These questions lead to an inescapable conclusion that any citizen who tries to move beyond partisan shouting and think clearly about bias should quickly reach: partisan-bias charges are easy to make but hard to get right. Any ideologically motivated critic can level a charge—and when enough of them do it over a long time span, they sound convincing. But do they really hold up to scrutiny? The conversation about media bias is in desperate need of a common language and framework, and this chapter provides it, beginning with understanding the concept of media bias.

Defining Bias

As the Clinton poll example shows, defining partisan bias is harder than it sounds. Nonetheless, credible analysis of bias charges must begin with a workable definition. Otherwise, journalists, scholars, critics, and critics of the critics risk talking over each other's heads.

The first task is to define the broader concept of "media bias." A common thread that runs through diverse uses of the term, or its synonyms like "distortion," is that bias occurs when *news content deviates from an ideal.* An ideal is an expectation for how the news product should look in a well-functioning free society. Scholars and critics hold news organizations and their output to a wide variety of standards—far beyond simply whether the press treats both sides equally—and are not shy about documenting the ways in which they fall short, to the detriment of informed deliberation and democracy.

For example, political scientist Lance Bennett identifies several "informational biases" that undermine the news media's ability to "advance the cause of democracy." These include the media's tendency to overdramatize political events and to tell stories in disconnected fragments that fail to show the bigger picture.[5] Scholars and media critics have identified numerous others, and chapter 4 highlights them.

Partisan bias is just one particular type of media bias, albeit the one that gets the most attention. It too involves an observed pattern of news coverage that allegedly violates good journalistic practice. Accordingly, partisan bias occurs when *news content deviates from an ideal, to the benefit of one side of the American political divide.*

At first glance, this definition may appear more complicated than necessary. After all, isn't partisan bias simply the press favoring one party or ideology? Indeed, when critics make the universal charge, they are in fact equating partisan bias with the press favoring one side of the spectrum.

However, commentators and media watchdogs simply are not equipped to provide evidence of a universal slant. Does CBS have a consistent, systematic leftward tilt? Is CNN's entire range of content unwaveringly liberal? Only scholars have the resources and analytical wherewithal to make that judgment—and, as chapter 2 showed, their findings are complicated. Instead, as discussed above, most popular discussions of bias are narrower. While these charges are generally intended as planks in a larger platform—that news content has an overall tilt to one side—they deserve to be evaluated on their own terms.

Importantly, the intuitive definition of partisan bias fails to describe the full range of common charges. It does work for some, such as when an outlet is accused of favoring the Democrat over the Republican in a presidential race. But what about when liberal critics accuse the media of having a conservative slant because they give equal coverage to both sides of the climate-change debate, even though the scientific consensus tilts overwhelmingly to one side? In this specific context, the charge is not that they favor one side; it is that they do *not* favor one side when they *should*. The standard to which critics hold the press here is that, when a contentious issue is underpinned by an observable factual reality (i.e., a clear scientific consensus), journalists are obligated to cover the factual reality rather than the political split. Hence, it is deviation from an ideal, and that deviation benefits one side of the political spectrum—in this case the climate-change deniers whose political power belies their dubious claim to the truth.

Thus, defining partisan bias as when "news content deviates from an ideal, to the benefit of one side of the American political divide," better accommodates the full range of charges.

The Components of a Bias Charge: The I-B-E Framework

As media bias is deviation from an ideal, it follows that an effective bias accusation should provide not only evidence of a shortcoming, but also a standard by which to measure the news content in question. Furthermore, the standard should have two parts: what would constitute unbiased news and why. Accordingly, a fully elaborated partisan-bias charge should take this form, known hereafter as I-B-E:

1. News should [live up to an *ideal*].
2. In this context, that means [*baseline*].
3. However, [*evidence*] shows deviation from the baseline to the benefit of one side.

Here is an example of how this might look in one common arena for bias charges—presidential elections:

1. News should give voters the information necessary to make competent electoral choices.
2. In a presidential election, this means giving the major-party candidates equal coverage.
3. However, a content analysis of 2012 election coverage shows Obama receiving more favorable coverage than Romney.

And here is how it might look for the climate-change example:

1. News should seek the best attainable version of the truth. If there is overwhelming scientific consensus on a politically divisive issue, journalists are obliged to adjudicate the political dispute by emphasizing the science.
2. As climate change carries an overwhelming scientific consensus, the press should not give significant coverage to those who dispute the consensus.
3. However, a content analysis of recent climate-change coverage shows that deniers received almost as much coverage as those who accept the consensus. This gives unwarranted benefit to the conservative side of the political divide.

These model charges contain the three components of a valid bias charge: ideal, baseline, and evidence (I-B-E). Each is discussed in turn. Now obviously, when cable TV or talk-radio commentators fling bias charges at the mainstream media, they seldom phrase them in exactly that form—nor do they need to. Still, a charge worthy of being taken seriously must explicitly state the evidence while providing enough clues about the other components to evaluate their validity. Also, some media critics might argue that the baseline and ideal are so obvious in many cases that articulating them amounts to an unnecessary academic exercise. However, as chapter 2 showed—and further examples here will corroborate—even simple-sounding charges, such as favoring a candidate across an entire presidential election, can fall apart under scrutiny if their baseline and ideal are not carefully thought out.

Ideal

The ideal is a belief about news's proper role in American representative democracy and its public sphere. For a given bias charge, it is the apparent belief about how news *should* look in that context, which in turn serves as the normative underpinning of the baseline. As the ideal is usually left unstated by the charger, this component of a charge may be tough to identify with any specificity. Fortunately, the ideal need not be explicitly articulated by the charger nor identified by an evaluator of the charge. Instead, the evaluator merely needs to infer whether the ideal is nonideological.

A "nonideological" ideal is a belief about how the news media should behave that derives from commonly accepted principles of good journalism. For example, the press should be a watchdog of the government, or it should aim to paint a comprehensive, undistorted picture of the world. While someone using a broad definition of ideology might point out that those too are ideological, the term's use is narrower here, referring only to the same liberal–conservative spectrum that is at issue in bias charges. Chapter 7 further discusses the importance of nonideological ideals and elucidates the criteria for recognizing them.

The gold standard for nonideological ideals is the widely lauded and influential book *The Elements of Journalism* (*Elements* hereafter) by longtime media analysts Bill Kovach and Tom Rosenstiel.[6] The authors show convincingly that American news reporters, editors, and producers subscribe to a set of broadly shared beliefs about the news media's proper function in society—beliefs that predate the nation's founding and are no less relevant in the digital age. The book is anchored around a first principle: "The primary purpose of journalism is to provide citizens with the information they need to be free and self-governing." This alone can serve as an ideal for a bias charge. For example, one could argue that, to give citizens the information they need to make informed choices about an election or a party-polarizing issue, its coverage must be balanced between the two sides.

The "elements" provide specific guidance as to what is expected of journalism in a well-functioning representative democracy. Among the elements most likely to underpin bias charges are the following:

"Journalism's first obligation is to the truth": The authors forcefully defend the notion of truth seeking, at least in its "functional" form whereby journalists must work toward telling the closest attainable version of it.

"The essence of journalism is a discipline of verification": If Democrats and Republicans make conflicting empirical claims, journalists are obligated to adjudicate the claims rather than merely writing a "balanced" story in which each charge is aired.

"Journalists must serve as independent monitors of power": This is essentially the well-known "watchdog" role, modified to include nongovernmental sources of power such as large corporations.

"Journalists must keep the news comprehensive and proportional": The aggregate news product should be like a good map: complete and undistorted. All topics of importance should be aired, and none should be disproportionately privileged simply because they comport with profit-driven news-selection criteria.

While many bias charges are grounded in nonideological elements of journalism, others will betray ideological motivation upon careful analysis. An extreme example of an ideological ideal is the belief that the ostensibly neutral news outlets should favor your side of the political divide. Although prominent bias cops are unlikely to state this openly, some specific charges reveal this assumption upon analysis.

Daily Kos, the flagship liberal community blog with a readership in the millions, makes frequent media-bias charges in its front-page and user-contributed stories. In November 2014, a front-page writer accused ABC of bias against the Democrat in Iowa's Senate race.[7] In that story, the ABC reporter asked three "Walmart moms" about their biggest concerns in the election, and they gave answers such as "the economy," "the price of gas," and "health care." The blogger questioned why the reporter failed to answer those concerns with the "factual realities" of Obama's first six years in office. He then enumerated those "realities" in a long list, taken from a monologue by liberal talk-show host Bill Maher, which included "63 straight months of economic expansion," "a health-care law, Obamacare, that's working and lowering healthcare cost," "Bin Laden is dead," and "unemployment down from 10% to 5.9%." But is that really a comprehensive portrayal of reality? In fact, it reads more like a list of the positive developments under Obama's presidency than an objective journalistic assessment of the state of the union. The latter surely would include equally true items such as stagnant wages, overseas turmoil, and controversy about the success of Obamacare. If this blogger truly thinks that news should convey only selective facts that help Democrats, then he appears to want ABC to favor the Democratic worldview. Hence the ideal is ideological.

There is also a gray area between ideological and nonideological ideals. Some ideals are rooted in values that, while not purely liberal or conservative, overlap one of the sides. For instance, a wide array of press criticism asserts that certain viewpoints—racism, sexism, homophobia, and radical Islam, to name a few—should be treated as deviant and thus should not be legitimized by media exposure. Though most partisans on each side reject all of those viewpoints, complaints about coverage of any given one are far more likely to come from either liberal (racism, sexism, homophobia) or conservative (radical Islam) media critics because of their side's more vocal aversion to those ideas.

As an example of this, MMfA criticized CNN in 2013 for letting "a virulently racist convicted criminal" appear on a news segment to defend George Zimmerman, the Florida man who made national headlines in 2012 after shooting black teenager Trayvon Martin.[8] The complaint was not that CNN failed to balance the guest's views with alternative viewpoints—instead, his *mere presence* on the air is what annoyed MMfA.

The argument that deviant or dangerous voices should be excluded from the news strays from agreed-upon elements of journalism and often takes on an ideological tenor. In this case, while many conservatives likely share the opinion that a properly functioning media should exclude overtly racist sources, liberal critics are far more likely to criticize the press for including them. In fact, the two sides frequently disagree about the scope and even the definition of "racism" in America. Therefore, the MMfA charge against CNN has an ideological tinge to it.

Baseline

The baseline establishes how the coverage would look if it were unbiased, according to the bias charger. A valid accusation must state, or clearly imply, criteria for unbiased coverage in that context. Otherwise, a charge against one or more news stories, with no apparent standard for what would have constituted unbiased coverage, is merely empty rhetoric with no logical heft.

The most common baseline is "balance." This simply means that the coverage in question would have been deemed unbiased by the charger had each side received the same quantity or quality of coverage. A classic example of a balance-baseline charge is when a media outlet is accused of favoring one candidate in a general election. Whether stated explicitly or not, the implication is usually clear that the charger expected balanced coverage between the Democrat and the Republican.

Balance is always the baseline for the universal charge of partisan bias. After all, if the accusation is that the traditional media consistently slant their content to one side across space and time, then this implies that coverage should be balanced. However, the baseline can be more variable for charges of narrower scope.

In fact, nonbalance baselines are surprisingly common. As discussed above, a frequent charge from liberal critics is that news outlets give too much coverage to global warming skeptics—with too much apparently meaning *any*. In their view, unbiased coverage is coverage indexed to the scientific consensus rather than balanced between the two sides of the political controversy.

Nonbalance baselines also appear when the accuser references the treatment of only one side. For example, conservative commentators and watchdogs complained repeatedly that Hillary Clinton's various alleged scandals before her 2016 presidential run were under-covered by the mainstream media. Headlines such as "Study: How the Broadcast Networks Have Deleted Hillary's E-Mail Scandal" and "ABC, CBS Fail to Cover Benghazi Committee's Request for Meeting with Hillary Clinton over E-Mails" were common at MRC throughout 2014 and 2015. There is no call for balance here, as they do not ask for the Republican side to receive equal coverage to Clinton's; nor do they allege a double standard between equivalent scandals, for example, "Clinton's e-mail-storage scandal received only one-fourth the coverage of former Republican secretary of state George Shultz's snail-mail-hoarding scandal."[9]

Of course, a tacit assumption of such charges is that, had Shultz really had such a scandal, it would have received more coverage than Clinton's scandal. But such hypotheticals are obviously impossible to evaluate with real data. Thus, in reality, the baseline here is not balance—it is simply that the Clinton scandal should have received more coverage than it did.

Evidence

The final component is the most straightforward: All bias charges must present concrete evidence of the alleged bias. The evidence consists of either excerpts from one or more stories or summary data from a content analysis of the accused stories.

A typical charge against a single news story will include key passages from the story in question that best illustrate its alleged bias. Helpfully, MRC includes the entire transcript of the story as an addendum to its criticism of it. Charges that cover a wider scope, such as accusations that the press favored one candidate over the course of an election season, either provide excerpts strategically drawn from the accused news content or conduct systematic content analyses of a large volume of news over the relevant time period. The latter is rare among nonscholarly media analysts. Also, for the common charge that the media gave too much or too little coverage to an issue or scandal, the evidence is often culled from a database search of news content. For example, if the three networks are accused of "ignoring" a story over a certain time period, the watchdog groups—some of whom have their own media-monitoring capabilities—will search the entire news product from the networks and determine whether they did in fact ignore it.

How to Evaluate a Bias Charge

The I-B-E framework suggests a series of hurdles that bias charges must clear if they are to be taken seriously as anything more than partisan sniping. Specifically, it yields a number of questions that should be asked of a bias charge to determine its logical and evidentiary robustness.

Recapping the essential points from the framework, a valid bias charge should (1) set a nonideological normative expectation for high-quality news content, (2) derive a clear standard for what would constitute unbiased coverage in that context, and (3) provide social-scientifically valid evidence of the alleged deviation from the standard. The following questions can be used to judge bias charges according to these criteria. The first identifies a basic threshold that charges must clear even to warrant further analysis, and the rest are questions to ask about charges that clear the threshold.

Does the charge accuse ostensibly neutral news content of slanting to one side?

This question has two parts. First, accusations of partisan bias are only worth analyzing if their targets are news outlets that market themselves as being neutral between the two sides of the American political spectrum. Is Fox News biased? Is the Daily Kos blog biased? Of course they are; it's their mission.

MMfA aims most of its fire at Fox News and other openly partisan outlets. When they level a charge such as "Fox News' Sean Hannity Feeds Donald Trump Fake Middle Eastern Refugee Claim from Hoax Website," the complaint is not that Fox is favoring the conservative side but rather that it is playing loose with the facts to do so.[10] Thus, while this may be a legitimate observation about Fox's practices, it is not a partisan-bias charge.

✳The second part is more important: the charge must accuse *news content* of bias. That is, a valid bias charge must make a direct accusation against the actual words or images printed or spoken in one or more news stories. This may sound obvious, but it is actually tough for many partisans to accept.

Critics from the left and right each have a common accusation that sounds plausible to like-minded partisans but that by itself fails as an analyzable bias charge because it doesn't address content. One of the most common pieces of evidence mustered to support liberal-bias charges is the observation that a majority of journalists are liberal. Many surveys over the past few decades have shown that American journalists self-identify as Democratic and liberal at a much higher rate than the public as a whole. Though some recent studies show a majority identifying as independent and moderate—perhaps because they are savvy to the surveyors' attempts to label them as liberal Democrats—the majority of those willing to identify a party or ideology still pick liberal and Democrat. No credible analysis has ever disputed this.

To a typical conservative media critic, this is a slam-dunk case for liberal bias. Surely, liberal reporters do what they can to slant the product toward their worldview. Or, even if they don't slant it consciously, they are only human, and fallible humans simply cannot leave aside their biases and give an untainted journalistic account of the world.

However plausible this sounds, it is an inferential leap from liberal reporters to liberal content. If that leap is warranted empirically, then the liberal slant will indeed appear when the content is measured. But it may not be. Perhaps reporters' biases are kept in check by their own professionalization, or by that of their editors. Or perhaps the tone is set by the owners, who have a large financial stake in not alienating half the potential audience. Indeed, as discussed in chapter 4, anyone familiar with the complex interplay of incentives and constraints that influence news organizations would find the "reporter ideology = news slant" model of newsmaking to be grossly simplistic.

Liberal critics have a radically different view of newsmaking. A recurring theme in the liberal-blogger worldview is that the mainstream media carry a conservative bias—particularly on economic issues—because large multinational corporations own nearly all newspapers and television networks. The heads of such companies—often conservative themselves, but always concerned with the bottom line—are assumed to slant the product toward the conservative issue positions that align with their direct financial stake in the political system, including low taxes, limited regulation, and the ability to spend millions of dollars to lobby or help elect lawmakers.

Indeed, multinational corporate conglomerates own all high-profile national news outlets, with the exception of nonprofit National Public Radio and the Public Broadcasting System. *Columbia Journalism Review*'s website is a helpful tool for following the ever-shifting and consolidating news-ownership landscape, in which a tiny number of companies own a mind-boggling array of news, TV, radio, cable, sports, movie, music, publishing, and entertainment brands.[11] As of now, National Amusements (formerly Viacom) is the majority shareholder in CBS. Comcast has a 51 percent interest in NBC (part of NBCUniversal), with former owner General Electric retaining 49 percent. ABC is owned by multiplatform entertainment behemoth Disney. Time Warner owns CNN, and Rupert Murdoch owns Fox broadcast and cable networks as part of his 21st Century Fox news and entertainment conglomerate. Meanwhile, many major newspapers are owned by a handful of large companies such as Gannett, McClatchy, and Tribune. The *New York Times* is large enough to be its own substantial multinational corporation, and the longtime family owners of the *Washington Post* recently sold it to Jeff Bezos, CEO of Amazon.

However, while the idea of financially interested owners influencing the slant of their own product makes intuitive sense and is not as structurally naive as the "reporter slant = content slant" theory from the right, it is still a major leap of inference. If news outlets do carry a consistent slant toward the parties, candidates, and issue positions most favorable to their bottom lines, this would show up in systematic analyses of their content. While theorizing about the relationship between ownership and content can aid in deriving testable hypotheses, the ownership status, by itself, fails as evidence of biased content. And thus the bloggers and other popular critics who swear that it must be so are falling into the same logical trap as the conservative critics who swear that liberal reporters must be slanting their output.

Incidentally, readers who are not affiliated with either camp may notice the potential for these two theories to cancel each other out. While it is simplistic to say "liberal reporters + conservative corporate incentives = balanced product," what is clear to anyone familiar with the actual operation of newsrooms is that those factors, plus many more, compete in a complex interplay that results in a product whose slant cannot be explained by just one factor.

The bottom line is this: however plausible the linkage between news producers and content, it is still a social-scientifically unacceptable inferential leap to draw conclusions about the content without actually attempting to evaluate it. Thus, a valid bias charge must show evidence of slanted content. Otherwise, it fails to pass this basic threshold and warrants no further analysis. The remaining questions concern content that clears this threshold.

For a Nonbalance Baseline

Balance and nonbalance baselines are fundamentally different and thus must be evaluated using separate criteria. Balance baselines are on firmer ground in many ways because balance is often an intuitively defensible standard for political news. Still, balance-baseline charges face considerable challenges, primarily in proving that balance was appropriate in that context. In contrast, nonbalance baselines run into trouble because they lack such a concrete standard.

The following questions must be asked of a charge without a balance baseline:

Can a baseline be ascertained?

Failure to specify a baseline is fatal to a bias charge. If you cannot tell us how NBC should have covered that scandal, then your accusation against them lacks merit. Although most charges do not explicitly state a baseline in an easy-to-spot manner such as "we believe that unbiased coverage would take the following form . . . ," a bias-charge evaluator should make a good-faith effort to figure out the charger's standard for unbiased coverage.

If the charger simply accuses the coverage of being biased without furnishing any explanation, then the charge is invalid. Though that is rare among prominent bias cops, vague baselines that severely cripple a charge's persuasive power are more common. For example, late in 2014 it was revealed that Republican US House representative Steve Scalise gave a speech to a racist organization. MRC complained that the revelation garnered too much coverage in the *New York Times* and *Washington Post*.[12] No similar Democratic scandal was invoked to give it a balance baseline, so the charge was simply that "a combined 3800 words and three front page stories" constituted "hyperdrive" coverage. In this case, the baseline is inferred to be: coverage should have been less extensive than 3,800 words in the two newspapers. But how much less? And by what standard did they determine that this particular word count was excessive? The lack of guidance given to answer these basic questions leaves the charge without much substance.

Charges that the media ignored an ostensibly important story surface nearly every day from MRC and other bias cops. For example, in October 2014, MRC called out the three broadcast networks for ignoring a controversial statement by Hillary Clinton:

> Speaking at the campaign event, Clinton told the audience: "Don't let anybody tell you that, you know—it's corporations and businesses that create jobs. You know, that old theory, trickle down economics. That has been tried, that has failed." . . . Since then, English-language networks ABC, CBS, and NBC and Spanish-language networks Telemundo and Univision have ignored this story in both their morning and evening newscasts.[13]

With no further elaboration in the charge, the baseline is inferred to be: her statement should have received *some* coverage. As a relatively precise standard, this serves as a better baseline than that of the previous charge. However, the plausibility of the charge comes down to the newsworthiness of Clinton's statement, which is assessed in the next step.

Is the ideal nonideological?

If the baseline is derived from a widely accepted principle of good journalism, then a bias charge demonstrating deviation from it is robust. However, to the degree that the bias charge's coherence depends on an ideologically loaded view of news, the charge is reduced to an ideological assertion, thereby weakening the standing of the charger to claim that the news outlet is doing something wrong.

Returning to the Clinton example, given the assertion that her statement is newsworthy, the strength of the bias charge rests on the question of why it is newsworthy. The only clues in the text of the charge are descriptions of her statement as "off-putting" and "antibusiness." The question then becomes this: What nonideological news-judgment standards would require that such a statement by a future presidential candidate be included in the networks' limited news hole? Being generous to MRC, one could argue that, in order to facilitate informed electoral choices, journalists need to expose all gaffes by leading candidates. However, this seems unrealistic given the wide array of comments that could theoretically be spun as gaffes by the opposition. This comment in particular appears to be more of a boilerplate Democratic talking point, perhaps sloppily worded, than any novel revelation about Clinton that would stand out among the cacophony of political rhetoric. Accordingly, the ideal seems to revert by default to the ideologically loaded notion that the incident should be covered because it makes Clinton look bad. This renders it unconvincing as objective media criticism.

For a Balance Baseline

The second set of questions concerns charges with a balance baseline. They stem from the fact that identification of a coverage imbalance is necessary but not sufficient for proving a balance-baseline charge. The charger must also rule out any obvious alternative explanations for the observed slant that are rooted in either objective reality or nonpartisan news-selection criteria.

Is the necessary equivalence really equivalent?

Balance-baseline charges attempt to demonstrate unequal coverage of entities that deserved equal coverage, such as candidates in a general election. However, the latter part of that formulation—"deserved equal coverage"—often goes unanalyzed. If the subjects of the unbalanced coverage are themselves unbalanced, either in an objectively measurable manner with implications for the quality of the coverage or with respect to the ideal—then the bias charge fails.

For example, a common charge is that a scandal on the charger's side of the political divide received more coverage than a scandal on the other side. For that charge to make sense, however, the under-covered scandal must be as important (or more important), from the perspective of a nonideological ideal such as monitoring power, as the more heavily covered scandal. While sometimes this is easy to demonstrate, scandals of different scope and kind—say, corruption versus sexual misbehavior, or a governor versus a high-ranking federal bureaucrat—quickly become difficult to compare.

This shortcoming can destroy an otherwise valid bias charge in a number of ways. A striking example came in September 2014 when MRC published a study comparing coverage of Obama's low approval numbers to those of his predecessor.[14] They analyzed the three broadcast networks for mentions of each president's approval rating from January 1 to August 31 of their sixth year, finding a dramatically higher rate of mentions for Bush than for Obama. With a balance baseline, an easily justifiable ideal, and a well-designed content analysis, this widely circulated charge seemed plausible at first glance. However, they failed to establish the equivalence of the presidents' approval ratings, thus not ruling out the possibility that the unbalanced coverage resulted from unbalanced ratings.

And indeed, though neither president was over 50 percent, their ratings were quite different in both level and trajectory.[15] Figure 3.1 shows the RealClearPolitics polling averages for each president during the two periods of analysis.[16] Obama's level was nearly always higher than Bush's, sometimes by as much as 10 percent. Also, perhaps more important, Obama's ratings were extremely stable, while Bush's suffered a long fall followed by a recovery. Among other things, this means that the coverage discrepancy might have been attributable to news-selection criteria such as the privileging of novelty and change over continuity rather than favoritism toward Obama.

Can the coverage imbalance be explained by nonpartisan news-selection criteria?

A bias charge essentially accuses a news outlet of using one particular criterion—the partisanship of the story subject(s)—to guide a news-judgment decision. However, political-communication scholars have documented a whole catalog of criteria—most of which can be derived from the media's need to operate frugally, meet deadlines, and gain and maintain a large audience—that influence coverage decisions. While it would be unrealistic to expect an individual bias charger to grapple with all possible explanations for the coverage pattern at issue, a robust charge should at least rule out any obvious alternate explanations. Regular news consumers should already be familiar with basic news-selection attributes—which are discussed in detail in chapter 4—such as

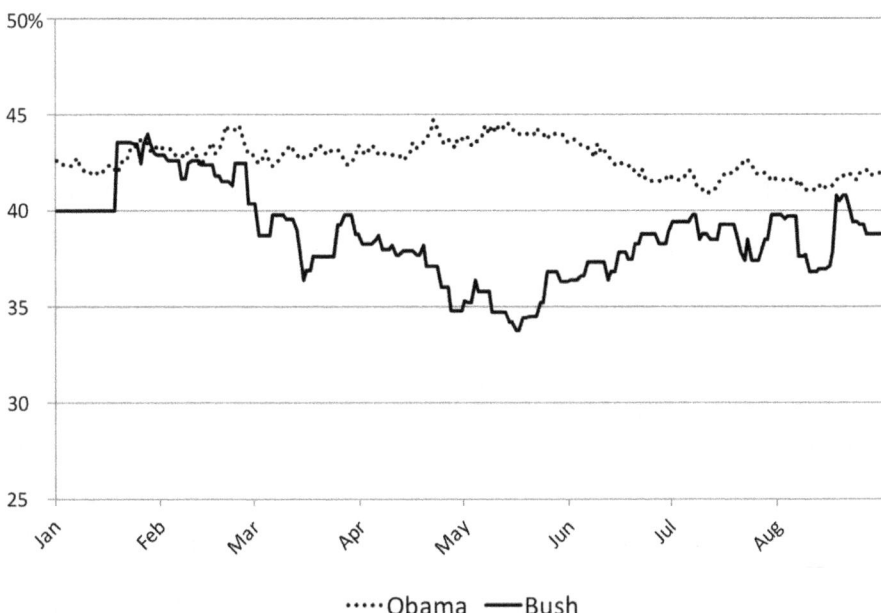

Figure 3.1 Job Approval for Bush and Obama during Their Sixth Year.
Source: Data from RealClearPolitics.

the tendency to cover stories that feature sex, violence, scandal, negativity, simplicity, and novelty, while ignoring equally or more important stories that lack those characteristics.

As an example of the need to rule out other explanations, consider a candidate for a low-profile state or local race who received more coverage than her opponent. Before attributing that to favoritism of her party, a bias charger must ask whether she was more experienced, charismatic, controversial, PR savvy, and so forth in ways that would have resulted in equally disproportionate coverage for a similar candidate of the other party. If the bias charger fails to grapple with that possibility in a relevant situation, it leaves an opening to attack the charge's credibility.

Evaluating the Evidence

For charges with either type of baseline, the evidence needs to be social-scientifically valid. While most bias cops are not social scientists, and thus it is unrealistic to expect peer-review-quality manuscripts to back up a talk-radio quip or watchdog item, it is nonetheless fair to ask whether the charger was reasonably diligent in avoiding the most common inferential errors that plague bias charges.

Does the evidence constitute the universe, or a random sample, of the accused content?

Nonscholarly bias cops are almost never disinterested parties. Rather, bias charges are an important weapon in the rhetorical arsenal of partisan talk-show

Spotlight: CNN's Pervasive Pro-Dog Bias

CNN continued to earn its nickname as the Canine News Network in 2015, as slobbering hydrant humpers enjoyed one glowing story after another, while their feline superiors were mercilessly attacked.

In June CNN ran numerous stories about two escaped fugitives, several of which effusively praised police dogs. In one story, Anderson Cooper's show quoted a local DA: "The dogs are still on the scent. They are working it very hard." Working it hard? Were they shakin' their tails, too?

In October they reached all the way back to World War I to find something nice to say about dogs. In a long feature story, they discussed how "terriers were commonplace in the trenches of the western front. They killed rats by the millions. Many became legendary among the soldiers they protected." Legendary for killing rats? Cats do that for breakfast.

The mainstream media's perennial glorification of guide dogs is bad enough. But CNN compounded the bias in a story about a "hero" guide dog that saved his trainer's life by alerting him to an out-of-control car in the road.

Meanwhile, the cat coverage was predictably negative. In June, a flight instructor in South America made headlines for flying with a cat stuck in the fabric of the plane's wing. Of course they blamed the cat for crawling into it rather than the instructor for failing to check his plane before takeoff.

August brought the bizarre tale of a cat that allegedly held two adult women hostage in their own bedroom. "Mom tells me her daughter went to the bathroom in the middle of the night and the family cat cornered her for hours. When the daughter would move, he would swat shredding up her nightgown." Something tells us there's more to this story—but of course CNN failed to air the cat's perspective.

Correspondent Jeanne Moos even took a cheap shot at cats in an unrelated story about a catfish that attacks pigeons with a 28 percent success rate. "That's better than a real cat could do," she snarled. But what do you expect from a network that continues to employ someone named "Wolf" Blitzer?

hosts and activists—their only weapon in the case of specialized groups such as MRC. While this does not automatically negate the validity of their claims, it does call for careful scrutiny of one aspect in particular.

Individual bias charges mostly present evidence from a single news story. The problem here is that such anecdotes are cherry-picked—that is, they are selected from among the vast universe of news content because they conform to the charger's expectations. Meanwhile, the chargers ignore any anecdotes to the contrary. Even if a charger compiles hundreds or thousands of anecdotes, they still do not add up to systematic analysis. As social scientists are apt to say, the plural of anecdote is not data.

Special Report: CNN Continues to Favor Cats

As any well-informed dog will tell you, CNN's reputation as the Cat News Network is well deserved. A review of its dog and cat coverage in 2015 shows a consistent favoritism of antisocial, allergenic fuzzballs over their lovable rivals.

It was another banner year for overhyping Internet cat videos. In October, correspondent Jeanne Moos took it to a nauseating new level by citing a "study" claiming that "watching those videos was probably good for your health." The findings relied on the dubious premise that such videos are pleasurable to watch.

In October, CNN celebrated the media fiction known as "National Cat Day" with gushing stories, across multiple shows, about the International Cat Video Festival (yes, that's a thing). The story bent over backward to make cat banalities like "the cat and the lamb, the cat trying to catch its tail . . . or cat versus printer" sound interesting.

Meanwhile, the coverage featured its usual share of overblown dog-attack hysteria, such as a December story about a nine-year-old child killed by a dog and a September piece about a pit bull attack in New York, which included the unnecessary detail that the survivor's injuries "were so severe that police gave him his last rites." In March, dogs were portrayed in an unflattering light in a story about the Ferguson, Missouri, police department's misuse of dogs to attack African American citizens.

They even managed to disparage dogs in unrelated stories. In a January debate over a father who lets his baby daughter play with a python, the pro-python guests took gratuitous swipes at dogs: "Last year, 20 children were killed by big dogs . . . 4.6 million people each year in the United States alone are attacked by dogs."

They also continued their offensive use of dog attacks as a metaphor in their political coverage. Before an October Democratic debate, panelists wondered whether Bernie Sanders would play the role of "attack dog" against Hillary Clinton. Also, when Lindsey Graham dropped out of the Republican race, a commentator suggested that "he's going to have a larger role in playing attack dog rather than surrogate for a particular candidate."

Cherry-picking is easy to accomplish in the contemporary media environment. Given the massive amount of daily news output, an interested party could compile anecdotes to demonstrate nearly any pattern imaginable, stringing together a formidable compendium of individual examples until the case seems unimpeachable by sheer volume. This can be difficult for casual consumers of news criticism to detect without stepping back to see the big picture. To illustrate how easy this is to do in our media-saturated environment, two sidebars cherry-pick CNN stories from a single year to make opposite claims about the network's treatment of dogs and cats. The organizations and arguments are contrived, but all CNN stories cited are real.[17]

The small subset of charges that cover an entire election cycle or the life span of a controversial issue usually avoid this problem. For example, charges that claim a topic has been covered too much or too little typically search the entire universe of relevant content to tabulate the total number of stories mentioning the topic.

Is the charge subjective?

"Bias is in the eye of the beholder." This commonsense insight has academic corroboration in the form of the so-called hostile media effect.[18] Researchers have shown repeatedly that partisans on both sides of the political divide are more likely to view the *same news content* as biased against their side.[19] When the "beholder" runs an organization or hosts a talk show known for its bias charges, then obviously they are motivated to find bias in every nook and cranny of mainstream news. This does not mean they are wrong, of course. But it does mean they cannot be trusted to make their own subjective judgments about news slant.

Many charges use objective evidence such as counting the number of times each side is mentioned in a story, and thus such charges can be trusted as long as the chargers are honest and transparent about their data gathering. However, many charges involve subjective assessments of news content. In particular, this describes nearly all charges that a news outlet gave more positively or negatively toned coverage to one side. If the charger fails to outsource these assessments to independent parties with no stake in the outcome, the charge fails—or at the least, it is highly vulnerable to challenges.

Conclusion

Partisan-bias charges are easy to make but hard to get right. The I-B-E framework arms media consumers with the tools to evaluate individual bias charges from any source and any ideological origin. From an offhand remark in a blog's comment section to a large-scale study published in a top academic journal, all accusations of partisan bias in the mainstream press—or, for that matter, assertions of a lack of bias—are subject to scrutiny under the framework.

In short, a valid bias charge should (1) set a nonideological normative expectation (the "ideal") for high-quality news content, (2) derive a clear standard (the "baseline") for what would constitute unbiased coverage in that context, and (3) provide a social-scientifically valid demonstration (the "evidence") of the alleged deviation from the standard. Chargers expecting something other than "balance" in news content must justify the standard to which they are holding the news. Charges using a balance baseline, though avoiding many of the pitfalls of nonbalance charges, nonetheless fail if balance is not an appropriate standard in that context.

Bias charges succumb to many pathologies. Among the most common are that the charge attacks journalists or owners rather than their product, the charger fails to specify a standard, the standard is ideologically loaded and thus is more of a partisan talking point than a valid media criticism, the charger expects balance between unbalanced phenomena, an alleged imbalance can be explained by factors other than media bias, the charger cherry-picks confirming evidence and ignores disconfirming content, or a charger with a vested interest in a particular conclusion makes a subjective assessment of news slant. Consumers of news criticism should also be on the lookout for blatantly dishonest argumentation such as misrepresentation of the accused content. Though rare, even the mainstream bias-watchdog organizations will occasionally stoop to this level. Chapter 5 gives an example.

Partisan bias is simply one type of media bias, and chapters 2 and 3 have demonstrated that the popular obsession with it is largely misplaced. Recognizing this insight is an important but incomplete part of the task of understanding and evaluating media bias. Attention now turns to the "real biases," meaning the deviations from ideal news that (1) have more consistent empirical support in the scholarly literature than partisan bias and (2) arguably undermine the media's ability to inform citizens about politically relevant topics to a greater degree than the effect of an occasional tilt in one ideological direction.

Notes

1 Lisa Lerer and Emily Swanson, "AP-GfK Poll: Clinton's Standing Falls among Democrats," Associated Press, July 16, 2015, accessed July 25, 2015, http://ap-gfkpoll.com/featured/findings-from-our-latest-poll-21.
2 Eric Boehlert, "The Press' Latest Double Standard for Democrats," Media Matters for America, July 20, 2015, accessed July 25, 2015, http://mediamatters.org/blog/2015/07/20/the-press-latest-double-standard-for-democrats/204487.
3 Boehlert, "The Press' Latest Double Standard."
4 Kyle Drennen, "Networks Ignore Hillary Clinton's Favorability Plummeting to 39%," MRC NewsBusters, July 16, 2015, accessed July 25, 2015, http://newsbusters.org/blogs/kyle-drennen/2015/07/16/networks-ignore-hillary-clintons-favorability-plummeting-39.
5 W. Lance Bennett, *News: The Politics of Illusion*, 9th ed. (Boston: Longman, 2012), 45.
6 Kovach and Rosenstiel, *Elements*.
7 Egberto Willies, "ABC News Segment a Classic Illustration of Media Republican Bias," Daily Kos, November 2, 2014, accessed November 10, 2014, http://www.dailykos.com/story/2014/11/02/1341153/-ABC-News-segment-a-classic-illustration-of-media-Republican-bias.
8 Ben Dimiero, "CNN Still Welcomes George Zimmerman's Racist Defender," Media Matters for America, November 22, 2013, accessed July 10, 2015, http://mediamatters.org/blog/2013/11/22/cnn-still-welcomes-george-zimmermans-racist-def/197022.
9 In case it's not obvious, there was no such scandal.
10 Brendan Karet and Tyler Cherry, "Fox News' Sean Hannity Feeds Donald Trump Fake Syrian Refugee Claim from Hoax Website," Media Matters for America, October 27, 2015, accessed November 12, 2015, http://mediamatters.org/research/2015/10/27/fox-news-sean-hannity-feeds-donald-trump-fake-s/206449.
11 "Resources," *Columbia Journalism Review*, accessed February 1, 2016, http://www.cjr.org/resources.
12 Scott Whitlock, "Wash Post, NYT Devote over 3800 Words to Hyping Scalise Scandal," Media Research Center, December 31, 2014, accessed January 5, 2015, http://mrc.org/biasalerts/wash-post-nyt-devote-over-3800-words-hyping-scalise-scandal.
13 Curtis Houck, "Networks Ignore Hillary Clinton's Claim That Businesses Don't Create Jobs," Media Research Center, October 28, 2014, accessed November 12, 2015, http://www.mrc.org/biasalerts/networks-ignore-hillary-clintons-claim-businesses-dont-create-jobs.

[14] Rich Noyes, "MRC Study: TV Buries the Bad News on Obama's Collapsing Polls," MRC NewsBusters, September 8, 2014, accessed July 13, 2015, http://newsbusters.org/blogs/rich-noyes/2014/09/08/mrc-study-tv-buries-bad-news-obamas-collapsing-polls.

[15] To its credit, the conservative blog Hot Air brought up this possibility in its coverage of the charge and even linked to the discrepant poll numbers. Allahpundit, "Study: Nightly Network News Covered Bush's Crumbling Job Approval 124 Times to This Point in Year Six—versus Nine Times for Obama," Hot Air, September 16, 2014, accessed July 13, 2015, http://hotair.com/archives/2014/09/16/study-nighty-network-news-covered-bushs-crumbling-job-approval-124-times-to-this-point-in-year-six-versus-nine-times-for-obama.

[16] "Polls: President Bush Job Approval," RealClearPolitics, accessed October 2, 2014, http://www.realclearpolitics.com/epolls/other/president_bush_job_approval-904.html; "Polls: President Obama Job Approval," RealClearPolitics, accessed October 2, 2014, http://www.realclearpolitics.com/epolls/other/president_obama_job_approval-1044.html.

[17] Stories were selected from a LexisNexis search of CNN broadcast content (web content was excluded) during 2015.

[18] Also known as the hostile media phenomenon.

[19] See, for example, Robert P. Vallone, Lee Ross, and Mark R. Lepper, "The Hostile Media Phenomenon: Biased Perception and Perceptions of Media Bias in Coverage of the Beirut Massacre," *Journal of Personality and Social Psychology* 49 (1985): 577–85; Albert C. Gunther and Kathleen Schmitt, "Mapping Boundaries of the Hostile Media Effect," *Journal of Communication* 54 (2004): 55–70.

CHAPTER 4

The Real Biases

In the dark ages of 2004, before the advent of basic creature comforts such as YouTube and embeddable video, it took significant effort to make something go viral. Yet the video and transcript of *Daily Show* host Jon Stewart's now-legendary appearance on CNN's *Crossfire* "ignite[d] a net frenzy," as one report called it.[1] Within days, the video was downloaded more than 670,000 times from early video-hosting site iFilm, it was shared widely on Bit Torrent systems, and its transcript was the most linked-to content by bloggers.[2]

When the hosts of CNN's long-running arguetainment show—Paul Begala from the left and Tucker Carlson from the right—gave Stewart a platform to promote his new book two weeks before the election, they expected a light-hearted exchange with hilarious one-liners and jabs at the candidates. Given Stewart's fast-growing popularity with young citizens, that by itself might have gone viral. Instead, Stewart used the platform to attack the show's hosts, format, and values, and it broke the pre-breakable Internet.

He set the tone early in his appearance:

> STEWART: I made a special effort to come on the show today, because I have privately, amongst my friends and also in occasional newspapers and television shows, mentioned this show as being bad. . . . And I wanted to—I felt that that wasn't fair and I should come here and tell you that I don't—it's not so much that it's bad, as it's hurting America. . . . So I wanted to come here today and say. . . . Stop. Stop, stop hurting America.[3]

As the flabbergasted hosts failed to steer him back on topic and floundered miserably in attempting to match wits with him, he presented the core of his argument:

> STEWART: See, the thing is, we need your help. Right now, you're helping the politicians and the corporations. And we're left out there to mow our lawns.
>
> BEGALA: By beating up on them? You just said we're too rough on them when they make mistakes.
>
> STEWART: No, no, no, you're not too rough on them. You're part of their strategies. You are partisan, what do you call it, hacks.

During several exchanges, the conservative Carlson made an implied partisan-bias charge by accusing Stewart of being too soft on Democratic candidate John Kerry during his *Daily Show* appearance. Carlson repeatedly hammered this point, only to be humiliated by Stewart:

> STEWART: It's not honest. What you do is not honest. What you do is partisan hackery. And I will tell you why I know it.
>
> CARLSON: You had John Kerry on your show and you sniff his throne and you're accusing us of partisan hackery?
>
> STEWART: Absolutely.
>
> CARLSON: You've got to be kidding me. He comes on and you—
>
> STEWART: You're on CNN. The show that leads into me is puppets making crank phone calls. What is wrong with you?

While few remember that addition to the canon of liberal-bias charges—aside from Stewart's puppet-assisted takedown of it—his attack on *Crossfire* for staging political theater rather than fulfilling its journalistic obligations resonated with many news consumers.

Stewart may have won the battle—a victory that extended to *Crossfire*'s cancellation shortly thereafter—but he is losing the war. Current dinner-hour and prime-time shows on CNN frequently borrow elements from the *Crossfire* template, pitting left versus right in long segments of shouted talking points. In 2016, the dominant format for its general-election coverage featured candidate "surrogates" seated at two long, symmetrically aligned tables, intermingled with network analysts. Sometimes the surrogates calmly recited their talking points in turn, while other times the conversation devolved into chaos. On the August 25 episode of *Erin Burnett OutFront*, a four-minute and six-second segment with six guests featured one minute and forty-one seconds of unintelligible crosstalk in which at least two panelists were speaking simultaneously. Guest host Jim Sciutto lost control of the panel, asserting his authority only when it was time for a commercial break.[4]

Though the two partisan cable networks don't worry about balance, they frequently employ the same shouted-talking-points aesthetic—either just their own talking points or their own shouted loudly enough to drown out the overmatched guest from the other side. Following Stewart, abundant critics have decried these artificial nondebates as falling woefully short of the media's obligation to be an independent monitor of power and to provide useful information to the electorate.

This is just one example of what we might call the "real biases"—the patterns, constraints, and shortcomings plaguing American political news that do far more harm than an occasional slippage to the left or right. They also afflict openly partisan news every bit as much as straight news—and, given that partisan outlets comprise a larger proportion of popular discourse every year, the gap between the importance of partisan bias and the real biases will only expand in the future.

Each of these biases could fill an entire academic book. In fact, many do. However, all of them combined receive far less popular attention than the ubiquitous partisan-bias charge. This chapter briefly reviews some of the most consequential.

A Note on Standards

Thus far a high logical and evidentiary bar has been set for partisan-bias charges, beginning with the definition of media bias as *deviation from an ideal*. Other types of bias charges are, of course, subject to the same scrutiny. As with partisan bias, any accusation that the news product harms democracy or informed discourse must be grounded in a nonideological ideal.

Fortunately, most accusations of press shortcomings highlighted in this chapter flow logically from agreed-upon tenets of journalistic best practices, which is why they carry such cachet among media scholars, critics, and politically aware citizens. It is easy to draw a straight line from the first principle of *The Elements of Journalism*—"The primary purpose of journalism is to provide citizens with the information they need to be free and self-governing"—to the expectations that are disappointed every time cable news turns politics into a trivial spectator sport or ignores an important story in favor of a celebrity scandal.

However, a normative ideal is, by definition, contestable. Any given news consumer or producer is entitled to hold the media to as high or low a standard as desired. If you genuinely do not believe that the press should prioritize useful information over what is perceived to be entertaining, then dramatization and horse-race election coverage are not biases to you.

Even some prominent scholars dissent from the standards set by *Elements* et al. Political scientist John Zaller argued that it is neither realistic nor necessary for news to "provide citizens with the basic information necessary to form and update opinions on all the major issues of the day, including the performance of top officials."[5] Instead, news should act as a "burglar alarm," whereby news consumers should be "alerted to problems requiring attention and otherwise left to private concerns."[6] He also sees the media's tendency to dramatize important events as a feature rather than a bug. After all, a burglar alarm grabs people's attention through "excited and noisy tones."[7]

While acknowledging such differences of opinion, this book ultimately sides with the higher standard. The press is the only industrial sector in America with a constitutional amendment guaranteeing that it can do whatever it wants, within certain limitations such as malicious lying or revealing national-security secrets. With this unique protection comes a heightened obligation to serve the public interest. The First Amendment was not written to protect sports reporting, news helicopters hovering over gruesome car crashes, or celebrity gossip from government interference—and, while no serious critic argues that there is no room at all for soft news, most agree that news organizations worthy of constitutional protection should prioritize citizen informational needs.

The Real Biases

With the exception of NPR and PBS, nearly all major news outlets operate as for-profit businesses, either standing alone or, in most cases, as one holding of a large corporate conglomerate. News production is also an inherently fast-paced undertaking, particularly in the modern twenty-four-hour news cycle where the real-time nature of the Internet exacerbates the already-urgent need to break news quickly.

Most of the real biases flow from these two insights. Like any business, a news organization must keep costs low while generating as much revenue as possible. In fact, merely generating revenue that exceeds expenses, such that the lights stay on and the employees get paid, is insufficient. Keeping the share value of publicly traded companies at an acceptably high level requires steady, long-term growth and profit generation.

This puts pressure on both sides of the ledger. On the cost side, news organizations—even the prestigious national TV outlets owned by multinational, Fortune 500 corporations—are under constant pressure to keep their costs as low as possible, using the minimum resources necessary to fill the airtime and relying on shortcuts whenever possible.

A particularly harmful manifestation of this arose in the 1990s and 2000s when corporate owners attempted to increase their healthy profit margins by cutting expenses, notably personnel. For newspapers, this created a vicious cycle such that a product steadily diminishing in both size and quality was purchased by ever fewer consumers, which in turn forced even more cuts and then an even less desirable product. Although many casual observers blame newspapers' woes on the Internet—stealing their readers and their classified-ad revenue—a careful examination by communication scholar Robert McChesney and journalist John Nichols showed the decline of newspapers to be long and steady, far predating the advent of the Internet, and not timed exclusively to disruptive technological innovations such as cable television.[8]

On the revenue side, news organizations are obsessed with maximizing audience size. Even though direct payments by consumers provide a small portion (newspapers, cable) or even no portion (broadcast) of an outlet's revenue, their ad rates are calibrated to audience size. This is nothing new, of course. At the turn of the twentieth century, newspaper barons fought ruthless circulation wars in the largest cities, turning newspapers into hubs of scandal- and sensation-obsessed "yellow journalism" and setting the eventual template for modern television news.[9] However, competition arising from the unprecedented array of news choices—and, for that matter, ways to entertain ourselves that have nothing to do with news—forces contemporary news producers to shout at the audience to gain its attention above the fray. In the process, they commit many of the biases highlighted here with greater frequency and intensity.

In addition to financial concerns, unavoidable logistic and medium constraints shape the news product in ways that cause it to diverge from ideals. While deadline pressure has plagued American newspapers since the colonial era, Ben Franklin would be shocked by the immediacy of the Internet and twenty-four-hour cable news. When important news breaks, the need to be first tends to trump all other concerns. Even for routine news, the sheer volume required to fill a cable channel or a constantly updated website shrinks the window for necessities such as fact checking and keeps reporting at a relatively shallow depth.

All of those factors conspire—with audience maximization being the chief culprit—to shape the news product through a series of predictable, routine-driven patterns. These patterns often cause a deviation from the ideals of high-quality news, turning them into consequential biases. For our purposes, these biases are broken into three categories: skewed news judgment, limited perspectives, and informational shortcomings.

Skewed News Judgment

In a 2005 online essay, an army lieutenant colonel named Tim Ryan blasted the American news media for its overly negative coverage of the Iraq War.[10] The thoughtful essay, from a voice not usually heard in public debate over war, made him an instant national celebrity. Several national news outlets interviewed him, and talk-radio hosts such as Rush Limbaugh and Michael Savage read the essay on their shows.[11]

Conservative commentators were quick to spin the piece as a scathing attack on the liberal media, but he carefully avoided references to the partisan or ideological slant of the outlets he criticized. Instead, his argument converges with several of the media criticisms highlighted in this chapter. One of his key points involved a telling parallel with local television news:

> Much of the problem is about perspective, putting things in scale and balance. . . . What if you combined all of the negatives to be found in the state of Texas and used them as an indicator of the quality of life for all Texans? Imagine the headlines: "Anti-law Enforcement Elements Spread Robbery, Rape and Murder through Texas Cities." For all intents and purposes, this statement is true for any day of any year in any state. True—yes, accurate—yes, but in context with the greater good taking place—no! After a year or two of headlines like these, more than a few folks back in Texas and the rest of the U.S. probably would be ready to jump off of a building and end it all. So, imagine being an American in Iraq right now.[12]

What if Texas news focused on robbery, rape, and murder? It does! And, while there is no direct evidence that consuming too much local news leads to jumping off buildings, it does cause unwarranted fear of people in one's own community.

In one of the more peculiar puzzles of contemporary American life, citizens became more afraid of violent crime during the 1990s and 2000s, even as the crime rate dropped. Gallup often asks whether there is "more crime in the U.S. than there was a year ago," and in all but two years between 1989 and 2011, a majority of respondents said "yes"—typically by margins of more than fifty points over "no."[13] Meanwhile, the violent crime rate fell during nearly all of those years, until it was less than half of its 1980s levels.[14] It is not a stretch to posit a prominent role for violence-obsessed local television news in explaining this disconnect. Indeed, a multimethod study by three communication scholars provided compelling evidence that fear of crime is correlated with heavy local-news viewership, irrespective of local crime rates.[15]

Just how bad is local television news? In a groundbreaking study, Tom Rosenstiel (of *Elements* fame) and coauthors analyzed thousands of newscasts from 154 stations in the late 1990s and early 2000s.[16] They found a remarkable uniformity of content across media markets. Newscasts have similar structures and topic emphasis, from the largest metropolitan areas down to small, safe, and homogenous cities.

The lead story slot—also the longest on average, at over two minutes—is dominated by murder and mayhem, with "crime, accidents, disasters" comprising more than 60 percent of all stories. Crime continues as the most common topic through the sixth story—about seven to eight minutes into the twenty-two-minute news hole, on average—when "politics/government, social issues, business, defense/foreign affairs" briefly takes its place as the most common topic. A newscast usually ends with soft news.[17]

For those who leave their couches at least occasionally to explore their metropolitan areas, it is easy to see the blatantly distorted picture local news paints of the community. This bias represents a profound deviation from the ideal that news should be comprehensive and proportional.[18] However news quality is defined, it is impossible to square it with local TV news's prioritization of mayhem and its minimal, superficial treatment of consequential civic issues.

At this point, even the most idealistic readers might say, "Though your criticism sounds nice in theory, we all know that local stations are just giving viewers what they want." But this is where the study really shines—it shows that, in fact, this is *not* what viewers want. The authors merged a content analysis of thousands of stories with viewership ratings data. They consistently found that higher-quality news earned higher ratings.

Defining high quality as adherence to the principles of good journalism—such as "covering the whole community," "presenting significant and substantive stories," "demonstrating enterprise and courage," and avoiding excessive sensationalism—their findings debunked several myths about what viewers desire from local news. For one, viewers reward stations for running long stories about substantive issues. They also found that viewers aren't merely voyeurs who want to be "titillated," nor do they watch the newscast with one finger on the remote control waiting to change channels as soon as the topic switches away from flashing sirens and "live from the scene" reports.

The pathologies of local television news, while perhaps more extreme than elsewhere, are not unique to the medium. Cable news fills an exorbitant amount of its news hole with celebrity gossip, scandal, and salacious crime stories. Even crimes involving private citizens can garner sustained prominence on cable news if they contain the right combination of lurid factors. For example, Casey Anthony, the Orlando mother accused of killing her child in 2008, received massive amounts of coverage from 2008 to 2011. Combine sex, violence, celebrity, and one or more hot-button social issues, and you have a perfect storm of newsworthiness, as in the case of the genre-defining O. J. Simpson murder saga of 1994–95. While prestigious newspapers like the *New York Times* attempt to avoid some of these biases, they are susceptible to most of them to varying degrees.

News-Judgment Criteria

Scholars and critics have identified myriad "news-judgment criteria" (NJC)—also known as "news values"—which are the attributes of an event or phenomenon that make it more likely to earn a spot, or a more prominent spot, in an outlet's limited news hole.[19] Although NJCs are not automatically biases, they become biases when they pull news content away from an ideal. So, for instance, if the perception that news needs to be timely causes an outlet to break an important story quickly, such as a rapidly moving fire, thereby giving citizens the information to act on it while the problem is still solvable, then timeliness is not a bias. However, if the rush to be first causes an outlet to get the story wrong, then timeliness has trampled the principle of truthfulness, leading to biased output.

A prominent criterion is bias toward the *negative*, in which bad news often merits more attention than comparable good news. This corresponds with, and is perhaps caused by, the fact that humans are hardwired to pay more attention to negative stimuli in our environment than positive stimuli.[20] That our primary source of social and political information devotes more attention to negative phenomena worsens the asymmetry inherent in our perceptions of the world.

This is seen in a wide variety of contexts. For instance, several studies have shown that bad economic news receives more prominent coverage than equivalent good news.[21] In the medical realm, scholars examined news coverage of two studies published back-to-back in the same issue of the *Journal of the American Medical Association*—one that found a link between radiation and cancer and one that found no link. The study that found a link received far greater coverage than the one that didn't.[22]

Political news has been overtaken by a negative and cynical tone in its day-to-day coverage of elections and governing. "Attack journalism" is now as integral a part of the Washington landscape as appropriation bills and August recesses.[23] The impulses born of the mandate to monitor power, and the alleged audience draw of vitriol and dysfunction, have combined to push coverage of national politics into relentless negativity. The proliferation of openly partisan outlets such as Fox News, MSNBC, and blogs exacerbates this trend, as they pursue alleged wrongdoing—whether bona fide scandals or mere ideological disagreement—with ferocious vigor, as long as it reflects negatively on the other side.

Nowhere is this negativity more pronounced than in scandal coverage. In fairness, covering scandals can obviously serve a crucial function. As any student of history, journalism, or Oscar-winning movies knows, uncovering the Watergate scandal was perhaps the premiere showcase moment for effective watchdog journalism. However, many critics argue that the post-Watergate pendulum has swung too far in the direction of publicizing the private. As a leading textbook notes, "although the U.S. press is entitled to probe the lives and reputations of . . . public persons and the U.S. public has a right to know about matters that are politically relevant, there is widespread agreement that the press is often overzealous in such investigations and destroys reputations needlessly."[24]

Beyond an obsession with scandals, coverage of politics and society is shaped by other NJCs that privilege colorful, visceral, or prurient attributes that are arbitrary with respect to a potential story's importance: sex, violence, disorder, humor, and hot-button social phenomena such as race, just to name a few. To be clear, it's not that disorder, race, etc., are never important—in fact, they play a role in some of the most consequential political issues. However, their status as NJCs means that their presence will always give a potential story a leg up on the competition, regardless of the importance of that story.

A crucial criterion that lends staying power to a topic is whether it can be shoehorned into a dramatic arc. As observant fans of Shakespeare, *Fifty Shades of Grey*, and all known shades of gray in between are aware, most works of dramatic storytelling follow a predictable template: exposition, the introduction of conflict, rising action with (hopefully unpredictable) twists and turns, a climax, and finally a resolution.

News is no different. Potentially newsworthy issues, events, and phenomena vary greatly in their dramatic potential. A useful way to judge a real-world story's dramatic value is by the degree to which it resembles the plot of a single episode or full-season arc of a popular television drama. The quintessential dramatic arc belongs to sensational crime stories that mimic episodes of the dramas that have dominated prime-time television for more than twenty-five years: the various iterations of *Law and Order*, *CSI*, *NCIS*, and so on.

The O. J. Simpson murder saga, though hardly the first crime event to be serialized into sustained news coverage, smashed all previous records for volume and intensity of news attention. It contained nearly every imaginable prurient and sensational component short of a Martian invasion: sex, murder, race, celebrity, sports, corruption, and the like. And the apparent public appetite for it created incentives to chase after every potential new O. J., whether it was celebrity scandals such as Michael Jackson's molestation trial or lurid private-citizen murder trials like Scott Peterson and Casey Anthony.

The bias of television news toward these serial dramas arguably leaves politics under-covered. But it also affects the types of political stories that are able to garner sustained coverage. Parallels with television drama are again instructive.

Dramatic events such as those portrayed in the acclaimed Netflix soap opera *House of Cards* are rare in real politics—but of course high-stakes scandals like the Clinton-Lewinsky affair dominate the news for months or years when they do occur. The closest thing to a popular drama about day-to-day politicking was *The West Wing*, which nonetheless required creator Aaron Sorkin's flowery prose and unrealistically fast-paced action to make appropriation bills seem sexy, and even then there was disproportionate emphasis on conflict and scandal.

Unfortunately, politics is undramatic when it works well. Hence, the types of political phenomena that do fit a dramatic arc receive excessive coverage. Scandals, of course, fit this bill. Battles over budget stalemates and looming government shutdowns do as well, but smooth budgetary processes do not. This bias not only contributes to cynicism and distrust of government; it also represents a narrow, incomplete rendering of the press's watchdog role. As *Elements* argues,

> the press should recognize where powerful institutions are working effectively as well as where they are not. How can the press purport to monitor the powerful if it does not illustrate successes as well as failures? Endless criticisms lose meaning, and the public has no basis for judging good from bad.[25]

Of all the political phenomena that follow a dramatic arc, the one that arguably most deserves sustained coverage is a presidential election. Even so, the length of time during which each election receives saturation coverage and pushes all but the most important nonelection political stories off the news agenda is astounding. Heavy coverage can begin immediately after the midterm election, as it did for the 2008 election, and by the summer before election year it is locked in as the big political story. Other political stories simply cannot compete with an election, with its steady stream of both scheduled mileposts—nomination contests, conventions, debates—and spontaneous newsworthy events.

Other NJCs merit a mention. First, whether fairly or not, the public is perceived as having a short and ever-shrinking attention span. As a result, news must be timely. In the short run, this results in fierce competition to be the first outlet to break a story, often at the expense of accuracy. The long-term consequences are even more damaging, as the need for timeliness means that topics become stale quickly, particularly those that cannot be developed into a dramatic narrative. The most consequential political and social problems are often extremely complex, and the formulation of realistic and palatable solutions may take months, years, or even decades. However, the media seldom allow issues to remain on the public agenda long enough to provide the necessary forum for mobilizing an informed public response.

Closely related is the concept of novelty. The old newsroom adage, "if dog bites man then it's not news, but if man bites dog then it's news," highlights the privileged position held by things new and unusual. Novel events such as a stock-market crash or terrorist attack on the homeland are obviously newsworthy. However, on a day-to-day basis, the prioritization of novelty pulls news away from being comprehensive and proportional, almost by definition, as it exaggerates the dog biters while downplaying the dog-bitten. A common lament in this genre is, "Why does every plane crash make the news, but they never cover any of the millions of flights that land safely?" While uneventful flights fail to constitute news by any reasonable definition, the disproportionate coverage of disasters nonetheless affects public perception of flight safety. The same can be said of the bills that land safely while the media obsess over congressional gridlock and acrimony.

Another NJC is simplicity. Americans are among the busiest people in the world, and few have the luxury of following politics as a vocation or serious hobby. As such, political discussion aimed at a general audience must be kept reasonably simple. This results in complex topics either being left out of the discussion altogether or shoehorned into simple frames like good versus bad, personality conflict, or authorities trying to solve a problem. This makes sense in many regards, as pitching news above the head of its audience would be pointless. However, important topics can be left off the table if news organizations believe they are too complicated for the audience. Oversimplification can also unwittingly benefit one side of an issue if its arguments comport better with journalistic storytelling styles.

Limited Perspectives

The partisan-bias charge captures the public imagination in part because it speaks to the belief that an informed citizenry is only possible if both sides of the major political divide are given a fair opportunity to air their arguments, theories, and preferred facts. Chapter 2 showed that both sides are generally given a fair shake—and even the most fervent bias cop would have trouble making a case that conservative (or liberal) voices are shut out entirely from national nonpartisan outlets, even if their ratios fall short of the desired parity.

However, if we recast the belief more broadly—that a fully informed citizenry is only possible if *the complete array of relevant perspectives* is heard—then a different picture emerges. Looking beyond left versus right toward the diverse cast of stakeholders and viewpoints required for intelligent decision making, the news media fall far short of their ideals for many important political topics. Most of these biases can be subsumed by two key insights with considerable overlap: (1) the scope and tenor of news coverage tends to be calibrated to the range of debate among influential government officials, and (2) ideas must fall within the boundaries of "acceptable" discourse to be taken seriously by the media.

Consensus and Conflict

As political scientist Timothy Cook put it, "the most abiding political bias of the news is, of course, its primary concentration on the events, ideas, preoccupations, strategies, and politics of powerful officials."[26] Among other things, this translates into a tendency to rely heavily on government officials as sources.[27]

Accordingly, top officials with the power to set the policy agenda are also able to set the parameters of political coverage for the allegedly independent press. Political scientist Lance Bennett's "indexing" theory spells this out in a widely cited framework:

> The core principle of the mainstream press system in the United States appears to be this: the mainstream news generally stays within the sphere of official consensus and conflict displayed in the public statements of the key government

officials who manage the policy areas and decision-making processes that make the news. Journalists calibrate the news based on this dynamic power sphere.[28]

This reliance on the power sphere privileges actors with "political power and spin capacity"—typically key White House officials and congressional leaders.[29] Other voices are mostly shut out, even if they carry a crucial alternative perspective that could aid citizen or official decision making.

Indexing was influenced by an earlier theoretical framework. In the 1980s, the nation's wounds from the Vietnam War were still open. Among other things, it was one of the most contentious moments in the history of American press–state relations, with many war supporters in and out of government blaming negative media coverage for the American defeat. Political scientist Daniel Hallin sought to shine a systematic scholarly light on this controversy by studying television-news coverage of the war. His findings upended previous understandings and led to an important theory.

Hallin's content analysis discerned two distinct phases of war coverage. Prior to the 1968 Tet Offensive, national television stories were overwhelmingly favorable to the war. Fewer than 5 percent of all quoted sources were war critics, with representatives of the Johnson administration (26 percent) and American soldiers in the field (49 percent) making up a large majority of the sources. Likewise, journalists' editorial comments were nearly 80 percent favorable to the administration.[30]

The administration appeared to lose control of the message in the wake of the Tet Offensive as the tone shifted. The editorial comments regarding the administration nearly reversed their positive/negative ratio, while war critics jumped to 26 percent of all quoted sources—nearly on par with the administration (28 percent).[31] Does this mean the press shifted from a stenographic lapdog to oppositional watchdog as it soured on the war? Hallin argues no. Instead, a crucial continuity sat under the surface of the apparent shift in tone: a reliance on official sources. Opposition to the war was only taken seriously when government officials pulled it into the realm of acceptable discourse.

Grappling with the tension between the press norms of objectivity and monitoring power led Hallin to his framework for understanding press standards. In it, coverage of a topic can fall into one of three spheres: consensus, legitimate controversy, and deviance. The middle sphere, legitimate controversy, encompasses the topics that divide officeholders and other elites along party or ideological lines.[32] Coverage of these topics endeavors to be balanced, invoking the common rendering of "objectivity" as neutrality and equal treatment of the competing official perspectives.

For issues that fall outside the realm of legitimate controversy, media coverage follows a markedly different model. Opinions shared by both sides of the American divide fall into the sphere of consensus. Here, the media "do not feel compelled either to present opposing views or to remain disinterested observers. On the contrary, the journalist's role is to serve as an advocate or celebrant of consensus values."[33] The third sphere, deviance, describes issues and actors that fall outside the boundaries of acceptable opinion. In this case, the press "plays the role of exposing, condemning, or excluding from the public agenda those who violate or challenge the political consensus."[34]

These aspects of newsmaking violate all sorts of journalistic ideals. First, they can compromise the search for truth. As Bennett and colleagues explain, "the prominence of various perspectives in the news does not have so much to do with whether they are supported by available facts, but whether they have powerful champions, and whether they go unchallenged (or survive challenges) by other powerful players."[35] This turns into a catastrophic bias when journalists fail to call out government officials for lying. Also, monitoring power requires more than simply quoting those who have it and allowing their frames and perspectives to set the boundaries of acceptable debate.

The buildup to the Iraq War serves as a compelling example. While there was elite conflict—a minority of Democrats opposed the Bush administration's months-long campaign for invasion—the opposition was relatively weak and ineffectual. Not only was the country caught up in a patriotic fervor after the attacks of September 11, 2001, making Democrats hesitant to oppose the war, but also the Bush administration was ruthless and effective at controlling the narrative and using the press to tell its story.[36] As a result, even the most respected American news outlets reported the administration's sales pitch uncritically while mostly ignoring opposition from scholars, activists, allied governments, and international organizations. Most infamously, the *New York Times* felt compelled to apologize to its readers in a long editor's note about a year after the war began, after a thorough internal review of its coverage showed a complete failure to question the administration's dubious claims about Iraq's weapons capabilities and ambitions.[37]

False or Manufactured Balance

While critics of the press's indexing habits complain most about perspectives left off the table, a corollary effect of calibrating news to power has been gaining attention recently: actors who possess the skills and resources to take advantage of the media's routines and incentives can earn undeservedly prominent seats at the table.

Around the same time that liberal-bias charges ascended to a deafening level during the 2000s, a different press criticism gained currency among academic and popular-press watchdogs as well as liberal Internet denizens. The essence of the complaint—known by many names, including "he said, she said journalism" and "false equivalence"—is that, in attempting to be balanced between the two sides, journalists were increasingly failing at their primary duty of getting at the truth.[38]

A self-aware newspaper editor once gave this description at an academic symposium: Suppose Democrats say it's raining and Republicans say it isn't raining. The news report will read, "Democrats claim it's raining, while Republicans dispute this"—but at no point will the reporter look out the window to see if it's raining.[39]

This tendency stems from a combination of bias aversion and expediency, as it is both quicker and safer to say, "Democrats say this, Republicans say that; now you decide," than to adjudicate the dispute. It is also aided by the evolving definition of objectivity. When the concept first appeared in newsrooms in the early twentieth century, it referred to a quasi-scientific method of truth seeking. Now, however, it is most commonly conflated with ideas such as "fairness" and "balance," which were never intended to be core principles of journalism.[40] Many contemporary political journalists fear that looking out the window violates the norm of objectivity, when in fact it was key to the original notion of truth seeking.

Critics of global-warming coverage level this charge frequently, complaining that climate-change skeptics are treated as the "other side" of an issue that, were news calibrated to scientific consensus rather than political balance, would not even be a two-sided issue. Although it overlaps conceptually with charges of partisan bias, especially when expressed by liberal commentators or activists, its central critique is a more substantive and evidence-based attack on the media's treatment of the science/politics nexus.

By any reasonable definition of "consensus"—short of an etymologically incorrect conflation of it with "unanimity"—there is overwhelming agreement among credentialed climate scientists that recent human industrial activity has altered the climate in potentially catastrophic ways. Yet, as media-content studies continue to show, the coverage portrays it as a scientific controversy. Environmental scientist Maxwell Boykoff, who has published several studies of climate-change media coverage, finds that "media depictions consistently framed discussions of anthropogenic climate science as contentious, despite the aforementioned consensus."[41] He attributes this to several NJCs, including novelty and dramatization, and also to the norm of balance.[42]

However, as balance is only sought within the sphere of legitimate controversy, how did the climate-change divide become legitimized in the face of a scientific consensus? Science historians Naomi Oreskes and Erik Conway elucidate this process in a book titled *Merchants of Doubt*.[43] They document the considerable resources and coordination required to create the appearance of scientific controversy where there is none as they expose the interested stakeholders such as fossil-fuel producers who are eager to expend the resources to do so. An army of media- and government-savvy think tanks and institutes dispatched scientists-for-hire—nearly always credentialed in fields other than climatology—to dispute the consensus, circulate their own data analysis, and even orchestrate smear campaigns against the most prominent climate scientists. Their actions paid off not only in earning balanced media coverage, but also in thwarting governmental action on environmental regulation through several presidential administrations.

Notably, the authors showed a remarkable parallel between the campaign against climate science and prior corporate-funded campaigns, over the course of several decades, to muddy the scientific waters for issues such as the environmental effects of acid rain, the pesticide DDT, and aerosol-propellant CFCs, as well as the health effects of tobacco. In fact, some of the *same people* have played key roles in these diverse efforts.

In fairness, science reporting is difficult. Perhaps it is a tall order for busy, deadline-constrained journalists, not trained in the technicalities of science, to sort through competing claims and rise above the manufactured controversy. That is what the merchants of doubt count on, of course. And regardless of the cause, the press's failure to adjudicate these disputes in a manner consistent with science's best approximation of the truth represents a severe lapse in the ideals of healthy journalism.

While the intersection of politics and hard science is controversial enough, most political phenomena lack a recognizable expert consensus to which journalists could calibrate their output if so desired. Thus, the question of whether the media should "look out the window" to adjudicate typical political issues is downright perilous. This was never more apparent than during the 2016 general election, when "false balance" suddenly became an urgent talking point among liberal writers and activists. They argued that, in a unique election characterized by profound imbalances between the candidates in qualification, temperament, and truthfulness, the news media were obligated to reflect this imbalance in their output. Chapter 7 explores this controversy.

Informational Shortcomings

The third category of biases encompasses several well-documented patterns in political news coverage that shortchange citizens on the information necessary to be competent democratic participants. Their causes can stem from the norms and constraints of for-profit journalism and from other patterns and biases discussed above.

First, as Bennett explains, the coverage of policy topics tends to be personalized, as news "downplay[s] the big social, economic, or political picture in favor of the human trials, tragedies, and triumphs that sit at the surface of events."[44] This results in a number of patterns, including focusing on the politicians battling over policy issues rather than the issues themselves, and finding heartstring-tugging personal anecdotes to illustrate a story rather than explaining the bigger picture.

A closely related pattern in American news—usually called "fragmentation" or "episodic news"—occurs when social and political topics are covered as isolated events, divorced from any meaningful context that could help citizens accurately understand causes and attribute responsibility.[45]

To see this pattern in action, think about typical crime coverage. Monday: "A man was killed near downtown." Tuesday: "Two people were killed on the south side." Thursday: "A woman was stabbed to death in her apartment." And so on, over weeks, months, and years. Some episodes do become serialized over a long time period if they fit in a dramatic arc, and even the most isolated crime usually receives a follow-up or two upon a suspect's apprehension, trial, verdict, etc. But serialization of a drama is not the same thing as context or explanation.

Missing are the underlying social themes that put the crimes in context and provide citizens useful information, in proper perspective, about criminal justice issues in their community: What causes some individuals to be violent criminals? What causes the violent-crime rate to peak and ebb over time? What are the benefits and drawbacks to various law-enforcement and crime-prevention techniques? How does the justice system work, and is it fair to all citizens? Hype aside, how dangerous are our communities in actuality? These questions mostly fail to penetrate the episode-dominated news product.

It is even worse for political news. According to Bennett, "the news generally comes to us in sketchy, dramatic capsules that make it difficult to see the causes of problems, their historical significance, or the connections across issues."[46] Conflict- and personality-obsessed political news tends to give short shrift to the contextual facts, ideas, and processes that could help citizens navigate the political landscape and aid democratic responsiveness.

Early twentieth-century journalist and writer Walter Lippmann identified this pattern in newspaper coverage of politics nearly one hundred years ago, describing it with an oft-quoted image accompanied by a dreary prognosis for democracy:

> The press is no substitute for institutions. It is like the beam of a searchlight that moves restlessly about, bringing one episode and then another out of darkness into vision. Men cannot do the work of the world by this light alone. They cannot govern society by episodes, incidents, and eruptions.[47]

Although many critics believe Lippmann was too pessimistic, political scientist Shanto Iyengar identified a troubling consequence of the predominance of episodic news. Through a series of studies, he showed that, when television news is framed episodically, viewers tend to attribute responsibility for social problems such as poverty, terrorism, and crime to individual citizens rather than to system-level actors such as political leaders.[48]

The bias toward individual attribution results in a "pro-establishment" tilt to political news. Ideally, citizens evaluate officeholder performance retrospectively, rewarding them for keeping their promises and for positive policy outcomes while punishing them for failures. However, as news fails to give citizens the contextual information necessary to see the connections between policy output and social outcomes, political actors are insulated from accountability. Meanwhile, news viewers blame "lazy poor people" or "deviant criminals" for social ills.[49]

One type of episodic coverage that perennially comes under fire from scholars and news critics is "horse-race coverage" of elections. The complaint—so common now that most news viewers have probably heard it—is that election coverage focuses mostly on the latest twists and turns in the contest: campaign strategies, personnel shake-ups, and, above all, polls. With new polls released constantly—several per day during the late phases of a general election—news organizations have a constant stream of horse-race developments to fill the news hole. Meanwhile, largely missing from the conversation is in-depth discussion of the candidates' policy positions and proposals: What are they? What are their pros and cons? Who benefits and who loses if they are enacted? How realistic are they?

Worse, when policy issues do manage to sneak into the coverage, they are mostly framed in a way that limits their usefulness to citizens. Political scientist Thomas Patterson notes that the press covers issues from either a "game" or "governing" framework, with a heavy bias toward the game.[50] A CNN report from June 2016 illustrates the two frames. Correspondent MJ Lee previewed a Hillary Clinton speech in Denver, beginning with this:

> What Hillary Clinton has been doing over the last few weeks is rolling out specific policy prescriptions, whether it's on foreign policy or the economy, and in just a few minutes she is going to speak at a small-business incubator here in Denver. And according to campaign aides we're going to hear her talk about plans like bringing high-speed Internet to most households by 2020, ensuring that students have access to computer science education; she'll be discussing student loans, ways to give young entrepreneurs a leg up.[51]

Were this narrative to be elaborated with sufficient detail for viewers to form opinions on those topics, this would be the governing frame, which emphasizes policy details and consequences. Instead, Lee not only pivoted to the game frame but actually apologized for the governing preface:

> Now all of this of course sounds a little wonky, but keep in mind that the big-picture strategy here is to draw a contrast between herself and Donald Trump. This is something that we have seen her do over and over again over the last few weeks, and in doing this, Clinton's goal is to paint herself as a serious candidate with a comprehensive policy agenda while making sure that voters know that she believes Donald Trump is temperamentally unfit to be president on almost every front. So we can expect that this kind of rhetoric from Clinton will continue over the next couple of months.

And thus the dominant game frame takes over, in which policy proposals are mere instruments of candidate strategy rather than ideas about how to govern.

The game frame goes well beyond election coverage, dominating stories about policy, politics, and governing even when an election does not loom on the horizon. The next chapter shows evidence of this regarding coverage of the Affordable Care Act.

Conclusion

Media bias occurs when news content deviates from an ideal. Though most popular charges of media bias are of the partisan variety—in which the deviation results in a slant toward one side of the political spectrum—careful observers of the American media have documented a much wider array of deviations that hamper the public's ability to gain the information necessary for competent democratic citizenship. When the daily news-judgment choices of what stories to cover, whose voices to allow in them, and how to present the information become entangled with the for-profit media's need to minimize cost and maximize audience size, the media's role of structuring political information in a complex democratic society gets pushed aside.

This catalog of complaints against the mainstream news media, though far from encyclopedic, might come off as its own form of negativity bias. After all—to co-opt the plane-crash analogy—why focus on the news stories that crash without discussing all of the stories that land safely every day? This criticism would be fair if this book were a systematic attempt to characterize the overall quality of the aggregate news product. However, the topic here is media *bias*, defined as deviation from ideals.

The discussions of partisan bias in chapters 2, 3, 5, and 6 mostly defend the press against the loudest and most damaging charge leveled against it. On the other hand, the "real biases" are indeed real—well documented and sometimes pervasive—and attempts to catalog, measure, and criticize them are a necessary part of understanding the broader challenges to effective democratic citizenship and representation in this increasingly polarized, hostile, and dysfunctional political environment.

The next two chapters document political arenas in which critics are distracted by partisan-bias charges while the real biases take their toll on public discourse. In the case of the Affordable Care Act, news coverage fell short along a number of dimensions. And in the early phases of the 2016 Republican nomination contest, the media played a crucial role in one of the most remarkable political developments of our lifetime.

Notes

[1] Matt Hines, "Jon Stewart 'Crossfire' Feud Ignites Net Frenzy," CNET, accessed March 2, 2016, http://www.cnet.com/news/jon-stewart-crossfire-feud-ignites-net-frenzy.

[2] Hines, "Jon Stewart."

[3] Transcribed from my copy. The video can be found at https://www.youtube.com/watch?v=aFQFB5YpDZE.

[4] I watched the show as it aired and timed the crosstalk from a DVR rewind.

[5] John Zaller, "A New Standard of News Quality: Burglar Alarms for the Monitorial Citizen," *Political Communication* 20 (2003): 110.

[6] Zaller, "A New Standard," 121.

[7] Zaller, "A New Standard," 122.

[8] Robert W. McChesney and John Nichols, *The Death and Life of American Journalism* (Philadelphia: Nation Books, 2010), 30–33.

[9] See, for example, Darrell M. West, *The Rise and Fall of the Media Establishment* (Boston: Bedford/St. Martin's, 2001).

[10] Tim Ryan, "Media Coverage Distorts Iraq Reality," *FrontPage Magazine*, September 21, 2005, accessed March 4, 2016, http://archive.frontpagemag.com/readArticle.aspx?ARTID=7222.

[11] "Western Grad Slams, Attracts National Media Attention in Iraq," Western Carolina University Office of Public Relations, accessed March 4, 2016, http://www.wcu.edu/pubinfo/news/Ryan05.htm.

[12] Ryan, "Media Coverage Distorts."

[13] Lydia Saad, "Most Americans Believe Crime in U.S. Is Worsening," Gallup, October 31, 2011, accessed March 10, 2016, http://www.gallup.com/poll/150464/americans-believe-crime-worsening.aspx.

[14] Saad, "Most Americans Believe."

15 Daniel Romer, Kathleen Hall Jamieson, and Sean Aday, "Television News and the Cultivation of Fear of Crime," *Journal of Communication* 53 (2003): 88–104. For a comprehensive discussion of the link between the news media and crime perception, see Sara Sun Beale, "The News Media's Influence on Criminal Justice Policy: How Market-Driven News Promotes Punitiveness," *William & Mary Law Review* 48 (2006): 397–481.

16 Tom Rosenstiel et al., *We Interrupt This Newscast: How to Improve Local News and Win Ratings, Too* (Cambridge: Cambridge University Press, 2007).

17 Rosenstiel et al., 32–34.

18 See Kovach and Rosenstiel, *Elements*, ch. 9.

19 I prefer the more precise "news-judgment criteria" because the term "values" has many potentially confounding definitions within political science, particularly within the study of public opinion.

20 For a thorough review of the negativity bias literature and its application to political science, see John R. Hibbing, Kevin B. Smith, and John R. Alford, "Differences in Negativity Bias Underlie Variations in Political Ideology," *Behavioral and Brain Sciences* 37 (2014): 297–350.

21 Brian J. Fogarty, "Determining Economic News Coverage," *International Journal of Public Opinion Research* 17 (2005): 149–72; David E. Harrington, "Economic News on Television: The Determinants of Coverage," *Public Opinion Quarterly* 53 (1989): 17–40.

22 Gideon Koren and Naomi Klein, "Bias against Negative Studies in Newspaper Reports of Medical Research," *Journal of the American Medical Association* 266 (1991): 1824–26.

23 Graber and Dunaway, *Mass Media and American Politics*.

24 Graber and Dunaway, *Mass Media and American Politics*, 344.

25 Kovach and Rosenstiel, *Elements*, 174.

26 Timothy E. Cook, *Governing with the News: The News Media as a Political Institution* (Chicago: University of Chicago Press, 1998), 111.

27 See, for example, Leon V. Sigal, *Reporters and Officials: The Organization and Politics of Newsmaking* (Lexington, MA: D.C. Heath, 1973).

28 W. Lance Bennett, Regina G. Lawrence, and Steven Livingston, *When the Press Fails: Political Power and the News Media from Iraq to Katrina* (Chicago: University of Chicago Press, 2007), 49. The theory was originally articulated in W. Lance Bennett, "Toward a Theory of Press-State Relations in the United States," *Journal of Communication* 40 (1990): 103–27.

29 Bennett, Lawrence, and Livingston, *When the Press Fails*, 49.

30 Daniel C. Hallin, "The Media, the War in Vietnam, and Political Support: A Critique of the Thesis of an Oppositional Media," *Journal of Politics* 46 (1984): 8–10.

31 Hallin, "The Media," 8–10.

32 Hallin, "The Media," 21.

33 Daniel C. Hallin, *The "Uncensored War": The Media and Vietnam* (New York: Oxford University Press, 1986), 116–17.

34 Hallin, *The "Uncensored War,"* 117.

35 Bennett, Lawrence, and Livingston, *When the Press Fails*, 50.

36 Bennett, Lawrence, and Livingston, *When the Press Fails*, chs. 1 and 5.

37 "From the Editors; The Times and Iraq," *New York Times*, May 26, 2004, accessed March 14, 2016, http://www.nytimes.com/2004/05/26/world/from-the-editors-the-times-and-iraq.html.

38 One of the most widely circulated forms of this argument was Brent Cunningham, "Re-thinking Objectivity," *Columbia Journalism Review*, July–August 2003, accessed March 14, 2016, http://www.cjr.org/feature/rethinking_objectivity.php. Press scholar and critic Jay Rosen has written extensively about it. For a nice primer, see Jay Rosen, "He Said, She Said Journalism: Lame Formula in the Land of the Active User," PressThink, April 12, 2009, accessed March 14, 2016, http://archive.pressthink.org/2009/04/12/hesaid_shesaid.html.

39 Jack Z. Smith of the *Fort Worth Star-Telegram* conveyed this analogy during a 2003 panel on the Texas Christian University campus.

40 Kovach and Rosenstiel, *Elements*, 103.

41 Maxwell T. Boykoff, "From Convergence to Contention: United States Mass Media Representations of Anthropogenic Climate Change Science," *Transactions of the Institute of British Geographers* 32 (2007): 481.

[42] Maxwell T. Boykoff, *Who Speaks for Climate? Making Sense of Media Reporting on Climate Change* (Cambridge: Cambridge University Press, 2011).

[43] Naomi Oreskes and Erik Conway, *Merchants of Doubt* (New York: Bloomsbury Press, 2010).

[44] Bennett, *News*, 45.

[45] "Fragmentation" comes from Bennett, *News*. "Episodic news" comes from Shanto Iyengar, *Is Anyone Responsible? How Television Frames Political Issues* (Chicago: University of Chicago Press, 1991).

[46] Bennett, *News*, 47.

[47] Walter Lippmann, *Public Opinion* (New York: Free Press Paperbacks, 1922).

[48] Iyengar, *Is Anyone Responsible?*

[49] Iyengar, *Is Anyone Responsible?*, 140–43.

[50] Patterson, *Out of Order*, ch. 2.

[51] Transcribed from DVR rewind, June 28, 2016, 11:01 CDT.

CHAPTER 5

Coverage of the Affordable Care Act

The previous two chapters provided the tools to analyze news content, and criticism thereof, in accordance with the book's two-part thesis: (1) most partisan-bias charges fail to be convincing, while (2) a litany of other biases undermine the quality of political news. This chapter employs these tools to analyze coverage of the Patient Protection and Affordable Care Act (ACA) debate in 2009 and 2010.

Partisan Bias Charges

To no one's surprise, media coverage of the effort to pass health-care reform during Obama's first term garnered many accusations of partisan favoritism. In particular, MRC issued numerous charges—most often against network news—which were summarized in two long reports.

Shortly before the Supreme Court's 2012 ruling on the law, MRC released a long compendium of charges against various news outlets.[1] The tone-setting headline—"Selling Socialism: The Media's Campaign for ObamaCare"—already raises questions about their ideal and baseline. Do they expect the media to parrot factually tenuous Republican talking points such as "socialism"? The second sentence of the narrative further bolsters this concern: "During its coverage of the health care debate, the liberal press never permitted questions about ObamaCare's legality to interfere with their dream of a government takeover of the health care sector." As discussed below, the "government takeover" line is a gross mischaracterization of the ACA that a truth-seeking press should have debunked rather than affirmed. Still, giving MRC the benefit of the doubt and assuming they desired balance between the competing sides, the specific charges deserve a hearing.

They compiled an extensive list of quotes from mainstream news stories, including from MSNBC. Twenty-seven quotes were showcased from ostensibly neutral outlets such as the three broadcast networks and the *New York Times* front page.

Many nits can be picked about the quotes. For example, ABC's Diane Sawyer was called out for equating ACA opponents with "violent thugs" (MRC's description in "Selling Socialism") when she said, "Opponents of the bill have been out today, and some of them pulled out all the stops. Protesters roaming Washington, some of them increasingly emotional, yelling slurs and epithets." First, to equate that description with "violent thugs" is a stretch. Also, while those sympathetic to the protesters may object to terms such as "emotional" and "slurs," this is merely boilerplate language used to describe protesters of all political stripes. While this may be troublesome for other reasons—and indeed, the minimization of citizen-activist voices is a perennial complaint of media critics—no evidence is provided that it disproportionately impacts conservative protesters.

Nitpicks aside, though, the report succumbs to one flagrant flaw: it is nothing more than a cherry-picked list of quotes that purports to add up to systematic bias but instead carries no greater intellectual heft than the dog and cat charges in chapter 3. Each of these quotes could, with little effort, be matched to quotes from the same outlets that tell a different tale, often within the same story. Here are a couple:

On the March 5, 2009, edition of ABC's *World News*, medical editor Tim Johnson—a frequent target of MRC criticism—told anchor Charlie Gibson that he was "blown away by President Obama's grasp of the subject, how he connected the dots, how he answered the questions without any script." By itself, that might suggest affection for Obama and his health-care plan. However, the next quote in the same segment is not so reverent, as a reporter opines on the likelihood of Congress agreeing to raise taxes to pay for the program: "Charlie, it may not be dead on arrival, but it is pretty close. In my reporting across Capitol Hill today, I couldn't find any strong support for the plan. And it is strongly opposed by several key Democrats on the key Senate Finance Committee, including the chairman."

Another target was a *CBS Evening News* story from December 31, 2010. The following is the complete excerpt MRC gave of correspondent Sharyl Attkisson's report:

> Millions of seniors are about to get their first taste of health care reform, and a lot of them will probably like it. For the first time, the 45 million seniors on Medicare can get free annual physicals, no more co-payments. They'll get free screenings for diabetes and cancer. . . . Advocates say most of these first provisions taking effect are quite popular and will be hard for anyone to take away.

That sure sounds like a one-sided focus on the law's benefits, shamelessly glossing over its drawbacks in the name of partisan bias. Or at least it does until you peek at the transcript and see what the ellipses replaced:

> ATTKISSON: There are also less popular provisions. Medicare patients will pay higher premiums for prescription drugs if they make over $85,000. $170,000 for couples. Non-prescription drugs like cold and allergy medicines can't be reimbursed through tax-free flexible spending or health savings accounts. And perhaps the biggest worry . . .
>
> DR. HERBERT PARDES, PRESIDENT AND CEO, NEW YORK PRESBYTERIAN HOSPITAL: I think there's a very real concern about having adequate numbers of Medicare doctors.
>
> ATTKISSON: That could mean long waits to see the doctor.

PARDES: I think they will see delays in the timing of their appointments. I think a number of doctors who have been frustrated because of the Medicare fee level will actually stop taking Medicare. So that's a real worry for all of us.

This example of cherry-picking-through-ellipses is so blatant that it borders on dishonesty. That aside, even the quotes that were not deceptively spliced are still mere anecdotes that fail to add up to convincing evidence of pro-ACA bias.

The other report, published in mid-2009, outlines several complaints against the three networks during the early phase of the ACA debate.[2] It is more thematic than anecdotal, and it even includes a systematic content analysis. Thus, while not immune to the charge of cherry-picking, it is not fatally encumbered by it like the other report. However, a close examination reveals contested or ideologically loaded assertions, as well as patterns that are better explained with nonideological theories of news judgment. While the report contains too many charges to analyze here, three will be highlighted.

First, the report complained that "only 5 percent (11 out of 224) of the health care stories mentioned Medicare and critical remarks were rare." This was suggestive of bias because "Medicare's in ruins," and the "public option" being debated at the time bore similarities to it. Leaving aside the contested assertion that Medicare is "in ruins," this charge is weakened without a baseline. How many stories about the vast, multipronged issue of health-care reform *should have* mentioned Medicare? And why is 5 percent too few?

Another charge was that the networks persistently exaggerated the number of uninsured citizens. "While the Census Bureau said that there are 45.7 million uninsured people (including nearly 10 million non-citizens) in the U.S., network reporters and anchors continue to falsely claim that there are 47 million to 50 million Americans uninsured." While no one would disagree that networks should strive to the get the numbers right, this charge is substantively trivial. Forty-seven million uninsured—or fifty at worst—rather than forty-five million? That sounds more like rounding than ideological malice.

A final charge exemplifies the failure to consider more obvious explanations for the apparent slant. MRC complains about Obama's ability to set the "tone and timing of networks' health care coverage." To bolster this claim, they show a correlation between coverage spikes and key Obama moves such as a prime-time address to Congress and the public. This is wholly unconvincing as a partisan-bias charge, given the well-documented power of all presidents to sway the national conversation. In fact, a more interesting task would be to find an instance when a president's most important actions on his signature legislative priority did *not* cause a coverage spike.

As for their systematic content analysis, the main takeaway was that "in 224 stories on ABC, CBS and NBC, the networks favored proponents to critics by a margin of more than 2-to-1 (243 to 104)." This is a serious, data-backed charge that merits careful consideration. However, it is weakened by the uncritical use of a balance baseline.

To illustrate this point—and in the process produce a more thorough accounting of network sourcing—I asked a research assistant to categorize every outside source quoted or paraphrased in every broadcast-network evening news show from January 2009 through the bill's passage into law in March 2010. Although we avoided subjective assessments of tone, the unambiguous partisan affiliation of most sources lends insight into the coverage tilt. The unit of analysis was a "statement," meaning each uninterrupted direct quote or distinct paraphrase—thus, there could be more than one statement from a given source in a story. While this is not an exact replication of MRC's study, it yields similar enough findings to facilitate a discussion of baselines.

Table 5.1 separates the sources by partisanship/ideology and by phases of the ACA process: the introductory phase (January–May 2009), the beginning of congressional debate (June–July), the contentious town halls and continued debate (August–September), the long slog toward adoption (October 2009–February 2010), and finally the intense burst of action before adoption (March).

TABLE 5.1 Ideological Distribution of Outside Sources on Network Evening News, ACA Coverage, January 2009–March 2010

	Jan–May 09	Jun–Jul 09	Aug–Sep 09	Oct 09–Feb 10	Mar 10	Total
Obama administration	69	192	265	214	149	**889**
House Democrat	5	23	60	46	123	**257**
House Republican	6	12	37	51	53	**159**
Senate Democrat	11	28	109	134	1	**283**
Senate Republican	15	25	50	112	36	**238**
State Democrat	1	0	7	12	1	**21**
State Republican	1	6	7	17	4	**35**
Other liberal	0	4	26	8	14	**52**
Other conservative	5	3	30	9	32	**79**
Total liberal	86	247	467	414	288	**1,502**
Total conservative	27	46	124	189	125	**511**
Total liberal (minus Obama administration)	17	55	202	200	139	**613**

Source: LexisNexis search.

Altogether, Democratic/liberal sources outnumbered Republican/conservative sources by a ratio of 3 to 1, which is even more lopsided than MRC's analysis of the earliest period. The Democratic dominance varies a bit by time period, but not enough to glean any consequential trends. The most important contributor to the imbalance is the dominance of President Obama, White House spokespersons, and members of the executive branch, which are combined into the "Obama administration" category.

The crucial question here is whether a balance baseline is appropriate. In one sense, it is easy to justify normatively: coverage of a closely divided and polarizing policy controversy should feature equal voices from both sides. But there is also the empirical question of whether a lack of balance might be explained by factors other than favoritism toward that side of the issue and/or the party pushing it.

In this case, a clear alternative explanation can be constructed, beginning with a crucial question: When a new administration—whose party also controls both houses of Congress—pushes its top legislative priority and the opposition party offers no explicit alternative, is it realistic to expect a balanced source count? As with the conundrum of finding a baseline for election coverage (see chapter 2), this is nearly impossible to answer without examining an equivalent issue with the shoe on the other partisan foot.

President George W. Bush's attempt to reform Social Security in 2005 is probably the closest recent equivalent, and it can serve as the mirror-image issue for comparison (in the mold of Niven's "comparable performance" design—see chapter 2). While differing in some important ways, it shares enough attributes with Obama's health-care reform to serve as the other side's equivalent issue. Both presidents enjoyed a relatively high approval rating at the beginning of their terms, they each had majorities in both congressional chambers, and they both decided to spend their political capital on a major reform proposal. Also, while unified against the reform plans, the opposition party offered almost no concrete alternatives. They did, however, rally citizens and allied groups to try to stop the reform.

As for the most important differences between the issues, all of them arguably should have generated better coverage for the pro-ACA side than the pro–Social Security reform side: Bush was entering his second term and was less popular than Obama. Bush also had a tougher task because, while nearly everyone believed that the health-care system was broken, Social Security is one of the most popular government programs ever. Most important, the ACA eventually passed, while Bush's effort—failing to secure key support from his own party—fizzled. So, if the source count nonetheless tilted in Republicans' favor, then that would be strong evidence that a key presidential initiative under unified government cannot realistically expect balanced sourcing.

And indeed, the pro–Social Security reform side enjoyed even more lopsided coverage than the pro-ACA side. Table 5.2 presents the results in a similar format to the ACA results. The coverage is divided into three phases: Bush's introduction of the reform effort prior to and during his inauguration (January 2005), his national tour to promote reform (February), and the slow unraveling

TABLE 5.2   **Ideological Distribution of Outside Sources on Network Evening News, Social Security Reform Coverage, January–August 2005**

	Jan 05	Feb 05	Mar–Aug 05	Total
Bush administration	48	77	100	225
House Democrat	4	8	12	24
House Republican	8	14	9	31
Senate Democrat	4	15	19	38
Senate Republican	3	12	22	37
Other liberal	5	17	10	32
Other conservative	5	16	13	34
Total liberal	13	40	41	94
Total conservative	64	119	144	327
Total conservative (minus Bush administration)	16	42	44	102

Source: LexisNexis search.

of the effort (March–August). Though the reform was mostly dead by summer, the content analysis extends through the week before Hurricane Katrina.

The Bush administration utterly dominated the partisan voices, comprising an even higher proportion than the Obama administration during the ACA effort. As with the ACA, the congressional and nongovernmental voices were reasonably balanced between the two sides. The conclusion is inescapable: a balance baseline is not appropriate for comparing source counts for a single issue because of the pervasive official-sources bias; thus, MRC's critique of ACA coverage is, at best, unconvincing.

The Real Biases

CNN seemed well prepared on the morning of June 28, 2012, as the US Supreme Court handed down its opinion on the constitutionality of the ACA.

For the task of producing immediate and stylish news, they had all the bases covered, with veteran Wolf Blitzer at the anchor desk, producer Bill Mears inside the Court chambers, rising star Kate Bolduan reporting from the steps of the Court, and longtime analysts John King and Dr. Sanjay Gupta providing commentary on the political and medical implications, respectively. The one thing they forgot to bring was whatever combination of expertise, patience, and judgment is required not to look foolish while the whole world watched.

At 10:07 a.m. eastern time, Blitzer interrupted King to let Bolduan deliver the breaking news:

BOLDUAN: This is our first reading. We're still going through the opinion, but I want to bring in the breaking news that according to producer Bill Mears, the individual mandate is not a valid exercise of the commerce clause. So it appears as if the Supreme Court justices have struck down the individual mandate, the centerpiece of the health care legislation.[3]

King joined the conversation, engaging in speculative banter such as this remark at 10:09:

So the justices have just gutted, Wolf, the centerpiece provision of the Obama health care law. The question now is, what else do they say in this ruling and can parts of the law be salvaged? . . . Without a doubt, the individual mandate, which has been the polarizing centerpiece of the political and policy debate over health care, the justices throwing that out is a direct blow to the president of the United States, a direct blow to his Democratic Party.

At 10:10 Gupta chimed in on the implications of the ruling, speaking for a little over a minute before Blitzer interrupted him to bring some uncertainty into the mix:

GUPTA: It's a very big deal here, Wolf, this particular of the 450 provisions, this one obviously was the centerpiece on which so many of those other ones were riding.

BLITZER: Yes, if in fact that's the final word on the individual mandate. It could be a little bit more complicated. John King, you're getting some more information as well. We're watching all of this unfold. We're still trying to dissect what this additional report we're getting from inside the Supreme Court means.

KING: Wolf, that is the key point in the details. If they rule the mandate part unconstitutional, if the federal government has that authority, what about the other provisions?

Can it stand as a taxing provision so we'll get—the headline from the court tells us one thing, but we have to get deeper into the decision to find out whether they left all or part.

The "headline from the court" remark—as if the justices teased journalists with a click-bait-style headline that didn't match the opinion—foreshadowed the next couple of minutes, during which Blitzer tried to spin CNN's uncertainty as some sort of dynamic battle occurring within the Court chamber. This was at 10:13:

BLITZER: Yes. As we say, there's some confusion out there, conflicting reports coming in from inside the Supreme Court. . . . Initial suggestion that perhaps the mandate, the individual mandate not a valid exercise of the commerce clause of the Constitution, but now there are, now there are other reports saying perhaps the tax that would be imposed on those who refuse to purchase health insurance, but could get—

We're now getting more information. I just want to update our viewers. The chief justice John Roberts, saying potentially, potentially the individual mandate could be upheld as a tax, but we're getting some conflicting information on what leads up to that. So let's take a deep breath and let's see what the justices actually decide. All of this unfolding, if you're watching Twitter, you can get some of the confusion as well because we're getting widely different assessments of what the United States Supreme Court has decided.

By that time, though, the "confusion" on Twitter consisted mostly of tweets like "CNN, you're wrong! The mandate was upheld." In fact, if one knew where to look, there was no confusion at all. SCOTUSblog—a website founded by longtime Supreme Court litigator Tom Goldstein—live-blogs and tweets Supreme Court decisions in real time. Their pathway to an accurate account of the decision was much less circuitous than CNN's:

10:07 Amy Howe: We have health care opinion.
10:08 Amy Howe: Parsing it ASAP.
10:08 Amy Howe: The individual mandate survives as a tax.
10:08 Amy Howe: It's very complicated, so we're still figuring it out.
10:09 Tom: So the mandate is constitutional. Chief Justice Roberts joins the left of the court.[4]

No "breaking news" sound effects or banter between well-dressed correspondents—they simply sat down, read it quickly, and reported what it said. Meanwhile, a full six minutes after Howe's pithy and wholly accurate summary, CNN descended into self-parody:

BOLDUAN: Well, I've got to tell you. This is a very confusing, very large opinion. But I want to make sure we are very clear on the second read, we found here, and I'm going to read you the exact line. Chief Justice John Roberts delivered the opinion of the court with respect to part 3, that is the individual mandate, concluding that the individual mandate may be upheld as within Congress' power under the taxing clause. . . . As you can see this is very thick and we're reading through it. It's very legally dense. I'm going right back to it to find out about the rest of it.

The juxtaposition of the two accounts is telling. While surely CNN was aware of SCOTUSblog and its excellent track record, their insistence on not only being first but also getting there through the fruits of their own high-production-value spectacle caused them to rely on their staff's tenuous expertise rather than the publicly accessible expert commentary.

As a side note, Fox News—while also blowing the call initially—corrected course more quickly, with Megyn Kelly chiming in at 10:09: "Wait, we're getting conflicting information. If you follow SCOTUSblog.com, which covers the high court, they say that . . . the individual mandate is surviving as a tax."

One might argue that this error, while embarrassing, is relatively trivial in the context of media bias. After all, CNN got the story right within eight minutes. However, this was no ordinary story. High-stakes breaking news is the Super Bowl for cable networks, and choking for "only" the first eight minutes is no more a consolation for them than it would be for a quarterback who did so in the real Super Bowl. So many of cable news's pathologies can be explained, at least in part, by the privileging of immediacy—and it is especially disappointing when they fail to get it right during those rare instances when vital breaking news unfolds at a predetermined moment for which they can prepare.

It was also a fitting capstone to the mainstream media's coverage of the ACA, which failed to satisfy the public's informational needs by succumbing to several of the "real biases" afflicting political news. The rest of this chapter exposes them.

Official Dominance

While it would be tough to set an agreed-upon baseline for what would constitute a normatively satisfying mix of sources, it seems reasonable to expect that government officials should not dominate the source count. Although the legislation's progress through Congress is newsworthy, especially during the critical steps along the bill's journey toward law, partisan warriors in Congress and the White House are among the least plausible sources of credible information about the substance of the complex legislation. Any actual informational content in their strategic spin is purely coincidental, as neither side has a material or political interest in disseminating neutral assessments of the benefits and costs of the debated options. Also, as the plural of "deceptive spin" is not "knowledge," getting it from both sides isn't helpful either. In contrast, independent experts, while never entirely free from ideology, at least have an incentive to provide useful information. Research institutes like Brookings and especially the Kaiser Family Foundation are well regarded for their thorough and informative analysis of health-care policy.

To show the degree of official domination, the findings from the ACA content analysis (described above) are presented in table 5.3, this time with the two sides combined and the rest of the categories added. This shows all sources used in every network evening-news story from January 2009 through March 2010.

In total, government officials comprised 65.7 percent of the sources cited in network stories. Congress and the Obama administration had similar shares, which together accounted for most of the government sources. The rest were mostly state governors and legislators.

The dearth of experts is striking. This category was defined generously, including think tanks (ideological or otherwise), research institutes, and any academically affiliated source—in other words, people with some claim to subject expertise. These voices are sorely needed to provide informational signal above the partisan noise. Yet such experts were only 6.1 percent of the sources, never amounting to even 10 percent during any of the time periods. This adds up to one quote—usually one sentence long—every two and a half days, or one every seven and a half days per network. By no reasonable account is this enough volume to enable informed decision making. Remarkably, the Kaiser Family Foundation was quoted a mere five times during the entire process, and Brookings fared only slightly better with nine. Only twenty-eight quotes came from academic experts.

TABLE 5.3 **Outside Sources on Network Evening News, ACA Coverage, January 2009–March 2010**

		Jan–May 09	Jun–Jul 09	Aug–Sep 09	Oct 09–Feb 10	Mar 10	Total
Government		61.9 (117)	73.4 (290)	54.3 (553)	69.7 (589)	78.1 (368)	**65.7 (1917)**
	Obama administration	36.5 (69)	48.6 (192)	26.0 (265)	25.3 (214)	31.6 (149)	**30.5 (889)**
	Congress	19.6 (37)	22.3 (88)	25.1 (256)	40.6 (343)	45.2 (213)	**32.1 (937)**
	Other	5.8 (11)	2.5 (10)	3.1 (32)	3.8 (32)	1.3 (6)	**3.1 (91)**
Stakeholders		28.6 (54)	21.8 (86)	33.9 (345)	21.8 (184)	9.1 (43)	**24.4 (712)**
	Doctors	3.7 (7)	5.6 (22)	2.5 (25)	3.6 (30)	1.1 (5)	**3.1 (89)**
	Citizens	9.5 (18)	10.9 (43)	28.3 (288)	14.1 (119)	5.9 (28)	**17.0 (496)**
	Other	15.3 (29)	5.3 (21)	3.1 (32)	4.1 (35)	2.1 (10)	**4.4 (127)**
Experts		3.7 (7)	4.3 (17)	8.7 (89)	6.5 (55)	1.9 (9)	**6.1 (177)**
Other		5.8 (11)	0.5 (2)	3.0 (31)	2.0 (17)	10.8 (51)	**3.8 (112)**
	Interest groups	2.1 (4)	0.5 (2)	3.0 (31)	1.3 (11)	9.8 (46)	**3.2 (94)**
	Media	3.7 (7)	0.0 (0)	0.0 (0)	0.7 (6)	1.1 (5)	**0.6 (18)**
Total		**100 (189)**	**100 (395)**	**100 (1,018)**	**100 (845)**	**100 (471)**	**100 (2,918)**

Source: LexisNexis search.

The stakeholder category is divided into citizens, medical doctors, and all others. "Citizens" are sources with no health-care expertise identified in the story and no apparent stake other than as individual consumers, and they are typically quoted for their person-on-the-street opinions or anecdotes. The "other" category includes sources identified as being affiliated with insurance, health-care provision, and health administration and law. Ordinary citizens dominated this category and garnered 17 percent of the total mentions. They reached nearly 30 percent during the August–September 2009 period, which featured heavy coverage of the contentious town-hall meetings held by many members of Congress during the August recess.

Just two sets of actors—government officials and ordinary citizens—add up to 82.7 percent of the source mentions. This coverage duopoly of strategic actors and the mostly uninformed recipients of their spin leaves little room for information that could help viewers make sense of the issue. The official dominance is neither unexpected nor hard to explain. The citizen numbers might seem surprisingly high, but they comport with NJCs in important ways.

The August town-hall meetings were loud, contentious, and often unruly. As members of Congress of both parties went home to explain the tenets of the proposed legislation, they were met with angry constituents—catalyzed by conservative media and organized by newly formed Tea Party organizations—who wanted answers regarding rumors about tax increases, care rationing, and other allegedly pernicious features of the reform. The persistent shouting, which even led to a couple of minor physical altercations, made for great television spectacle. In August, town-hall attendees were quoted 148 times on the networks, which is almost as much attention as all experts combined received during the entire period of analysis.

Personalization

Beyond the August melees, citizens also found their way into news via personalization, as anecdotes often introduced or added color to stories. Of the 348 non-town-hall mentions of individual citizens, ninety-seven of them referenced the person's insurance status (forty-one uninsured, fifty-six insured but worried about changes in coverage and rates). Individuals in various stages of illness served as a popular peg as well.

While introducing a story with a representative anecdote can serve a useful narrative function, such vignettes are seldom developed into informative stories. As Lance Bennett points out, "American news often stops at the character development stage . . . and leaves the larger lessons and social significances, if there are any, to the imagination of the audience."[5] Also, even if the quoted citizens are not cherry-picked to confirm the reporters' preconceptions about public opinion—and in many cases they probably are—they introduce an inescapable skew to the array of opinions heard, as they surely are not representative of either public opinion as a whole or of activists.

Personalization took an additional, more idiosyncratic twist in the years following the law's passage. The ACA itself was personalized when the law was given the nickname "Obamacare" by its opponents, who hoped to mobilize opposition by associating it with the president they loathed. Journalists, while generally calling it the "health-care law" or "Affordable Care Act" in their own voices, let opponents use the nickname uncritically until it became wedded to the law.

While Obamacare was not the first policy to take a president's name in public discourse—"Reaganomics" was a common descriptor of the fortieth president's economic program—it was perhaps the strangest and is thus a particularly apt example of why personalization can be a bias. Reaganomics described a general economic philosophy—consisting of policy preferences such as tax cuts and spending reduction—espoused from the bully pulpit of the presidency. It never became synonymous with any one bill or law. As a summary descriptor of Reagan's economic priorities, and the bills he pushed to make them happen, it made sense.

Obamacare, on the other hand, was one specific bill/law. Its crafting was a massive undertaking involving many authors—and, importantly, Obama was never central to it. Though it reflected some of the broad principles he advocated in the campaign, he consciously put congressional Democrats—who initially thought they would garner Republican cooperation—in charge of the details. For many good reasons, Social Security is not called Roosecurity, nor is NAFTA called Clintrade. In this light, Obamacare was surely an odd coinage, born of hostility to a president who took a backseat in its crafting.

Yet, with the media's acquiescence, Obamacare slowly took over as a dominant moniker. Figure 5.1 shows the number of monthly mentions of the terms "ACA" (or "Affordable Care Act"), "Obamacare," and "health-care law" on CNN from late 2009, when the bill began being referred to by name, through the end of Obama's first term. The "health-care law" trend peaked and ebbed with real events in the law's early life span and thus serves as a good baseline for the other terms. The biggest burst, of course, was March 2010 when the law passed. Two other large bursts came in 2012 when the Supreme Court heard oral arguments regarding the individual mandate (March) and then upheld it (June).

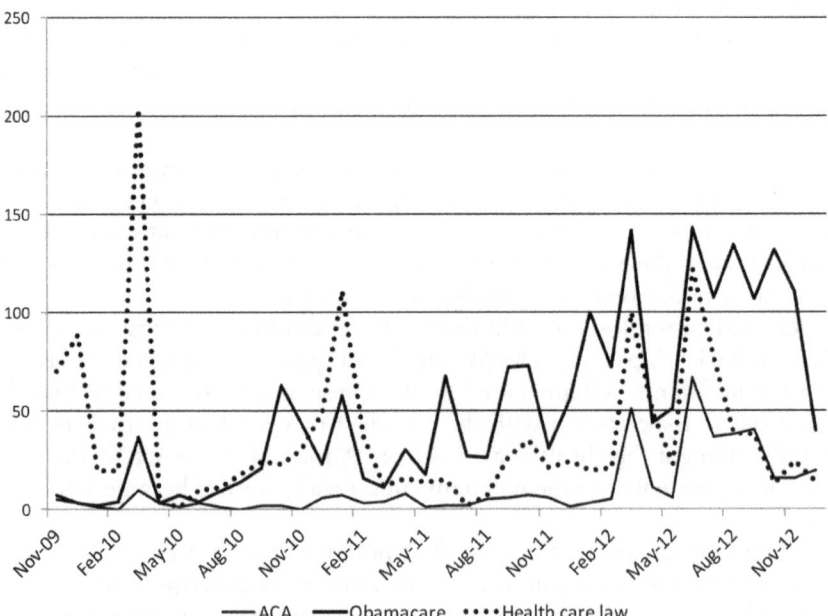

Figure 5.1 Monthly Count of Health-Reform Names on CNN, November 2009–December 2012.
Source: LexisNexis search.

The "Affordable Care Act"—perhaps a mouthful for broadcast, though it came with a concise acronym—languished in obscurity until the two Court-related bursts in 2012. By contrast, "Obamacare" slowly gained cachet until it consistently towered above the others. Unlike the other two terms, its usage did not let up after the June decision. This is easy to explain: Republicans made repeal of the law a centerpiece of their 2012 presidential and congressional campaigns. The effectiveness of this strategic oppositional tactic, coupled with a lack of pushback on the moniker from the other side, introduced an element of unintentional slant to the coverage.

Substantive Coverage: Sparse and Sketchy

Given the officials/citizens source duopoly on network television, it is difficult to imagine that the coverage left much room for substantive policy discussion. Indeed, studies confirm an emphasis on the "game," at the expense of policy specifics, across multiple outlets. Pew studied ACA coverage in more than fifty news outlets across broadcast and cable television, radio, newspapers, and the Internet from June 2009 through March 2010:

> Most of the coverage of the health care reform bill focused on the politics as opposed to reporting on what the bill would do or the state of health care. Fully 49% of the coverage focused on politics and strategy, as well as the legislative process. Less than a quarter of the coverage (23%) outlined what the various proposals would do, and 9% of the coverage focused on the state of the health care system in the U.S.[6]

The study also contained a finding relevant to the question of partisan bias: ACA opponents appeared to win the "messaging war," in that concepts and terms preferred by opponents were much more likely to appear in news stories than those favored by supporters. For example, the three most common concepts pushed by opponents—"more government involvement," "more taxes with health-care reform," "and rationing health care"—appeared a combined 18,181 times. Supporters' concepts—"more competition," "insuring preexisting conditions," and "greedy insurance industry"—appeared only 10,883 times.[7] This alone is not conclusive evidence of anti-ACA bias, as it may instead reflect the better messaging coordination of opponents or the relative simplicity of their "big government is bad" frames. However, it certainly throws further complications into any story of alleged liberal bias.

Another well-placed concept of note was the idea that the ACA included "death panels." The Pew study found 2,500 appearances of this phrase, nearly all after Sarah Palin popularized it in an August 2009 Facebook post:[8]

> And who will suffer the most when they ration care? The sick, the elderly, and the disabled, of course. The America I know and love is not one in which my parents or my baby with Down Syndrome will have to stand in front of Obama's "death panel" so his bureaucrats can decide, based on a subjective judgment of their "level of productivity in society," whether they are worthy of health care. Such a system is downright evil.[9]

This preposterous statement, which fact checker PolitiFact deemed a "pants on fire" falsehood, entered the ACA canon with the aid of the media. Many news reports were critical of it, but they nonetheless amplified its utterances to the point that it appeared in news stories about five times as often as references to greedy insurance companies.[10] And of course right-leaning partisan media were eager to disseminate it, which had an effect beyond their core audience. Communication scholar Patrick Meirick used survey data to show that non-Republicans who watched Fox News were more likely to believe the death-panels lie than those who didn't.[11]

Speaking of falsehoods, another concept favored by ACA opponents penetrated mainstream media coverage thoroughly without much resistance: the idea that Obamacare constituted a "government takeover" of the health-care sector. The talking point—introduced into the Republican vocabulary by consultant and spinmeister Frank Luntz—was anointed PolitiFact's "lie of the year" for 2010. Although the ACA added new regulations of health provision and especially of insurance, nothing in it moved America's mostly free-market system substantially in the direction of single-payer (government-run) insurance or government-owned health-care providers, which are common throughout the world.

PolitiFact found a lack of adjudication of this claim. "In most transcripts we examined, Republican leaders used the phrase without being challenged by interviewers. For example, during [Representative John] Boehner's Jan. 31 appearance on *Meet the Press*, Boehner said it five times. But not once was he challenged about it."[12]

Conclusion

As with any high-stakes, polarizing issue, media coverage of the ACA debate was bound to attract partisan-bias charges. But those charges not only fail to withstand scrutiny, they also distract from more serious complaints about the character of coverage. The media's obsession with the political game and its key players left little room for educating citizen stakeholders about the bill and its passage into law.

And this mattered. Several studies showed pervasive ignorance and misunderstanding of the most important provisions as they were taking effect. For example, a 2014 survey by the Urban Institute's Health Policy Center asked respondents whether they had heard of various ACA provisions.[13] Only a small majority knew of the most heavily touted features—the elimination of exclusion for preexisting conditions and the ability of dependents to stay on insurance until age twenty-six—and far fewer were familiar with other crucial features such as the ability to obtain preventive care without co-payments (30 percent). Also, the least knowledgeable respondents predominated in the demographic groups most likely to benefit from the provisions, such as lower-income and uninsured individuals.

Blame for this cannot be placed solely in the news media's lap, as citizen knowledge about a law as complex as the ACA will inevitably vary. Still, as the press is the only source of policy information for most citizens, it is reasonable to surmise that its failure to take that job seriously has negative repercussions for citizen knowledge. For example, one of the many drawbacks of game-oriented coverage is that it reduces citizens to mere spectators of ostensibly participatory democracy.[14] This becomes especially detrimental when the participation (or lack thereof) is related to crucial quality-of-life issues such as knowing whether one is eligible for perks like subsidized insurance and free preventative care.

The next chapter illustrates the consequences of the media's inability to tame complexity in another consequential arena: presidential nomination contests.

Appendix

ACA Study

A research assistant and I collaborated on a codebook that put all outside sources used in broadcast-network coverage of the ACA into an exhaustive and mutually exclusive set of categories. Even though the coding decisions were relatively objective, we trained until I was confident that the coding would attain nearly unanimous agreement regarding the consolidated subcategories presented in the findings.

The universe of content studied was composed of all stories on the *CBS Evening News*, *NBC Nightly News*, and ABC's *World News*, during all of 2009 and 2010, that mentioned the effort to reform the US health-care system. April–December 2010 was not used in the analysis.

The stories were found on LexisNexis through the following search query:

BODY(healthcare OR health care) AND BODY(Obamacare OR Affordable Care Act OR legislation OR reform)

All returned stories were read, and those with no relevance to the topic were discarded. The rest were coded in accordance with the codebook.

The recording unit was described as follows:

For a direct quote: record each statement enclosed in quotation marks. If a quote is interrupted by nonquotation text or a paragraph break and then resumed, the second quote is a separate entry.

For an indirect quote: record each statement that contains an attribution to a source. If a source is referred to more than once within a story, each reference should be recorded separately.

A "statement" is a direct quote or paraphrase unambiguously attributed to the source. If a source fits more than one category (e.g., a former senator who is now in the cabinet), use the one identified in the story. If more than one is identified, use the current (or most recent) one.

Social Security Study

We modified the codebook to reflect the relevant categories for Bush's attempt to reform Social Security in 2005. For example, "Obama" was changed to

"Bush," and health-care stakeholders were replaced with those relevant to Social Security.

The procedure was the same as for the ACA study, except that the search window was January–August 2005, and the LexisNexis search term was BODY(Social Security).

Notes

1 Geoffrey Dickens, "Selling Socialism: The Media's Campaign for ObamaCare," Media Research Center, March 20, 2012, accessed May 6, 2016, http://www.mrc.org/media-reality-check/selling-socialism-medias-campaign-obamacare.

2 "Uncritical Condition," MRC Business, November 4, 2010, accessed May 6, 2016, http://www.mrc.org/special-reports/uncritical-condition.

3 Transcribed from my recorded copy of the video.

4 Kali Borkoski, "Live Blog of the Health Care Decision (Sponsored by Bloomberg Law)," SCOTUSblog, June 28, 2012, accessed May 4, 2016, http://www.scotusblog.com/2012/06/live-blog-of-the-health-care-decision-sponsored-by-bloomberg-law.

5 Bennett, *News*, 45.

6 "What Americans Learned from the Media about the Health Care Debate," Pew Research Center: Journalism & Media Staff, June 19, 2012, accessed June 12, 2016, http://www.journalism.org/2012/06/19/how-media-has-covered-health-care-debate.

7 "What Americans Learned." They used expansive search terms to ensure that they captured all appearances of the concepts.

8 "Six Things to Know about Health Care Coverage," Pew Research Center: Journalism & Media Staff, June 21, 2010, accessed June 12, 2016, http://www.journalism.org/2010/06/21/six-things-know-about-health-care-coverage.

9 Angie Drobnic Holan, "Sarah Palin Falsely Claims Barack Obama Runs a 'Death Panel,'" PolitiFact, August 10, 2009, accessed June 14, 2016, http://www.politifact.com/truth-o-meter/statements/2009/aug/10/sarah-palin/sarah-palin-barack-obama-death-panel.

10 "What Americans Learned."

11 Patrick C. Meirick, "Motivated Misperception? Party, Education, Partisan News, and Belief in 'Death Panels,'" *Journalism & Mass Communication Quarterly* 90 (2012): 39–57.

12 Bill Adair and Angie Drobnic Holan, "PolitiFact's Lie of the Year: 'A Government Takeover of Health Care,'" PolitiFact, December 16, 2010, accessed June 15, 2016, http://www.politifact.com/truth-o-meter/article/2010/dec/16/lie-year-government-takeover-health-care.

13 Sharon K. Long and Dana Goin, "Most Adults Are Not Aware of Health Reform's Coverage Provisions," Urban Institute Health Policy Center: Health Reform Monitoring Survey, February 6, 2014, accessed July 25, 2016, http://hrms.urban.org/briefs/awareness-of-provision.html.

14 See Patterson, *Out of Order*, ch. 2.

CHAPTER 6

The Media and the 2016 Republican Nomination

No, no, you're not too rough on [presidential candidates].
You're part of their strategies.

—Jon Stewart to CNN *Crossfire* hosts, October 15, 2004[1]

I thought by this time I'd have forty to fifty million dollars spent,
and I've spent very little because I haven't had to, because
people like you put me on all the time.

—Donald Trump to *Meet the Press* host Chuck Todd, February 7, 2016[2]

Although most 2016 election postmortems focus on President Trump's surprising general-election victory, in many ways his capture of the Republican nomination is the real historical anomaly. This chapter examines the media's role in it.

A presidential nomination contest, lacking the distraction of worries about balance and party favoritism, is an optimal venue for exposing the real biases plaguing political news. In the remarkable 2015–16 nomination process, these biases played a starring role and probably helped shape the outcome. As previous chapters have shown, however, professional bias cops are capable of finding partisan bias in any corner of the media/politics nexus, and this nomination season was no exception. Our attention thus turns there first.

On October 28, 2015, business-themed cable-news network CNBC hosted the third debate of the 2016 Republican nomination contest. The first two Republican debates had been the most viewed primary debates ever for Fox and CNN, respectively, and conventional wisdom attributed their massive appeal to the bombastic, confrontational style of celebrity candidate Trump. Perhaps hoping to provoke viral-ready fights between the candidates, the moderators of the CNBC debate relied heavily on combative questions about their records and character.

Unfortunately for the moderators, what they actually provoked were viral-ready bias charges. When Florida senator Marco Rubio was asked about a newspaper editorial urging him to resign from office, he blasted it as "evidence of the bias that exists in the American media today." Later, after Trump criticized the other candidates' reliance on super-PACs, Rubio said, "I know the Democrats have the ultimate super-PAC—it's called the mainstream media."

Empowered by the candidates' high-profile, real-time call out of the mainstream media, the conservative commentary sphere exploded in righteous rage over the moderators' questions and dug deep into its bank of dramatic rhetoric to describe the alleged injustice. Rush Limbaugh called the debate a "kill show" that was "designed to take them all out" and "grease the skids for Hillary Clinton."[3] Sean Hannity called it "the single worst example of media bias in a debate in, like, intergalactic history."[4]

Among the questions that generated the most backlash were the following:

- Mr. Trump, you've done very well in this campaign so far by promising to build a wall and make another country pay for it, send eleven million people out of the country, cut taxes $10 trillion without increasing the deficit, and make Americans better off because your greatness would replace the stupidity and incompetence of others. Let's be honest. Is this a comic-book version of a presidential campaign?

- Dr. Carson, let's talk about taxes. You have a flat-tax plan of 10 percent flat taxes, and—I've looked at it—and this is something that is very appealing to a lot of voters, but I've had a really tough time trying to make the math work on this. . . . So what analysis got you to the point where you think this will work?

- This one is for Senator Rubio. You've been a young man in a hurry ever since you won your first election in your twenties. You've had a big accomplishment in the Senate, an immigration bill providing a path to citizenship the conservatives in your party hate, and even you don't support anymore. Now, you're skipping more votes than any senator to run for president. Why not slow down, get a few more things done first or at least finish what you start?

The partisan-bias charges tended to take one of two forms, one with a balance baseline and one without. Neither withstands scrutiny.

On the first count, many commentators criticized what they perceived as overly negative and confrontational questions from the three moderators, which they attributed to partisan bias. MRC even attempted to quantify the degree of negativity, analyzing the tone of each question to conclude, "Nearly two-thirds of [unique questions posed by one of the three moderators] included negative spin, personal insult or attack."[5]

Without a balance baseline, a reader is left guessing to what standard the critics are holding the moderators. In fact, liberal commentators wondered whether Republicans expected the moderators to coddle the candidates and act as conduits for their spin rather than asking tough questions. Indeed, a movement spread through conservative social media to demand that the Republican National Committee let talk-radio hosts such as Limbaugh, Hannity, and Mark Levin moderate a debate after Texas senator Ted Cruz suggested it in an interview. Requesting that hyperpartisan commentators moderate a debate is perhaps the best example of an ideological ideal in, like, intergalactic history.

Still, let's give critics the benefit of the doubt and assume that their main objection to the moderators' tone was that it deviated from the nonideological ideal of culling information from the candidates that would promote informed decision making by the Republican electorate. The charge still fails because, without a balance baseline, there is no logical connection between negativity and partisan bias. What if the moderators of Democratic debates were equally negative? Then, irrespective of whatever criticisms can be leveled at the moderators for deviating from an ideal, the deviation did not systematically favor one side.

The second form of the charge solves this problem, at least in theory. Many conservative critics used a balance baseline to attack the CNBC Republican debate, alleging a discrepancy between its negative tone and the tone of the first Democratic debate, hosted earlier that month by CNN and moderated by anchor Anderson Cooper. Cruz leveled this charge during the debate, decrying "the contrast with the Democratic debate, where every fawning question from the media was, 'Which of you is more handsome and why?'" Conservative commentators echoed this after the debate. For example, while interviewing candidate Chris Christie, who complained of a "total double standard," Hannity characterized CNN's questions to Democrats as "What's your favorite color? What's your favorite dog name? What's your favorite cat name?"[6]

Were there evidence to support this charge, it would be on more solid ground than the nonbalance version, as critics now have a clear and noncontroversial standard: treat the sides equally. But, alas, it is wrong.

To counter cherry-picking with cherry-picking for a moment, even a cursory glance at the transcript of CNN's Democratic debate refutes Cruz's claim that every question was "fawning." Here are a few:

* Secretary Clinton, I want to start with you. Plenty of politicians evolve on issues, but even some Democrats believe you change your positions based on political expediency. You were against same-sex marriage. Now you're for it. You defended President Obama's immigration policies. Now you say they're too harsh. You supported his trade deal dozens of times. You even called it the "gold standard." Now, suddenly, last week, you're against it. Will you say anything to get elected?
* Senator Sanders, a Gallup poll says half the country would not put a socialist in the White House. You call yourself a democratic socialist. How can any kind of socialist win a general election in the United States?
* The Republican attack ad against you in a general election—it writes itself. You supported the Sandinistas in Nicaragua. You honeymooned in the Soviet Union. And just this weekend, you said you're not a capitalist. Doesn't that ad write itself?

It would require industrial-strength partisan-tinted goggles to see those as any less negative than the most-complained-about Republican questions. Still, perhaps a higher proportion of the Republican questions were negative or combative.

To ascertain the actual degree of imbalance, I asked two research assistants to replicate MRC's analysis and then apply exactly the same criteria to

CNN's Democratic debate. The technical details of the study—including how it obtained the social-science requirement of "intercoder reliability" (evidence of adequate training and a sufficiently clear standard)—are in the appendix.

First, recall that MRC found twenty-eight of the forty-three questions (65 percent) in the CNBC Republican debate to contain "negative spin, personal insult or attack." The student coders found that twenty-seven of the questions (63 percent) fit those criteria, a close enough match to MRC's study to allow reasonable confidence that we replicated it successfully.

So, how did Anderson Cooper's questioning of the Democrats compare in its propensity toward negative spin, personal insult, or attack? Fifty-five distinct moderator questions were identified from that debate, and the students coded thirty-six of them as negative. This is 65 percent, roughly the same as the students' (63 percent) and MRC's (65 percent) negative scores for the CNBC Republican debate.

Thus, the balance-baseline, "double-standard" charge levied by many prominent commentators and politicians was simply false—and the loudest partisan-bias charge of the year was utterly lacking an empirical foundation.

The Real Biases

Although the alleged partisan bias in the CNBC debate got the usual partisan wheels turning, Cruz leveled by far the most impactful media criticism of the evening, earning boisterous applause, countless social-media shares, and the most favorable reaction ever from a Fox News focus group.[7] Responding to moderator Carl Quintanilla's tough question, he said,

> You know, let me say something at the outset. The questions that have been asked so far in this debate illustrate why the American people don't trust the media. This is not a cage match. And, you look at the questions: Donald Trump, are you a comic-book villain? Ben Carson, can you do math? John Kasich, will you insult two people over here? Marco Rubio, why don't you resign? Jeb Bush, why have your numbers fallen? How about talking about the substantive issues the people care about?[8]

In addition to providing a clever pretext for describing his opponents' weaknesses, Cruz's complaint about the lack of substance in debates resonated widely with citizens and critics. It was cited approvingly by mainstream observers, including Politico, and even many liberals expressed reluctant agreement with the far-right senator. Comedian Patton Oswalt tweeted, "I hate Ted Cruz with the power of a million chainsaws revving but I agree with everything he just said," while a Daily Kos front-page writer posted a piece headlined, "Ted Cruz got one thing right at the Republican Debate."[9]

The broader appeal of Cruz's remark parallels his Senate colleague Al Franken's quip likening the partisan-bias controversy to worrying about whether al Qaeda uses too much oil in its hummus. While Cruz did take a full serving of hummus later in his remarks by leveling a partisan-bias charge, his bipartisan viral moment—the cry for "talking about the substantive issues people care about"—echoes complaints from critics on all sides about how election news is trying to kill us, or at least kill informed vote choice in presidential nomination contests.

Thoughtful critics have warned for years that the nomination process could lead to disaster. Whether the 2016 Republican nomination was a "disaster" depends in part on one's view of President Trump and his relationship to the Republican Party. In so many ways, though, it unambiguously showcases the worst nightmares of anyone who expects the media to structure presidential nominations in an intelligible fashion. The rest of this chapter argues the following: The traditional news media, with its "real biases" cranked up to maximum settings, gave Trump a wildly disproportionate amount of coverage during the months in which they should have been helping the electorate vet the large field of Republican candidates. This likely helped him win the nomination. The story begins with parties, their nominations, and the media's role in the process.

The Party Usually Decides

Amid the chaos of debates, ads, rallies, polls, contests, and the breathless media coverage that accompanies all of it, a basic political-science truth is often lost: presidential nomination contests are *party functions*. They are not intrinsically electoral or democratic. Importantly, a party is far more than just the plurality of its electorate won by the nominee. A party is a multifaceted entity that combines three components: party in government (PIG), meaning the officeholders governing under the party label; party organization (PO), or the staff and resources of national, state, and local parties; and party in the electorate (PIE).[10] In fact, PIE is the most fluid and nebulous facet of a party, as its boundaries are impossible to delineate precisely. Should independents be part of a party's decision-making process? What about citizens who only weakly identify with the party and have no interest in, or knowledge of, the process?

Accordingly, for most of American history, the parties' marquee function of presidential-nominee selection gave no meaningful role to the mass electorate. Prior to the twentieth century, state parties chose their national convention delegates through state conventions. Even when states started holding primaries during the Progressive Era of the early twentieth century, most were nonbinding "beauty contests" used only to aid, rather than dictate, the party's decision making in proverbial (and literal) "smoke-filled rooms." After the disastrous 1968 Democratic convention—at which Vice President Hubert Humphrey won the nomination despite not running in a single primary, leading to protests that turned violent—the parties reformed their processes to give PIE a larger role.

Unfortunately, reformers ended up giving citizens a far too cognitively demanding task. In a general election, voters typically choose between only two major candidates, who are on opposite sides of nearly every hot issue. If nothing else, they can vote their party identification. However, nominations often involve a large candidate field, with many of them having identical positions on most or all hot issues. Even the most sophisticated voters struggle to parse the subtle distinctions among the candidates' views, and it is a lost cause for the average voter. Thus an external force will invariably fill the power vacuum and hold inordinate sway over primary voters.

Many scholars believe that party insiders serve as this force through numerous mechanisms for structuring the process and its outcomes. By controlling the rules of delegate allocation and contest type and order, helping to steer top staff and donors to preferred candidates, and endorsing their favorites before crucial primaries, state and national officeholders and other party elites exercise tremendous power over the outcome. A leading theory of party nominations, espoused in a book titled *The Party Decides*, argues convincingly that Republican insiders—defined broadly to include officeholders, party elders, and even "policy demanders" such as interest groups and citizen activists—have generally gotten their way in postreform nominations.[11]

However, the news media have always sat under the surface as an underappreciated force, waiting to be unleashed under the right circumstances. One scholar warned us about this more than twenty years ago.

Even More Out of Order

In 1993, political scientist Thomas Patterson published a widely acclaimed, now-classic critique of election coverage titled *Out of Order*. He blasted the patterns and practices of mainstream presidential-election coverage for a variety of sins, saving his toughest critique for their handling of nomination contests in a chapter called "The Miscast Institution." The institution, of course, is the news media, and they have been cast in the role of providing citizens with the information needed to play their part in postreform nominations:

> The de facto premise of today's nominating system is that the media will direct the voters toward a clear understanding of what is at stake in choosing one candidate rather than another. Whereas the general election acquires stability from the competition between the parties, the nominating stage is relatively undefined. It features self-starting candidates, all of whom clamor for public attention. . . . It is this confusing situation that the press is expected to clarify.[12]

Unfortunately, they do more muddling than clarifying—hence the "miscast." To serve the public's informational needs in a nomination contest, the media's norms and incentives would need to align with those of the party and the electorate. At the least, this would require detailed, substantive discussions of the policy differences between the candidates. But the media have only one incentive: to earn advertising revenue by telling good stories.

Patterson noted several consequences for the quality of information in nomination coverage. First, the media's obsession with trivia and their attention to the finest contours of public opinion render nominations volatile and impulsive. "With relatively small changes in luck, timing, or circumstance, several nominating races might have turned out differently."[13] Also, the overwhelming tendency toward horse-race and strategic-game coverage (see chapter 4) leaves voters with little useful information for making policy-relevant distinctions between the candidates.[14] Additionally, news-judgment criteria such as novelty and conflict create an emphasis on "issues" that reporters think are important for attracting eyeballs—such as gaffes, scandals, and food fights—rather than the issues about which attentive citizens care.[15]

If *Out of Order* were given a sequel, it could be called *Even More Out of Order.* Not only have its theses held up despite the ever-changing media landscape, but its insights are more accurate than ever. Recent nomination cycles have seen their share of the various media pathologies featured in Patterson's critique. An infamous gaffe during the 2004 Democratic contest aptly illustrates the media's tortured role in the process, in part because the gaffe itself was a media-technology artifact.

Late in 2003, former Vermont governor Howard Dean surged to the front of the Democratic pack on the strength of his opposition to the Iraq War and a groundbreaking Internet-based campaign. On January 19, 2004, however, he finished a surprising third in the Iowa Caucus. Hoping to rally his disappointed supporters, he gave a passionate speech to a raucous audience in a small West Des Moines ballroom. As the crowd noise turned into a deafening roar, Dean held the public-address microphone—which was also wired into the pooled-network television feed—closer to his mouth as his hoarse voice strained to be heard in the room. The climax of the speech was a list of upcoming primary states he desired to win, followed by an exclamation that is typically transcribed roughly as, "and then we're going to Washington, D.C., to take back the White House. Yeeeeeaaaaarrrrrggghhh!"

The last part, which sounded on TV like a bad horror-movie sound effect, quickly became known as the "Dean scream." By one count, it was replayed 633 times on national broadcast and cable news shows over the next four days.[16] Amateur remixers quickly went to work, and it became one of the most popular pre-YouTube Internet phenomena. The narrative congealed within hours: Howard Dean, former Democratic frontrunner, was now an unhinged national punch line, and any chance of a campaign rebound was diminished.

This event showcased numerous *Out of Order* pathologies as the press took a trivial, policy-irrelevant moment and exploded it into a defining episode. They also used the timeworn, self-referential rationalization that it "reinforced a narrative"—in this case the unsubstantiated, opponent-driven rumor that the passionate Dean had a bad temper.

But it was even worse than that. No one in the room—not Dean's staff, nor audience members, nor seventy-five print reporters—thought anything was amiss.[17] They heard what Dean heard: a candidate projecting over an increasingly loud crowd. However, his unidirectional microphone blocked the crowd noise and gave TV producers an isolated recording of the scream. As a sound engineer explained on a recent FiveThirtyEight podcast, producers would have had other microphones to pick up the crowd as well, and typically they mix the sound together to produce a realistic composite of a rally.[18] But in this case they broadcast the isolated audio and then played it on a continuous loop when they realized its comedy potential. Yes, perhaps Dean should have been more cognizant of the technology—but the whole episode was essentially a media creation.

2016: The Perfect Fit

The most recent campaigns, steeped in horse-race trivia, continued to lay the groundwork for Trump. The 2012 Republican contest featured a series of frontrunners—some, like Michele Bachmann and Herman Cain, with dubious claims to presidential qualification—each taking a turn in the spotlight before a scandal, gaffe, or fresher candidate pushed them aside. Political scientists John Sides and Lynn Vavreck called this the "discovery, scrutiny, decline" cycle.[19] Even though it was often driven by trivial events, one could at least argue that the process worked reasonably well as it exposed voters sequentially to several potential nominees before they settled on the less flashy but more serious Mitt Romney. The press's thumb was never overwhelmingly on the scale for any given candidate, as none of them singularly fit the most important NJCs such as novelty, conflict, and personalization. But their privileging of those criteria was ominous.

The competitive 2008 Democratic contest saw the media play its usual early role of winnowing the field. Only three candidates garnered any serious airtime: Barack Obama, Hillary Clinton, and 2004 vice-presidential nominee John Edwards. Among those ignored were more experienced candidates such as senators Joe Biden and Chris Dodd and multibranch career public servant Bill Richardson. The fact that the media elevated the young, telegenic candidates over other plausible nominees did not merit much mention among critics, as the serious and policy-knowledgeable Obama went on to unite and grow the party on the way to a landslide victory. Still, the apparent winnowing criteria— charisma, buzz, hype, and meaningless early polls—served in retrospect as an illustration of the power the media could wield if a buzzworthy candidate truly stands out from the pack.

And it happened on June 16, 2015, when Donald Trump rode down the escalator of his Trump Tower and announced his run in front of an enraptured national press corps, beginning a yearlong process of using media biases to gain an overwhelming share of the nomination coverage, even amid an extraordinarily deep and talented Republican field. As an intellectual exercise, one could quite possibly show that he benefited from every known quirk and pattern of the mainstream media. Here are just a few:

Novelty: Not only was his résumé unusual for a presidential candidate, nearly everything about his campaign style flouted the rulebook.

Conflict, negativity, sex/vulgarity: His campaign possessed these traits in abundance. Though his main slogans included "make America great again" and various platitudes about "winning," his tone was overwhelmingly negative toward Obama and Congress, the Republican Party, the news media, various social groups, his opponents, and even many foreign countries. He also fostered and escalated conflict at every possible turn with anyone who criticized him.

He got off to a fast start on the vulgarity front, making a crude comment about Fox anchor Megyn Kelly's menstrual cycle after she asked him tough questions at the first debate. By the middle of the contest season, when the usually dignified Marco Rubio made a last-ditch effort to be heard above the fray with a thinly veiled swipe at Trump's penis size—which Trump answered at the next debate by assuring the audience "there's no problem"—no one was even surprised.

Personalization: He was masterful at making the campaign about Donald Trump. Presidential campaigns are always about the candidate as a person to some extent, but his ego and his message melded into a single Trump-branded entity. Also, his attacks on opponents—in debates, tweets, and elsewhere—were brutally personal, as he gave them nicknames and variously attacked their appearance, speaking style, demeanor, and any other attribute that presented itself as fodder for his insult comedy. Whether this amused, offended, titillated, or horrified cable-news pundits depended on the comment and pundit—but his attacks seldom failed to become the story of the day.

Obsession with celebrity: This one is self-explanatory and self-evident.

Simplicity: Trump's orations were not hampered by gratuitous perspicacity. Similar analyses by the *Boston Globe* and Politico each showed that Trump's speeches and debate answers were pitched at about a fourth-grade level.[20] The *Globe* found his language to be the simplest of the nineteen candidates they analyzed, with others ranging from fifth to tenth grade. His avoidance of policy specifics in favor of short, declarative statements played well in the broadcast realm.

Horse-race coverage: His lack of policy knowledge was one weakness that he could not effortlessly spin into a strength. Fortunately for him, news coverage focused overwhelmingly on the horse race. Every new poll was an excuse to show surprise at his gain or endurance. In fairness, some might argue that the media often discussed him in policy-relevant contexts such as immigration and terrorism. However, "Wow, can you believe what he just said about [group]? Did he finally go too far this time?" is only "policy" coverage by the dumbed-down standards of contemporary election news, and it still falls within the "game" rather than the "governing" frame. The bottom line is that his vague, ever-changing, and often factually incorrect pronouncements—though frequently criticized by pundits—did nothing to dent his coverage-volume advantage.

Any given news quirk, pattern, or bias will exert maximum influence on news content when potentially newsworthy phenomena vary greatly with respect to it. For example, if all candidates in a race are white male governors and senators with decades of political experience, the criterion of "novelty" will not cause variation in the coverage because none is more novel than the others.[21] But if one stands out along that dimension, then the media will have a heightened incentive to give disproportionate coverage to the novel candidate.

Though other somewhat-interesting characters in the race had their moments—Carly Fiorina and Ben Carson come to mind—Trump was so far ahead of the others across such a wide array of NJCs that none of them stood a chance of beating him at the news-coverage game. As a result, his advantage in coverage volume was so overwhelming that it squeezed the other candidates out of the conversation.

Trump's Dominance of Television Coverage

How great was Trump's coverage advantage? It is difficult to find adjectives to do it justice, so the numbers will have to speak for themselves. The best measures are reported below, with some new data added to fill in the picture. The focus is on the months prior to the first contest, when the news media made crucial decisions that shaped the contours of the race.

While the cliché "all publicity is good publicity" is never completely accurate, it is functionally true during the earliest phases of a nomination contest. The foremost task of a campaign is to push its message—or, failing that, its mere existence—into the conversation. In a field as deep as the 2016 Republicans, press judgment about how to allocate scarce airtime was vitally important. Ultimately, they decided to give Trump coverage that was wildly excessive by any reasonable ideal.

As with any bias charge, the claim that Trump's coverage was excessive requires a baseline. Assuming a straightforward ideal—the media should give citizens sufficient information to evaluate the candidate field—then what is the proper allocation of coverage to the candidates? All members of the seventeen-candidate Republican field could make at least some plausible case that, with sufficient attention, they stood a chance of moving into the top tier. Even the lowest-polling candidates who never made a blip on the media or public radar—George Pataki and Jim Gilmore—were former governors of a large state and a crucial swing state, respectively.

This presented a tricky dilemma that was not the media's fault: How could they possibly balance covering the breadth of the field with covering each candidate in sufficient depth to inform voters? On the one hand, an argument could be mustered that all of them deserved equal coverage in the earliest weeks of the campaign. Once the polls began to sort them into tiers, though, then the coverage volume could stratify accordingly. On the other hand, some might argue that journalists should exercise judgment from the outset as to which candidates are "serious" contenders, however defined. Money? Experience? Early horserace indicators? A reasonable case could be made for a variety of approaches, some prioritizing equity while others favor more aggressive winnowing through editorial judgment. Although equity among seventeen candidates was probably unrealistic, even early on, any editorial winnowing that is consistent with the ideal would require clear and sensible criteria.

In short, there are many potential baselines here. However, it is largely irrelevant which one a given critic favors, because actual press behavior deviated radically from all of them. By some measures of the formative summer and early autumn 2015 phase, Trump received more coverage than his sixteen opponents combined.

Analysts took a variety of approaches to estimating Trump's media share. Although each technique has limitations, cumulatively they paint an unambiguous picture. The *New York Times*, using data and analysis from mediaQuant and SMG Delta, reported the candidates' total "free media"—meaning the dollar-value equivalent if every minute or column inch of coverage were instead an advertisement—from the beginning of the campaign through February 2016.[22] This widely discussed measure elegantly summarizes a vast amount of data by weighting each source by audience size.

Trump received the equivalent of $1.98 billion of media coverage, about twice the amount of all of his nomination opponents put together. Cruz was next with $313 million, then Bush at $214 million, Rubio at $204 million, and it dropped quickly from there. By comparison, Hillary Clinton had $746 million and Bernie Sanders $321 million.

As for specific outlets, MRC reported the number of minutes the broadcast networks devoted to each candidate at various stages of the campaign. From January to July 2015, Trump received an "avalanche" of coverage: 116 minutes. Next were Bush with 72, Chris Christie with 28, and Scott Walker with 18.[23] It became even more lopsided from August to October, with Trump gaining more coverage than all other Republicans combined: 266 minutes. Bush fell to 57, then Carson with 55, Fiorina with 26, and Rubio with 26.[24]

How does Trump's network advantage compare to previous cycles? While studying the 2012 election, I tallied the number of news-show segments in which a candidate was mentioned on the three broadcast networks during the precontest phase. This is a conservative measure, as it does not distinguish between a single mention and a whole segment devoted to a candidate. I replicated it for 2016 to enable direct comparison. Figures 6.1 and 6.2 show the two Republican contests, with the early phase divided into two parts. If anything, the 2016 race—with its larger and more experienced field—should have shown more parity. Instead, it showed Trump's dominance in contrast to the more evenly dispersed coverage in 2012. While the press clearly winnowed the twelve-person field in 2011 by delineating a top tier and ignoring the rest, Trump was in a category by himself in 2015. Even as the other candidates jockeyed for position, he had a solid, unwavering coverage chunk to himself. And this measure likely underestimates his share because it only credits one mention per segment.

Cable was even more lopsided. According to MRC's monitoring of CNN's prime-time shows, Trump received 580 minutes, or 78 percent of all Republican coverage, from August 24 to September 4. Bush got 88 minutes, Carson 41, and Walker 10. They also noted this striking tidbit: "Trump's 580 minutes of coverage averages out to more than 25 percent of total programming for the ten days analyzed."[25] This included complete coverage of three Trump rallies, with no other candidate earning the privilege of even one.

A broader measure confirms Trump's dominance of cable. The GDELT Project, using data from the Internet Archive Television News Archive, tallied the daily mentions of each candidate's name on the three major cable networks and other news channels such as CNBC, Fox Business, Bloomberg, and selected shows from Comedy Central.[26] Their count is based on the closed-captioning feed, which any hearing-impaired citizen or viewer of airport televisions knows is error prone. However, as there is no reason to believe the errors would be systematic or disproportionate, it is a serviceable measure over time and across candidates.

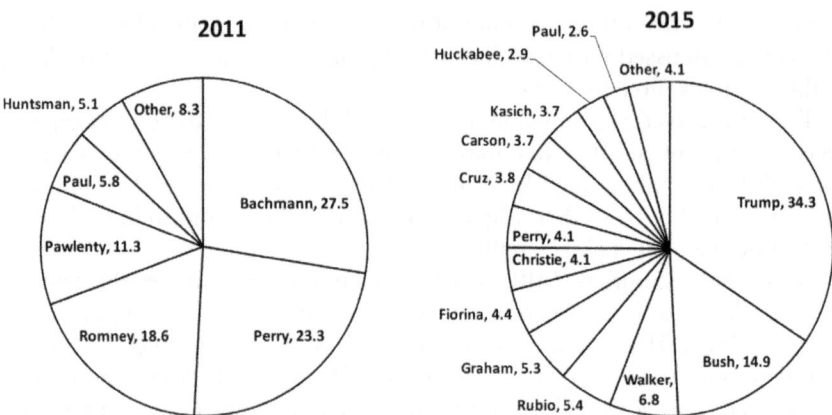

Figure 6.1 Republican candidates' share (%) of network news mentions, July and August.

Source: LexisNexis search.

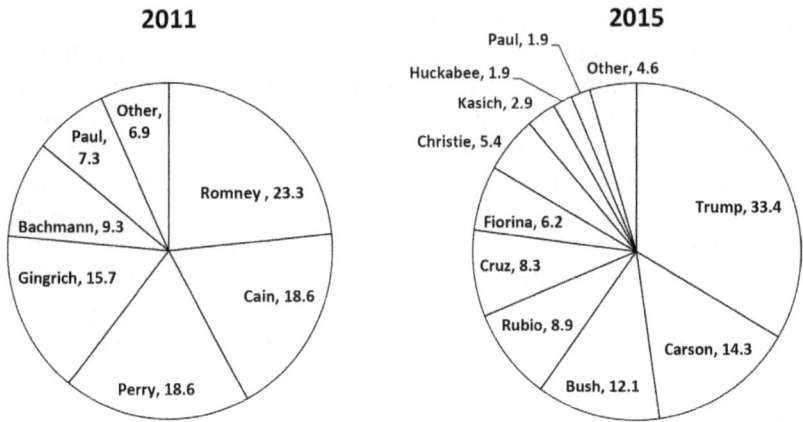

Figure 6.2 Republican Candidates' Share (%) of Network News Mentions, September–December.

Source: LexisNexis search.

Table 6.1 shows Trump's monthly share of the total Republican candidate mentions, beginning on June 16 when he announced his candidacy. After a relatively modest start in June—if we can call more than doubling his nearest opponent "modest"—the channels plunged into full Trump mode during the rest of the summer, giving him more than half of the mentions for the entire field. After a slight leveling off during the autumn—though never enough to bring his nearest rival anywhere close to his totals—he surged back to a position of absolute dominance during the critical last two months before the contests began. This metric probably underestimates his advantage, as it gives only minimal credit to uninterrupted coverage of an hourlong rally, a privilege that accrued mostly to him.[27]

Incredibly, Trump received more coverage than any opponent on the combined cable networks *every single day* between July 2 and October 29.

TABLE 6.1 **Trump's Proportion of Total Republican Candidate Mentions, June 16, 2015–April 30, 2016**

	All Channels	CNN	Fox	MSNBC
June (partial)	31.3	33.5	32.3	26.4
July	57.8	69.8	54.1	54.5
August	57.1	65.3	50.5	57.2
September	47.9	52.3	43.7	46.4
October	42.2	48.7	38.0	39.3
November	35.5	41.2	32.7	38.0
December	57.8	60.9	56.3	56.6
January	55.7	60.3	50.0	55.9
February	45.2	46.4	44.0	42.9
March	66.7	68.3	65.5	65.9
April	69.3	69.9	68.5	68.7

Source: Calculated from GDELT Project's data collection from the Internet Archive Television News Archive.

During that four-month stretch, there was literally nothing a Republican candidate could say or do to gain even one day in the spotlight. Were the rest of the field being treated with even a modicum of seriousness or respect, someone's campaign activity or policy views would have received more attention than Trump's *least* newsworthy day of tweets, boasts, and controversies. After a November that occasionally saw others—usually Ben Carson—have a day or two in the spotlight, Trump put together another unbroken streak of daily domination during all of December and January, commonly accruing ten times as many mentions as the second-place candidate.

CNN gave him more coverage than the two partisan networks, Fox and MSNBC, particularly over the summer. While bias cops sometimes accused CNN of playing up Trump because they thought he would be easier for Clinton to beat in a general election, the similarity of Fox's and MSNBC's volume— albeit with a different tone—raises doubts about using volume to measure party-driven coverage calculations. For whatever reason, Trump cast a heavier spell over CNN than over the partisan networks, though the latter still enthusiastically aided his dominance.

The Media's Role in Trump's Nomination

Did Trump's early coverage advantage help him win the nomination? This will be adjudicated for years, and the question is extremely tough to tackle with social-science rigor, as a truly satisfying answer would involve rerunning the election with different coverage patterns to see if he could still gain enough of a plurality to win pivotal early states. Having said that, there are many reasons to believe that the media will play a key role in history's judgment of the contest.

To be clear, the argument is not that the press bears *sole* responsibility for Trump's success. That reductionism would wrongly exclude the litany of factors that converged to enable such an extraordinary turn of events. Any story must include the attitudes, grievances, and fears of Trump's loyal supporters; underlying conditions such as globalization and rapid cultural change; deep and growing distrust of governmental institutions and the "establishment" that populates them; and various challenges facing the contemporary Republican Party, from its awkward post-Reagan coalition of free-market economics and social conservatism to the overstuffed candidate field and the repeated failure of the party elites to take Trump seriously and coordinate a response. However, none of those factors—individually or in tandem—comes close to telling the full story of Trump's nomination. Ultimately, in a thoroughly mass-mediated process such as a nomination contest, the press must figure prominently in the explanation.

This question can be tackled from various angles. First, scholars have been studying nomination contests for many cycles, accumulating a wealth of evidence of a significant media role in shaping outcomes. For example, numerous studies show a strong effect of news coverage on the degree to which candidates are able to generate momentum after a contest victory.[28] Indeed, it is almost self-evident that Trump benefited from momentum-generating coverage after his early victories. However, the contention here goes back a step: his domination of the *pre-primary* coverage enabled those early victories.

Research on the earliest phases of a campaign cycle, though relatively sparse, does suggest the potential for strong media effects. One study showed a consistent effect of network-news coverage volume on poll standing.[29] Another showed a correlation between the quantity and tone of newspaper coverage and the decisions of candidates—particularly long shots—to exit the race.[30] Summarizing the insights of numerous studies, political scientist Wayne Steger explains, "candidates who fail to attract media coverage are effectively off the radar screen and they are not given serious consideration by many potential caucus and primary voters."[31]

Turning to the 2016 contest, data can help answer an important question: did Trump's disproportionate coverage lead or follow surges in public opinion? If the press was merely noticing a groundswell of support rather than causing it, then that would undermine the contention that media biases were responsible for the coverage surge that made him the frontrunner.

Trump's social-media prowess is legendary, as cable news pointed out ad nauseam. Perhaps he built a grassroots army of supporters under the radar, which the press in turn felt obligated to cover as a genuine campaign phenomenon. On the other hand, maybe his social-media support grew primarily because of his saturation of television coverage. While it was likely some combination of each, statistical analysis can indicate the predominant direction of the flow.

The unwieldy world of social media is tough to quantify reliably. Some analysts measure the "conversation" about a given person or topic, and this can be useful in areas such as marketing. However, the conversation includes gawk-ers and haters as well as supporters, particularly with a polarizing figure such as Trump. Another measure—still noisy, but perhaps less so—is his growth in Twitter followers. Although many journalists, amused onlookers, and even fake accounts follow him, the relative daily growth in followers should serve as a rough proxy for when he is generating new support among the Internet-savvy subset of voters.

Using Twitter data from Trackalytics, I compared Trump's daily follower count to his cable-mentions count from GDELT/Internet Archive.[32] To assess whether the media tended to lead or react to Twitter surges, I used a statistical technique known as a Granger causality test. Common in political science and economics, it assesses whether previous values of one variable predict future values of another, and vice versa. Technical details are in the appendix.

The results were clear and consistent: during the pre-primary phase (June 2015–January 2016), spikes in news mentions led to spikes in new followers, but not the reverse. The same is true when the analysis is restricted to June through August 2015. As best it can be ascertained from looking at the daily dynamics, the media's obsession with Trump generated more social-media fol-lowers, but not vice versa.

Perhaps the most important relationship to analyze is that between Trump's coverage volume and his support among the Republican electorate. As polls are relatively sparse during the early pre-primary season, statistical tests are not appropriate for assessing the order of the flow. Instead, a close examination of the critical early days can shed light on the relationship.

Figure 6.3 shows Trump's daily share of the total Republican mentions on all cable-news channels in the GDELT data set from June to August 2015. The first big spike was obviously his June 16 entry into the race. Though he usu-ally held the coverage advantage over the next couple of weeks, other candi-dates such as Bush were able to earn significant airtime as well. Then something changed at the end of June. A series of spikes led to a new equilibrium whereby he seldom fell below 50 percent of the total coverage. In accordance with the common observation that he sucked the oxygen out of the field, let's call this the "suffocation phase."

Meanwhile, table 6.2 shows the polls that were released immediately before and during the first six weeks of his candidacy. The dates indicate when respon-dents were called. It is important to remember that all polls are subject to ran-dom sampling variation as well as the quirks of the particular pollster. Many were phone polls, while others—notably the frequent YouGov/Economist and Morning Consult polls—were Internet based. In gauging public opinion, then, more attention should be paid to the broader trends than the results of any one poll.

A couple of patterns immediately emerge. First, although it is impossible to determine the precise day on which Trump began to pick up significant support, the coverage burst from his announcement clearly led to his initial 11–15 percent level of support. In a seventeen-candidate race with no prior frontrunner, this was usually enough to put him within a few points of the lead.

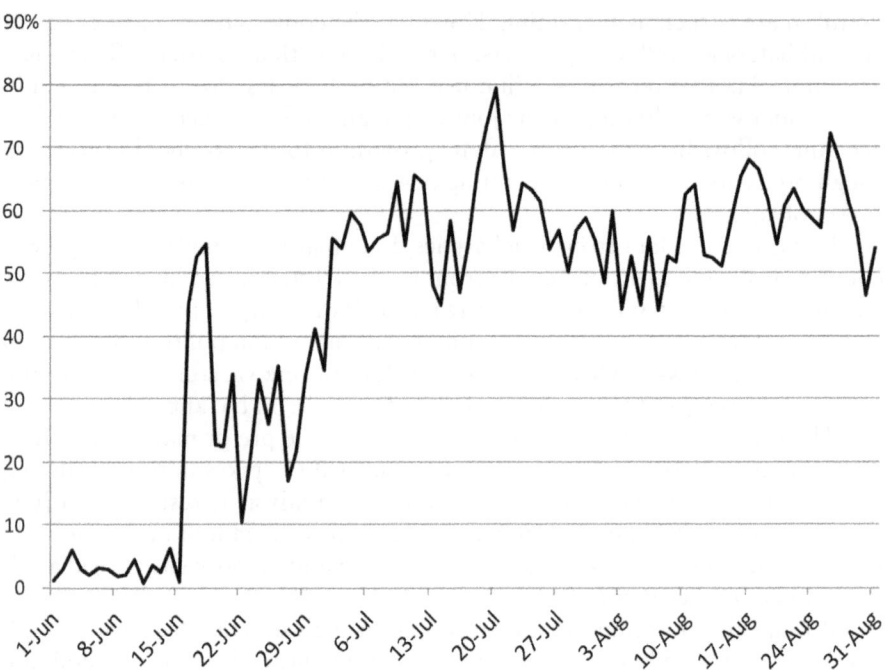

Figure 6.3   Trump's Percent of the Total Republican Mentions on All Cable-News Channels, June–August 2015.

Source: The GDELT Project, using data from the Internet Archive Television News Archive.

The pivotal period came when his support jumped into the 20s and he began to show a consistent lead—roughly during the second and third weeks of July. As this began about a week into the suffocation phase of news coverage, it lends further credence to the notion that the media pushed up his numbers.

What happened on the critical days when his coverage moved into the suffocation phase? If the coverage appeared to focus on his growing support, then that might complicate the "media caused his support" theory. Instead, however, the news judgment appeared to be driven by Trump's compatibility with media biases. That is, they began to realize what a great eyeball magnet he was.

The biggest single jump in coverage proportion during the move into the suffocation phase was July 2. He gained more than half of the total coverage for the first time since his announcement, and this quickly became a new equilibrium. Nearly every Trump-related cable news segment from that day concerned the continuing fallout from his two-week-old inflammatory comments about Mexican immigrants. The only news hook of note was that Serta Mattress Company became the latest firm—after NBC and Macy's—to sever business ties with Trump. Otherwise, it was pundit chatter about the controversy.

The July 2 transcripts also reveal why the mention counts may underestimate Trump's dominance. Pataki had one of his highest-volume media days of the year—but all of his mentions were about his comments denouncing Trump.

TABLE 6.2 **Trump's Poll Standing, June and July 2015**

Dates in Field	Company	Trump's Percentage	Trump's Lead (+) or Deficit (–)
6/11–6/14	Monmouth	2	–9
6/13–6/15	YouGov/Economist	2	–12
6/14–6/18	NBC/WSJ	1	–21
6/20–6/22	YouGov/Economist	11	0
6/21–6/23	Fox	11	–4
6/26–6/28	CNN	12	–7
6/27–6/29	YouGov/Economist	11	–3
7/4–7/6	YouGov/Economist	15	+4
7/9–7/12	Monmouth	13	–2
7/9–7/12	Suffolk/USAT	17	+3
7/8–7/13	Morning Consult	17	–2
7/13–7/15	Fox	18	+3
7/16–7/19	ABC/Post	24	+11
7/17–7/20	Morning Consult	22	+7
7/20–7/21	PPP	19	+2
7/18–7/20	YouGov/Economist	28	+14
7/22–7/25	CNN	18	+3
7/23–7/27	Morning Consult	24	+11
7/26–7/27	Rasmussen	26	+12
7/23–7/28	Quinnipiac	20	+7
7/25–7/29	Ipsos/Reuters	27	+16
7/26–7/30	NBC/WSJ	19	+4

Sources: HuffPost Pollster (http://elections.huffingtonpost.com/pollster) and RealClearPolitics (http://www.realclearpolitics.com/epolls/2016/president/us/2016_republican_presidential_nomina-tion-3823.html#polls).

Meanwhile, most of Bush's mentions on CNN that day were either about Trump gaining on him in the polls or his reaction to Trump's controversial statements. The only stand-alone Bush references were one sentence on his fund-raising prowess and a couple of mentions of a tweet in which he criticized a *New York Times* guacamole recipe for including green peas.

In summary, the available evidence strongly suggests that "the media created the Trump phenomenon" is a better description of the early campaign dynamics than "the media merely reported it."

Beyond what data can tell us, there is a more fundamental connection between Trump's coverage domination and his successful nomination run.

Perhaps the best entry into this broader argument, ironically, is through criticism of it. While many mainstream journalists acknowledge their role in the Trump phenomenon, others bristle at the suggestion that they bear responsibility for his success.[33] *Washington Post* columnist Eugene Robinson falls into the latter camp, as he made clear in a March 2016 column titled "No, the Media Didn't Create Trump."[34]

His lead sentence is as direct as the headline: "One of the more absurd things being said about the Donald Trump phenomenon is that the media created it. For the record, we didn't." Here is one of his key arguments:

> The news media operate in what should be every conservative ideologue's dream environment: an unfettered free market. Outlets compete every day—actually, in the Internet age, every hour—to provide consumers with information they need and want. Every editor and news director strives to beat the competition, and the fact is that audiences have decided they need and want to know about Trump.
>
> No one understands this better than Trump himself. To understate by miles, he knows how to draw attention to himself—the late-night Twitter rants, the fire-breathing rallies, the gold-plated jet, the ridiculous hair. After decades in the public eye, he had more than 90 percent name recognition when he began his campaign. So it was no surprise that hordes of media flocked to Trump Tower last June 16 and watched him descend the shiny escalator for his kickoff announcement. Who doesn't love a good sideshow?

While attempting to let the press off the hook, this instead shows why it deserves blame. The news media, through their commercially driven incentives and mandates, convey political reality through the warped prism of news-judgment criteria such as negativity, scandal, drama, novelty, simplicity, and personalization. Those are *media* biases.

Yes, they do stem in part from the media's perception of consumer taste. But "perception" is the key word. It is still the media not only perceiving but also deciding that such concerns override all others in news judgment. Even if such perceptions are accurate—which is not always true, as chapter 4 explained—and even if we leave aside the (news and entertainment) media's role in *creating* consumer taste, the power still rests with news organizations to decide how they will cover an election. As the long, exciting 2008 and 2012 cycles proved, cable networks hardly need an entertainment celebrity as a catalyst to cover nominations heavily and earn high ratings from them. Pushing the envelope further by helping a celebrity erase what was left of the line between electoral politics and reality TV is a conscious and fully autonomous decision by the news organizations. Sure, it may be difficult for most consumers even to envision an alternate universe in which politics is not covered in this fashion—but that itself is a damning indictment of the media's long-term role in shaping consumer tastes by withering their appetite for substance.[35] And it certainly does not make the press any less responsible for the content of its own product when it chooses to craft it this way.

Writer Neal Gabler made this point in an online essay in early 2016.[36] He argued that the media have been setting the stage for Trump over the long term by "systematically destroy[ing] our politics in the name of entertainment." He harkens back to historian Daniel Boorstin's decades-old coinage of the term "pseudo-events," which are things that are "increasingly staged expressly for the media without any intrinsic merit of their own—things like photo ops, press conferences, award ceremonies."[37] The human form of a pseudo-event is a "celebrity," defined as "a person who is known for his well-knownness."[38]

Gabler noted that Trump is a perfect candidate to take advantage of a media that "were spoiling for a pseudo-campaign" because they "had been growing increasingly bored with traditional politics." He added that "we only tolerate this state of affairs because the media have changed our expectations of a campaign. Having given us nothing in election after election but a show, we expect nothing but a show."

Conclusion

The general election rightly comprises a heavy proportion of scholarly and popular analysis of 2016 and the Trump phenomenon. However, the anomalous nature of the Republican nomination contest—and, in particular, the media's role in it—deserves a prominent place in the conversation as well. Individual reactions to its outcome are as polarized as any phenomenon in recent memory, and it is beyond this book's purview to step into that fray. However, well-functioning representative democracies require the ability to step back from outcomes and examine processes. And the media-dominated nomination process is a mess.

The "miscast institution" moved from a supporting to a starring role in 2016, when one candidate parlayed an unprecedented fit with the quirks and biases of the American news media—particularly cable television—into a suffocating domination of the conversation and process. By any reasonable standard, the media failed to meet not only the formidable challenge of structuring nominations in the direct-primary era, but even the minimal task of providing citizens with substantive information about the candidate field.

Appendix

Debate Content Analysis

I hired two students to replicate the MRC study of the CNBC Republican debate and then use the same criteria to code the questions asked at the CNN Democratic debate.

As the goal was to code the moderator questions using MRC's criteria, all relevant information on the criteria was culled from their write-up of the study. Specifically, they identified "negative spin, personal insults or ad hominem attacks" as the category of interest and gave the examples of "Harwood's question to Donald Trump asking if his was a 'comic book version of a presidential campaign,' or Quintanilla's question to Ted Cruz asking if his opposition to a just-passed spending bill showed that he was 'not the kind of problem-solver American voters want.'"

The only further elaboration was that the "category includes questions to one candidate inviting them to trash another, such as Harwood's question to Mike Huckabee asking whether Trump has 'the moral authority to unite the country.'" The other category was "positive," "involv[ing] personal questions without a negative slant, or policy questions that were phrased in a non-insulting way."

The coders were trained to distinguish between these two categories by practicing joint, and then independent, coding on debate questions from 2011–12. Given the vagueness and multidimensionality of the categories, they were split into three separate variables: positive or negative, personal or policy related, and invitation to attack another candidate or not. After training was complete, the coders were given a sample of older questions to code independently. They achieved agreement of 93 percent on forty-two coding choices.

The next task was to replicate MRC's study. MRC found forty-three "unique questions posed by one of the three moderators." While the line between "unique" and "follow-up" was sometimes blurry, I extracted the forty-three questions most likely to be deemed unique from the debate transcript and gave them to the coders. Their coding came closest to replicating MRC's work by using just the broader variable of "positive" and "negative." One coder found twenty-six negative questions and the other found twenty-seven, compared with MRC's twenty-eight. I adjudicated the disagreement and determined the count to be twenty-seven. The final step was to repeat the process for the CNN Democratic debate.

Network TV Graphs, 2011 and 2015

Mentions were found via LexisNexis. The network-news databases contain morning and evening news programs, divided into segments. A "mention" occurs when a candidate's name is mentioned at least once during a segment. They earn only one mention per segment, regardless of how many times their name was spoken.

Granger Tests

Vector autoregression (VAR) with Granger causality tests is a commonly used technique in political science and economics to model the dynamic relationship between two or more time-series variables. One variable is said to "Granger-cause" another if lagged values of the explanatory variable explain variance in a second variable, controlling for lagged values of the second variable.

In each analysis, each of the two variables—Twitter followers (Twitter) and cable-mentions count (cable)—served in turn as dependent and independent variables in VAR analyses. For each dependent variable, the independent variable was tested for whether it Granger-caused the dependent variable. To do this, two regression models were run: a full model with lagged values of the two variables and a reduced model that excludes the lagged values of the independent variable. The Granger test, reported below, determined whether the full model improved the prediction of the dependent variable over the reduced model to a statistically significant degree. The number of lags used in the models—eight—was determined using the Akaike information criterion (AIC).

June 2015–January 2016

	chi-2	df	p
Twitter → cable	2.17	8	.976
cable → Twitter	24.70	8	.002

June–August 2015

	chi-2	df	p
Twitter → cable	5.58	8	.694
cable → Twitter	17.96	8	.022

Notes

[1] Transcribed from my copy.

[2] Transcribed from a DVR rewind, February 7, 2016.

[3] Rush Limbaugh, "CNBC's Shameless Kill Show Debate," The Rush Limbaugh Show (website), October 29, 2015, accessed October 29, 2015, http://www.rushlimbaugh.com/daily/2015/10/29/cnbc_s_shameless_kill_show_debate.

[4] Sam Dorman, "Hannity: CNBC Debate Was 'Single Worst Example of Media Bias' in 'Intergalactic History,'" CNSNews, October 30, 2015, accessed October 30, 2015, http://www.cnsnews.com/blog/sam-dorman/hannity-cnbc-debate-was-single-worst-example-media-bias-intergalactic-history.

[5] "MRC Study Proves It: CNBC Agenda Was to Undermine GOP Candidates," Media Research Center, October 30, 2015, accessed October 31, 2015, http://www.mrc.org/press-releases/mrc-study-proves-it-cnbc-agenda-was-undermine-gop-candidates.

[6] "RNC's Priebus Speaks Out on Debate Reforms; Christie, Huckabee Weigh In on Issue," Fox News (website), November 2, 2015, accessed November 15, 2015, http://www.foxnews.com/transcript/2015/11/02/rnc-priebus-speaks-out-on-debate-reforms-christie-huckabee-weigh-in-on-issue.

[7] "This Line Got the Most Favorable Reaction Ever from a Luntz Focus Group," Fox News Insider, October 29, 2015, accessed October 29, 2015, http://insider.foxnews.com/2015/10/29/frank-luntz-focus-group-reacts-ted-cruzs-criticism-cnbc-gop-debate-moderators.

[8] "Transcript: Read the Full Text of the CNBC Republican Debate in Boulder," *Time* (website), October 28, 2015, accessed October 29, 2015, http://time.com/4091301/republican-debate-transcript-cnbc-boulder.

[9] Egberto Willies, "Ted Cruz Got One Thing Right at the Republican Debate," Daily Kos, October 29, 2015, accessed October 30, 2015, http://www.dailykos.com/story/2015/10/29/1442033/-Ted-Cruz-got-one-thing-right-at-the-Republican-Debate.

[10] This "tripartite view" of parties was based on ideas from V. O. Key Jr., *Politics, Parties, & Pressure Groups* (New York: Crowell, 1964). It was formalized by Frank J. Sorauf, "Political Parties and Political Analysis," in *The American Party Systems*, ed. William Nisbet Chambers and Walter Dean Burnham (New York: Oxford University Press, 1967).

[11] Marty Cohen, David Karol, Hans Noel, and John Zaller, *The Party Decides: Presidential Nominations before and after Reform* (Chicago: University of Chicago Press, 2008).

[12] Patterson, *Out of Order*, 35.

[13] Patterson, *Out of Order*, 42.

[14] Patterson, *Out of Order*, ch. 2.

[15] Patterson, *Out of Order*, ch. 4.

[16] Jack Holmes, "The Dean Scream: An Oral History," *Esquire*, January 29, 2016, accessed May 26, 2016, http://www.esquire.com/news-politics/a41615/the-dean-scream-oral-history.

[17] Holmes, "The Dean Scream."

[18] Jody Avirgan and Clare Malone, "Why the Dean Scream Sounded So Different on TV," FiveThirtyEight, February 4, 2016, accessed May 26, 2016, http://fivethirtyeight.com/features/why-the-dean-scream-sounded-so-different-on-tv.

[19] John Sides and Lynn Vavreck, *The Gamble: Choice and Chance in the 2012 Presidential Election* (Princeton, NJ: Princeton University Press, 2013).

[20] Matt Viser, "For Presidential Hopefuls, Simpler Language Resonates," *Boston Globe*, October 20, 2015, accessed May 28, 2016, http://www.bostonglobe.com/news/politics/2015/10/20/donald-trump-and-ben-carson-speak-grade-school-level-that-today-voters-can-quickly-grasp/LUCBY6uwQAxiLvvXbVTSUN/story.html; Jack Shafer, "Donald Trump Talks Like a Third-Grader," Politico, August 13, 2015, accessed May 28, 2016, http://www.politico.com/magazine/story/2015/08/donald-trump-talks-like-a-third-grader-121340.

[21] This idea first appeared in my book: Adam J. Schiffer, *Conditional Press Influence in Politics* (Lanham, MD: Lexington Books, 2008). It's called the invocation of constraints hypothesis, because that's the kind of name I gave things in my doctoral dissertation.

[22] Nicholas Confessore and Karen Yourish, "$2 Billion Worth of Free Media for Donald Trump," *New York Times*, March 15, 2016, accessed May 12, 2016, http://www.nytimes.com/2016/03/16/upshot/measuring-donald-trumps-mammoth-advantage-in-free-media.html.

[23] Rich Noyes, "TV's Campaign '16 News: An Avalanche of Trump Coverage, Not Much for Others," Media Research Center, August 4, 2015, accessed May 12, 2016, http://www.mrc.org/media-reality-check/tvs-campaign-16-news-avalanche-trump-coverage-not-much-others.

[24] Rich Noyes, "MRC Study: TV News Is Trying to Winnow the Field of GOP Candidates," Media Research Center, November 9, 2015, accessed May 12, 2016, http://www.mrc.org/media-reality-check/mrc-study-tv-news-trying-winnow-field-gop-candidates.

[25] Mike Ciandella, "CNN Spends 78 Percent of Prime Time GOP Campaign Coverage on Trump," MRC NewsBusters, September 16, 2015, accessed May 12, 2016, http://newsbusters.org/blogs/nb/mike-ciandella/2015/09/16/cnn-spends-78-percent-prime-time-gop-campaign-coverage-trump.

[26] "2016 Campaign Television Tracker," GDELT Project, accessed May 14, 2016, http://television.gdeltproject.org/cgi-bin/iatv_campaign2016/iatv_campaign2016.

[27] Aside from his tendency to refer to himself in the third person.

[28] See, for example, F. Christopher Arterton, *Media Politics: The News Strategies of Presidential Campaigns* (Lexington, MA: Lexington Books, 1984); Audrey A. Haynes and Sarah G. Murray, "Why Do the News Media Cover Certain Candidates More than Others? The Antecedents of State and National News Coverage in the 1992 Presidential Nomination Campaign," *American Politics Quarterly* 26 (1998): 420–38; Larry M. Bartels, *Presidential Primaries and the Dynamics of Public Choice* (Princeton, NJ: Princeton University Press, 1998); Ernest B. McGowen and Daniel J. Palazzolo, "Momentum and Media in the 2012 Republican Presidential Nomination," *Presidential Studies Quarterly* 44 (2014): 431–46.

[29] Andrew J. Dowdle, Randall E. Adkins, and Wayne P. Steger, "The Viability Primary: Modeling Candidate Support before the Primaries," *Political Research Quarterly* 62 (2009): 77–91.

[30] Audrey A. Haynes, Paul-Henri Gurian, Michael H. Crespin, and Christopher Zorn, "The Calculus of Concession: Media Coverage and the Dynamics of Winnowing in Presidential Nominations," *American Politics Research* 32 (2004): 310–37.

[31] Wayne P. Steger, *A Citizen's Guide to Presidential Nominations: The Competition for Leadership* (New York: Routledge, 2015), 74.

[32] "Donald J. Trump," Trackalytics, accessed May 24, 2016, http://www.trackalytics.com/twitter/profile/realdonaldtrump.

33 For an example of "acknowledging their role," see Nicholas Kristof, "My Shared Shame: The Media Helped Make Trump," *New York Times*, March 26, 2016, accessed July 3, 2016, http://www.nytimes.com/2016/03/27/opinion/sunday/my-shared-shame-the-media-helped-make-trump.html?_r=0.

34 Eugene Robinson, "No, the Media Didn't Create Trump," *Washington Post*, March 28, 2016, accessed July 1, 2016, https://www.washingtonpost.com/opinions/no-the-media-didnt-create-trump-covering-him-is-their-job/2016/03/28/11ffc554-f516-11e5-9804-537defcc3cf6_story.html.

35 See Kovach and Rosenstiel, *Elements*, 221.

36 Neal Gabler, "We Wouldn't Have Donald Trump if the Media Hadn't Helped Destroy the Democratic Process First," AlterNet, March 4, 2016, accessed July 5, 2016, http://www.alternet.org/election-2016/we-wouldnt-have-donald-trump-if-media-hadnt-helped-destroy-democratic-process-first.

37 Gabler, "We Wouldn't Have Donald Trump."

38 Daniel J. Boorstin, *The Image; or, What Happened to the American Dream?* (New York: Atheneum, 1962).

CHAPTER 7

Bias, Balance, and Ideals in the Trump Era

Partisan-bias charges against the mainstream American news media are as loud as ever, despite a news landscape that has changed markedly since the charge grew out of the conservative movement in the 1950s and 1960s. A talking point with this much influence and staying power demands rigorous analysis rather than the usual partisan, knee-jerk reactions.

The I-B-E (ideal-baseline-evidence) framework introduced in this book gives citizens and critics the tools to assess the validity of individual bias charges, from either side and from any source. As a corollary function, the framework also provides a template for bias cops to make more logically cogent bias charges, if such a thing were of interest. In short, a valid bias charge should (1) set a nonideological normative expectation for high-quality news content, (2) derive a clear standard for what would constitute unbiased coverage in that context, and (3) provide social-scientifically valid evidence of the alleged deviation from the standard. Although it would be impossible to take a representative sample of charges and assess what proportion fail the I-B-E stress test, anyone who incorporates I-B-E thinking into their engagement with bias charges will find that most charges fall short on logical and evidentiary grounds.

The best explanation for these common deficiencies is simple, though it has taken much scholarly effort to produce: the grand, universal charge of a leftward news tilt lacks merit. Although scholarship on this subject has its share of controversy and caveat, the overall conclusion is the fairest read of the literature.

While partisan-bias charges are as polarizing as any issue in the contemporary political landscape, more empirically grounded critiques of political news— the "real biases"—should transcend party lines. The real biases, which typically receive far less play in popular discourse than partisan-bias charges, explain a wide array of media-coverage patterns. Numerous examples were discussed in chapter 4 and elucidated in two case studies: coverage of the battle to enact health-care reform and the 2016 Republican nomination contest. Democrats concerned that the ACA did not receive a fair shake and Republicans alarmed at the process or results of their nomination may not agree on much—but they have common cause in decrying the state of political news.

Denunciations of the media reached a new level of intensity during and after the historic 2016 general election. The primary topics of this book—partisan bias and real biases—featured prominently in postelection commentary, which included strands of epistemic despair and grave concerns about the future of journalism. More than ever, analytical clarity is essential for making sense of the issues facing the news and its role in American democracy.

This concluding chapter draws lessons from the 2016 general election and takes a closer look at the *I* and the *B* in I-B-E to confront some of the challenges facing citizens, journalists, and critics in navigating the perilous political-media landscape.

Bias and Balance in the 2016 General Election

The breadth of news-media criticism has grown along with the Internet, and it flourished in the wake of the 2016 presidential election. Pitting the first female major-party nominee—a twenty-five-year veteran of national politics and an unrivaled lightning rod for scandals, both real and contrived—against an abrasive and fact-challenged outsider, this often nasty battle presented daunting dilemmas for national journalists, leading to coverage choices in which everyone found something to criticize. It is difficult to find a prominent commentator—left, right, or neutral—who did not opine in at least one column or segment about problems with the role of old or new media in the election.

In particular, the unique attributes of Donald Trump's candidacy were disorienting for media that depend on familiar frames and templates to tell the general-election story. First, although prevarication, evasion, and spin are endemic to politics, Trump spoke (or tweeted) verifiable falsehoods at a frequency unprecedented among major-party candidates. He also issued statements intended to insult, demean, or provoke a critic or adversary so often that it could fairly be called a principal strategy. Further, his awkward relationship with the Republican Party and its elders complicated the two-party symmetry from which the "balance" norm derives its ability to structure election coverage. Also, his simultaneous disdain for the media and incomparable ability to dominate coverage by playing to their biases created a target-rich environment for critics of all stripes.

Abundant Real Biases

Critics hoped that the reality-show aesthetic of the nomination phase would give way to more serious coverage as the question turned to which of the two candidates would be the next president. Instead, the nomination coverage flowed seamlessly into a summer and fall spectacle characterized by overwhelming negativity and a nearly complete absence of substantive discussions.

Out of Order's Thomas Patterson, in his role with Harvard's Shorenstein Center on Media, Politics, and Public Policy, conducted a thorough content analysis of 2016 election coverage in five top newspapers and five TV networks. The center issued several reports on the analysis, including one that covered the postconvention period from mid-August until Election Day.[1]

The bleak results were aptly described by the report's subtitle: "How the Press Failed the Voters." First, a negative tone predominated, as 77 percent of Trump's coverage was negative, compared to 64 percent for Clinton. If the time period is broadened to include the nomination—in which horse-race coverage of the winners should increase their proportion of positive coverage—the coverage was *still* negative, with Clinton getting the worst of it: 62 percent compared to Trump's 56 percent. During the general election, there was not a single week in which the coverage was net positive, nor was there any subcategory of coverage—horse race, controversies, issue stands, or personal qualities—for which the coverage was net positive.

The story topics were also out of line with the normative expectations of news critics, as policy stories were dwarfed by horse race, scandal, and game coverage. The horse race alone accounted for 42 percent of all coverage from mid-August through Election Day. "Controversies," such as Clinton's ongoing e-mail scandal and the leaked videotape of Trump bragging about sexually assaulting women, took up another 17 percent of the coverage. The category called "other," which included nonpolicy strategic considerations such as "upcoming events, staffing, logistics, etc.," received 24 percent. The miniscule news hole that remained was split between "personal traits" at 4 percent, "leadership/experience" at 3 percent, and finally "policy stands" at 10 percent.

The lack of substance in election coverage is an enduring lament that unites disparate critics. US senators Al Franken and Ted Cruz could scarcely be less alike, ideologically or temperamentally. Yet their news critiques highlighted in previous chapters were similar. Two paragraphs after his hummus quip, Franken complained that "almost all political coverage is about process and horse race and not about policy."[2] Meanwhile, after skillfully insulting his opponents in the CNBC debate, Cruz implored the press to talk "about the substantive issues the people care about." This convergence should bother journalists who comfort themselves with the notion that "if both sides are criticizing us, we must be doing something right." That notion does carry plausibility with partisan-bias charges, as ideologically divergent critics pound journalists with self-serving and contradictory complaints. But when Franken and Cruz are moved to say the *same thing*, self-reflection is warranted.

Partisan-Bias Charges

One charge that does not unite disparate critics is the ever-present liberal-bias charge. MRC and its allies dutifully screamed bloody bias and disseminated the charges around their vast network of influence throughout the general election. The uniqueness of the 2016 cycle aptly showcases the flaws in the liberal-bias charge.

The charges ran the gamut of I-B-E failures, including cherry-picking and a heavy reliance on the subjective "positive/negative" distinction. An example of cherry-picking is a twenty-eight-page MRC report, stringing together quote after quote purporting to show "more than a quarter century of positive treatment by the establishment media" of Clinton.[3] Needless to say, it failed to sample from the deep pool of attacks she endured during that same period.

On the coding front, MRC's most thorough studies depended entirely on the readers' trust that they used reasonable standards to determine positivity and negativity. Also, the key imbalance they found—that 91 percent of Trump's network-TV "mentions" were negative, compared to 79 percent for Clinton—came by way of a peculiar procedure:

> Our analysts ignored soundbites which merely showcased the traditional party line (Republicans supporting Trump and bashing Clinton, and vice versa), and instead tallied evaluative statements which imparted a clear positive or negative tone to the story. Such statements may have been presented as quotes from non-partisan talking heads such as experts or voters, quotes from partisans who broke ranks (Republicans attacking Trump or Democrats criticizing Clinton), or opinionated statements from the reporter themselves.[4]

While some of these choices are consistent with good scholarly techniques, the use of "partisans who broke ranks" potentially biases the findings, as a higher rate of Republican defection was one of the defining quirks of the general election. Nearly all major Democrats, even nomination rival Bernie Sanders, actively advocated for Clinton, while Trump had so many top Republicans speak in opposition—or, at best, sit in icy silence—that he had to turn to family members and obscure celebrities for many of his convention's prime speaking slots. It would be more surprising if this asymmetry in party-elite support did *not* unbalance the coverage.

More broadly, the most daunting issue facing partisan-bias charges was the use of a balance baseline. As the case study of the 2008 election showed (chapter 2), balance baselines are tenuous in presidential elections when "reality" is slanted. Normally, a reality imbalance results from underlying conditions such as the economy and approval of the current president. But in 2016, these factors predicted a close race. Instead, the imbalance stemmed from alleged asymmetry in the temperament, truthfulness, and qualifications of the candidates. While some of the imbalance is relatively noncontroversial—the claim above about the Republican elite's reluctance to support Trump publicly is easily verifiable—other aspects, such as the degree to which Trump's inexperience and petulance make him "unqualified" for the presidency, collapse hopelessly into the same partisan wrangling that neutral journalism aims to transcend.

Clearly, the unique attributes of this election put news organizations in a bind: they were damned if they did balance and damned if they didn't. The "if they did" part is discussed in the next section. Not surprisingly, MRC and others pounced on the media when they didn't, without recognizing the complications underlying the very concept of balance in the election. This uncritical use of a balance baseline, and failure to grapple with the I-B-E conditions for validity (equivalence, ruling out nonpartisan explanations), rendered their charges unconvincing.

The problem with establishing equivalence was pervasive in the series of MRC items that followed the common gatekeeping-bias template of "the networks cover *x* while ignoring *y*." For example, at an August 9 rally in North Carolina, Trump made waves when he said, "Hillary wants to abolish, essentially abolish, the Second Amendment. By the way, and if she gets to pick, if she gets to pick her judges, nothing you can do, folks. Although the Second Amendment people, maybe there is, I don't know." In addition to being factually incorrect in its characterization of Clinton's views on gun rights, the statement was widely interpreted as an encouragement to assassinate her. Trump's camp denied that interpretation, claiming that he was merely touting the power of gun-rights activists to organize politically. That same day in Florida, astute observers noticed an unusual attendee in Clinton's audience: the father of the man who killed forty-nine people at an Orlando nightclub in June.

MRC complained that the networks "squashed" Clinton's "terror woes" while playing up Trump's remark, documenting how the three broadcast networks "deluged viewers with more than five times more coverage—25 minutes and 35 seconds versus 4 minutes and 41 seconds—to Trump's 'Second Amendment people' remark than they did to the father of an ISIS-inspired terrorist sitting right behind Clinton at a rally in Orlando, Florida."[5] However, unless one believes the wildly implausible idea that Clinton *invited* the father, this comparison suffers from a serious equivalency lapse. By nonideological news standards, it is debatable whether the unwanted face among a crowd of thousands even merits a mention on network news. And even if it does, it is simply not comparable to a statement, directly from a candidate's mouth, that was heard by neutral listeners as an incitement to violence against his opponent.

The balance baseline also proved impotent in an MRC grievance from October, in which they complained about unequal coverage of two scandals that broke within an hour of each other. In what was perhaps the most sensational incident in a campaign full of them, a videotape from 2005 surfaced of Trump bragging to an *Access Hollywood* anchor, in vulgar and sexist language, about his sexual exploits and fantasies—including a now-infamous quip in which he appears to brag about sexual assault: "I don't even wait. And when you're a star, they let you do it. You can do anything—grab them by the pussy."

About an hour after the tape's appearance, e-mails stolen from Clinton's campaign chair John Podesta were released by WikiLeaks. The leaks provided excerpts of Clinton's speeches to Wall Street banks that she had refused to make public during the nomination contest. Among the most embarrassing revelations—particularly vis-à-vis Bernie Sanders supporters to whom Clinton needed to endear herself—were comments supporting free trade, praising big banks, and ruminating on the need to have "both a public and a private position" on contentious issues.

MRC's content analysis showed the Trump tape garnering 103 minutes of broadcast network airtime during the first three days of the scandal, whereas the Clinton revelations earned only 8 minutes. While notable, this imbalance is weak evidence of partisan bias.

The equivalence between the scandals is tough to establish, given the apples-to-oranges comparison between impolitic policy views expressed to bankers versus locker-room talk laced with a nonspecific confession of sex crimes. Even if we stipulate, for the sake of argument, that they were similar enough in magnitude to warrant more balanced coverage than a ratio of 13 to 1, nonpartisan alternative explanations for the imbalance abound.

First, the Trump tape wins on the "novelty" dimension by a landslide. The tape's 1980s movie-style vulgarity was unique in a presidential campaign.[6] But more notable than the tape's novelty was the *lack* of novelty in the Clinton revelations. While they provided red meat for her critics, they did so more by "reinforcing narratives"—everything from her secrecy in refusing to release the tapes to her long history of favoring free trade—than through any potential news hook. In fact, the passage most seized upon by critics—her admission of having "both a public and a private" position on key issues—is about the least novel revelation imaginable for a career politician and arguably belonged more in Trump ads than in ostensibly neutral news reports.

Also, the lurid nature of the Trump tape played directly into the media's privileging of prurient, emotional, and personalized stories. Finally, the circumstances surrounding the Clinton leak presented a dilemma for journalists. The information was made public by way of a felony—the hacking and theft of private correspondence. Russia's involvement in the hack—later proven by US intelligence agencies—was widely suspected as soon as the documents appeared on WikiLeaks.[7] Thus, news organizations had to balance the news value of the leak's content with the risk that they would be seen as pawns in Russia's attempt to influence the election. Meanwhile, the legally obtained Trump tape posed no such issue.

On the other side of the "damned if they did balance, damned if they didn't" conundrum, neutral and left-leaning commentators revived a media criticism that gained prominence during the George W. Bush administration.

The Special Case of "False Balance"

One of the loudest criticisms in 2016 was that the news media covered an asymmetric contest symmetrically. That is, they went out of their way to show balance and equivalence between the attributes, statements, and behavior of the two candidates, even when they were manifestly different. Given that Trump was the candidate who, according to critics, deserved more negative coverage than his opponent, it is not surprising that the charge was heard mostly from the liberal side. Throughout the general election, the Internet was awash in headlines such as "Media Should Stop Treating Clinton and Trump as Equals," "Does the *New York Times* Have a False Balance Problem?" "The Case against Journalistic Balance," "Stop the False Media Balance between Trump and Clinton," and "False Balance Is Ruining Campaign Coverage."

The fact that this argument comes from only one side does not, by itself, mean it is merely partisan sniping rather than legitimate press criticism. It does, however, require I-B-E scrutiny. When a charge strays from the balance baseline and in fact criticizes the press *for being balanced*, the need for a nonideological ideal becomes paramount. Those who make the charge carry a heavy burden to show that their criticism comes from a transpartisan concern for quality journalism rather than a mere desire to see the ostensibly neutral media pummel the opposition.

This burden is easily met for an issue such as global-warming coverage, where (1) the ideal tracks with the universally accepted norm that the press should get the facts right and (2) the facts can be demonstrated with quantifiable indicators and an overwhelming consensus of nonpartisan, scientific experts. However, the electoral realm is another story. For better or worse, the norm of balance carries tremendous clout not only among journalists who cover elections but among their customers, the candidates, and even—as chapter 2 demonstrated—many scholars who study election news. The key to being persuasive with such charges is to connect them to an agreed-upon standard. The connection between the ideal and the specific charge must be logical and convincing, not merely appended as an afterthought or a post hoc rationale.

An example from the 2016 "false balance" canon shows both the promise and difficulty of this approach. In September, *Boston Globe* columnist Michael A. Cohen urged his colleagues to "Stop Treating Clinton and Trump as Equals" because "there are a gulf of differences between [the candidates]."[8]

His list of differences was quite varied, and the variation is instructive. First, he argues that "Clinton shades the truth and exaggerates; Trump lies consistently and repeatedly in ways that are easily verifiable." The implication is clear: Trump violates journalism's most fundamental precept of getting the facts right, and he does so to such a greater extent than Clinton that treating them equally would violate the mandate of truth seeking. This critique is effective because he grounds the demand for unequal coverage in the relationship between an observable facet of reality—Trump's greater difficulty with facts—and a core principle of journalism.

His next sentence, however, goes in a different direction. "Trump is running on a nativist and racist platform that would bar adherents of an entire religion entry to America and would deport 11 million undocumented immigrants. Clinton is not." Like the previous passage, it is anchored around a real difference between the candidates. However, the peg to nonideological press norms is less clear. Certainly, many thoughtful observers would argue that policy proposals with shades of "nativism" and "racism" should be treated as deviant ideas by the establishment press rather than merely as one side of a general-election policy debate. However, that falls into the I-B-E "gray area" between ideological and nonideological ideals, as it strays from universal, *Elements of Journalism* norms and gets into sticky questions about the boundaries between acceptable and deviant, as well as the contested definitions of concepts such as racism.

He expands this idea later in the essay, lamenting the lack of heightened policy scrutiny for Trump by arguing that "Trump's ideas are, frankly, much more outside the historical realm of American politics." As evidence, he cites a number of policy positions, including

> violating the law by bringing back torture . . . tear[ing] up trade deals and negotiat[ing] better ones . . . weaken[ing] US support for its treaty-bound allies . . . push[ing] huge new investments in military, infrastructure and border security

spending, leav[ing] social insurance programs like Medicaid and Social Security untouched . . . all the while passing a massive tax cut. It's simply not possible for these numbers to add up and Trump has given no indication of how he'll pay for all this.

Again, while reasonable critics could make a case that some of those positions require unique scrutiny—particularly the promotion of illegal activity such as torture—the column risks reverting to a mere anti-Trump argument, rather than a cogent critique of the press, without solid grounding in universal press norms. As one example, Trump's plan to increase government spending while cutting taxes and disregarding the deficit, far from being "outside the historical realm of American politics," is as normal as it gets in the Reagan/Bush-era Republican Party. While the demand for policy scrutiny obviously comports with universal press norms, Cohen runs into rough territory when he argues that Trump's positions "merit far greater examination than what Clinton is recommending."

Beyond the Election

Both sides of the balance argument—the conservative bias cops and the mostly liberal "false-balance" lamenters—butt up against the extraordinary nature of the 2016 general-election contest. And yet their problems in evaluating election coverage pale in comparison to the challenges of making sense of news during the Trump presidency. During the election, news critics at least were able to anchor their analysis around the inherently symmetric features of a general election. Balance defenders in particular could draw upon Clinton's twenty-five years as a controversy magnet, her secrecy and occasional lack of honesty, and her contentious relationship with the press to downplay any alleged asymmetry between the candidates.

But once the election ended, neither President Trump nor press critics had Clinton to disparage any longer. As Trump's transition to the presidency progressed, and it became clear that the weight of the office would not sand down his rough edges, the media's relationship with him grew even more contentious, and the task of mapping media behavior onto existing templates became more daunting than ever.

CNN's postelection posture is a good example. As the presidency began, the network tried to retain the features of its campaign coverage that helped it earn record viewership. For example, they kept most of their Trump "surrogates"—the talking heads hired to provide balance to their liberal and anti-Trump-conservative analysts—as regular panelists on their news and arguetainment shows.[9] The interaction between this style and Trump's behavior led to a format—extremely common during the transition period—that became a Rorschach test for bias perception. The basic template of this format is as follows: (1) Trump says something false or provocative, (2) neutral panelists ("analysts") condemn the remark, (3) the anchor interrogates a surrogate, and (4) the surrogate spins and blames the media or opponents. An alternate form involves surrogates and analysts from all sides talking over each other until the segment becomes an incoherent cacophony.

A November 29, 2016, segment featured anchor Wolf Blitzer interviewing RNC strategist Sean Spicer—who later became Trump's press secretary—for nearly ten minutes. The main topic was a two-day-old tweet from Trump claiming that he would have won the popular vote "if you deduct the millions of people who voted illegally." This false statement lit up the Internet, so it predictably became an enduring topic of cable chatter. Blitzer asked tough questions—often interrupting Spicer to do so—including the following:

> Where is he getting that suggestion that millions of people voted illegally? . . . There have been studies that show there have been irregularities, but not millions of voters. . . . Are you saying he won the popular vote? Is that what you're saying? . . . The *Washington Post* gave him four Pinocchios for saying that, said it was totally, totally false. . . . But listen to the criticism from longtime supporters of his that he's getting [quotes from Newt Gingrich and Mitch McConnell]. . . . Is the president-elect going to move on, or is he going to continue to talk about millions of illegal voters?

In response to each query, Spicer spun and deflected.

This format frequently raised the hackles of MRC, who criticized similar interviews during the election and transition with headlines such as "CNN's Cuomo Presses [Trump campaign manager Kellyanne] Conway on Sessions, Trump's Tweets," and "Blitzer Badgers RNC Spox: Trump Needs to Refute Neo-Nazi Support 'More Dramatically.'" The complaint was simple: the CNN anchors showed tone bias by "pressing" or "badgering" the surrogates.

Liberal critics saw equally compelling flaws in the format. In a widely circulated article and accompanying video from late in the general election, MMfA argued that "CNN Has a Trump Surrogate Problem."[10] The chief complaint— which overlaps with the "false balance" narrative—is that the format "turned CNN's election coverage into a series of ridiculous, uninformative screaming matches that mainstream bullshit in the name of 'balance.'" The argument is not that Trump's position should go undefended on air, but rather that their style of defense—a "barrage of talking points, misdirection, and blind stubbornness"— violates the tenets of informative journalism.

Even though MMfA did a better job in this exchange of grounding its critique in nonideological norms, it is easy to see how the broader argument becomes intractable. Should CNN have hired surrogates to defend Trump in the name of balance? As noted above, there is a strong gravitational pull toward balance in a general election—but what about when the election ended? And if their continued employment was appropriate, did the hosts then have an obligation to treat them as equals to the other panelists—including thoughtful, nonpartisan analysts such as John King and Jeffrey Toobin—or should they have been aggressive about exposing the surrogates' "misdirection and blind stubbornness"?

Dilemmas like this abound for news organizations and their critics. Yet, at the same time, the flaws in the format should be readily apparent to anyone who subscribes to the *Elements'* foundational contention that the "primary purpose of journalism is to provide citizens with the information they need to be free and self-governing." At the extreme, simultaneous shouting—which transcription services often label as "unintelligible" or "crosstalk"—has no informational value. And even when the words can be deciphered, their content produces heat but little light. This may be good for ratings in the short run, and good for dismissing criticism as mere ideological squabble, but in an era when many observers see multiple threats to the "free and self-governing" ideal—both from the government and from a news media that has lost its way—it has never been more important for critics and consumers, regardless of their perspectives, to resist the temptation of partisan-bias charges and ground their expectations in the timeless values of a free press.

The Enduring Importance of Nonideological Ideals

Trepidation about the future of journalism runs rampant, in and out of the profession, as terms such as "existential crisis" are thrown around freely. The challenges of a president who is unusually hostile to the establishment news media—and at times even to the idea of a free press—join ongoing concerns about the financial viability of traditional outlets in the digital era, declining press credibility among a polarized electorate, and many others. These challenges are being taken up by numerous thoughtful writers and news professionals and are mostly outside the scope of this book. For those wanting to explore these issues in more depth, longtime press scholar and critic Jay Rosen's Twitter feed and blog PressThink provide sophisticated analysis of journalism's challenges and the most innovative potential solutions.[11] Also, to give credit where it is due to one of this book's most criticized news outlets, CNN's long-running weekly press-criticism show, *Reliable Sources*, has become a top-tier player under host Brian Stelter, joining NPR's *On the Media* as the best broadcast/cable venues for holding the press to high standards.

One prominent theme in postelection commentary that warrants discussion here is a fear that fragmented media, polarized politics, and the Trump phenomenon have ushered in a so-called post-truth era. That buzz phrase was anointed "word of the year" by Oxford Dictionaries, who defined it as "relating to or denoting circumstances in which objective facts are less influential in shaping public opinion than appeals to emotion and personal belief."[12] Although the phrase's usage showed a sudden surge in late 2016, the idea is not new. Instead, it overlaps with diverse strands of scholarly argument, most commonly associated with the movement known as postmodernism.

Elements authors Bill Kovach and Tom Rosenstiel seemingly anticipated this conversation with a passage in their "truth" chapter, present since the first edition of the book in 2001:

> Over the next fifty years [following mid-twentieth-century skepticism over the role of truth in newsmaking], after decades of debate and argument, sometimes by political ideologues and sometimes by postmodern deconstructionist academics, we came to the point where some denied that anyone could put facts into a meaningful context to report the truth about them. An epistemological

skepticism began to pervade every aspect of our intellectual life. . . . Columbia University historian Simon Schama suggested that "the certainty of an ultimately observable, empirically verifiable truth" was dead.[13]

Sentiments like this tend to erupt when events shake the foundation of common understandings of truth, so it is not surprising that 2016 nurtured a new term for this old concept. The fear, frustration, and even hopelessness felt by many citizens—particularly those in both parties who were taken aback by the Trump phenomenon—are understandable. "The facts were out there, but voters ignored them" was a common lament, sometimes leading to skepticism about the efficacy of even reporting facts in the first place.

However, challenges to truth have never gained traction in realms that require facts to function. Indeed, the perception of a "post-truth" epoch, and the implications some observers read into it for political journalism, would sound absurd in other contexts. For example, although weather forecasting is a probabilistic venture that often fails in its precise predictions, it nonetheless aids our comfort and convenience in tangible ways. If TV meteorologists began predicting the temperature using a random number generator or assembling panels with guests shouting conflicting forecasts at each other, they would quickly become laughingstocks. If sportscasters conveyed the wrong scores from the game we just watched, they would be out of a job.

Needless to say, these examples are not a perfect analogy to politics, a realm structured by values, ideology, and other concepts that cannot be factually verified or disproven. To a great extent, however, the separation of politics from these other areas is an artificial distinction, for two reasons.

First, even the most value-laden political statements typically have one or more factual assertions underpinning them. Only the purest normative statements—something like "I believe abortion is morally wrong"—are exempt from factual scrutiny. When Trump said, "We have the slowest growth since 1929," at the second general-election debate, he was incorrect by all known measures of economic growth.[14] While a hard-core skeptic could argue that "economic growth" is a social construct that does not exist outside of our definitions of it, the political world depends on the acceptance of shared and consistently measured concepts such as GDP growth, every bit as much as physics or engineering depends on the standard vocabularies of mathematics and measurement. Political journalism accomplishes nothing if it cannot recognize and adjudicate the factual foundations of political assertions.

Second, the *discussion* of values, ideologies, and opinions has factual dimensions. Straight-news reporting on opinions seldom involves a journalist merely stating an opinion, as that tends to be labeled "commentary." Rather, it involves conveying the tenets and nuances of an ideology, value, or opinion, as understood by the actor holding it. When conservatives accuse liberals of hating Christians because they favor separation of church and state, or when liberals accuse conservatives of wanting poor people to die of starvation because they support reducing social programs, those are strawman caricatures of complex ideological or value-based opinions. An informed citizenry depends on exposure not only to facts but also to the accurate description of normative arguments, without caricature, misrepresentation, or loaded language.

Ultimately, while the concerns of post-2016 skeptics are understandable, the goal of news has never been to stock every last citizen with a full armory of verified facts and cogent arguments to blow up all of their misconceptions and create a utopia of perfect information. The goal is more modest but no less crucial: to provide enough information, to whoever is receptive, to maximize the effective functioning of American democracy within its inevitable limitations.

A Framework for Post-Post-Truth News Criticism

To bypass the unproductive arguments over partisan bias and avoid succumbing to post-truth skepticism, critics should stay grounded in one of the key tenets of I-B-E: holding news content to rigorous, shared, nonideological standards. Doing so begins with asking a simple question, modified from the *Elements'* core principle in light of the above discussion: *Did the news content provide citizens with verified factual information and exposure to ideas that enable them to form opinions about, and participate in, their self-governance?*

To make this inquiry more concrete, the following checklist covers a wide range of story content that would be consistent with this foundational ideal, as well as the implicit ideals that follow from it such as the media's watchdog role:

Did the news content provide timely, accurate information about at least one of the following?

- The benefits and costs of policy proposals and outcomes:
  ○ Impact on individual citizens, municipalities, states, the nation, and the world.
  ○ The actual interests served (Who benefits? Who loses?).
  ○ Financial cost (and who bears it).
  ○ Background information necessary to understand the issue.
- The best arguments from all relevant actors and perspectives—not just from officeholders or others with effective communication capabilities—for a policy proposal or controversy.
- The veracity of statements by candidates, officeholders, and other influential actors.
- The degree to which public officials and other powerful entities are operating within the law, within the customs and norms of civil society, and in the public interest.
- Performance-relevant officeholder/candidate attributes:
  ○ Experience (expertise, track record, promises kept).
  ○ Details and consequences of planks in a candidate's platform.
  ○ Meaningful comparisons and contrasts between candidates.
  ○ How they voted and why they voted that way.
  ○ Their ideology, values, and other markers of their worldview.
  ○ Interests backing them (financial and otherwise).
  ○ Financial entanglements.

- ○ Key supporters/advisors/people with influence over them.
- ○ Scandals with potential effect on performance.
- The avenues of participation in the political process:
  - ○ Where/when/how to vote, volunteer, etc.
  - ○ Location of, and details about, events such as conventions and protests.
  - ○ Governmental meetings.
  - ○ Points of entry into the process for citizens of all social/economic statuses.
  - ○ Your rights as a citizen.
- Who actually has the power.
- How power is wielded in the real political world (e.g., how a bill *really* becomes a law, given current norms, rules, power structures, and political alignments).
- Updates on, and history of, potentially consequential local, national, and world events.
- Illumination—in proper context and proportion—of social phenomena with clear political/policy implications, such as crime, inequality, threats to safety, scientific findings, and macroeconomic indicators.
- Outcomes of elections and other vital processes.

Any valid bias charge—partisan or otherwise—against political news should have expected the news content to do at least one of these things. And the more clearly the expectation is set, the more robust the charge will be to accusations that it is politically motivated. Meanwhile, news organizations that remain tethered to these ideals, and the rest of the *Elements of Journalism*, will be better equipped to ride the current storm of acrimony and technological change.

Journalists: Mind Your Friends, Not the Bullies

The American news media take fire from many directions. While bias cops defy logic and evidence to scream about alleged partisan tilt, other critics denounce a wide array of patterns and shortcomings in news content. Journalists can thus be forgiven for tiring of the constant carping about the product of their high-stress and often thankless jobs, particularly when the carping comes in the form of hostile or even violence-threatening tweets and e-mails. These complaints are not equivalent, however, and it is crucial to remember that media criticism from academics—as well as from thoughtful, nonideological watchdogs—comes from a wholly different place than most partisan-bias accusations.

Politicians, watchdog groups, and partisan media often seek to destroy the traditional press's credibility for the purpose of scoring points with a party base, excusing their own wrongdoing, or undermining watchdogging. In contrast, critics of the real biases decry the press's failure to live up to its role as an independent monitor of power in a free society. Bias cops are like opponents trying to defeat a team, whereas scholars and other principled critics are like coaches frustrated with a team's underachievement. Accordingly, bias cops cheer the decline in the media's credibility and public esteem. Antibias groups and partisan news outlets do not even bother to hide their glee when reporting the latest "trust in the media hits a new low" poll. In contrast, scholars and students of the press lament it.

While it is understandable for even the thickest-skinned news professionals to be affected by the ever-present partisan-bias charge, there is probably nothing they could do to satisfy critics. When a strategic talking point is (1) highly effective at accomplishing its goal but (2) unmoored from empirical reality, any attempt to ameliorate it by modifying behavior—that is, trying harder to appear unbiased—is bound to fail. Recall the hostile media effect from chapter 3: a certain proportion of partisans will always view balanced news content as being biased against their side. And, in the increasingly polarized political climate in which an ever-growing number of citizens don the mantle of ideological warrior, the attitude toward the media's fairness and balance will, by definition, continue to grow more hostile.

Professional bias cops and the citizens who buy their spin are like playground bullies who told you that you're ugly and your mother dresses you funny. Coming back to school with a new haircut and a more fashionable wardrobe has never, in the history of the elementary-school social scene, caused such comments to cease. Instead, it merely wastes money that could have gone for other things, such as birthday gifts for your friends. Likewise, rather than trying to impress their antagonists by prioritizing the signaling of balance, news organizations should work to ameliorate the shortcomings that may eventually cause their friends—that is, customers who want and need a high-quality product—to tune out.

But why should news organizations—particularly the cable networks that enjoyed record-smashing audience numbers in 2016—care about academic criticism?[15] For his part, CNN's president Jeff Zucker forcefully pushed back against critics of the network's disproportionate coverage of Trump and its "shouting surrogates" format.[16] And why shouldn't he? After all, the Trump phenomenon brought CNN its best year ever.[17] However, there is cause to be mindful when well-intentioned observers notice that an organization has strayed from the primary mission that distinguishes it from other forms of communication.

Two insights from *Elements* bring this danger into focus. First is the "principle of 'the naked body and the guitar'":

> If you want to attract an audience, you could go down to a street corner, do a striptease, and get naked. You would probably attract a crowd in a hurry. The problem is . . . why should they stay once they have seen you naked? . . . There is another approach. Suppose you went to the same street corner and played the guitar. A few people might listen on the first day. Perhaps a few more on the second. Depending on how good a guitar player you are, and how diverse and intriguing your repertoire is, the audience might grow each day.[18]

The presidential campaign—which started with a comment about a journalist's menstrual cycle, escalated to taunts about penis size, and ended with boasts about grabbing genitalia—was like a long, profoundly unsexy striptease, with flourishes of insult comedy and reality TV. Of course viewers who were unaccustomed to the intrusion of those prurient elements into politics could not look away, and news organizations prospered. But what is the follow-up act now that we have seen politics naked? If political news ratings depend on a continuous escalation of entertainment, then diminishing returns are inevitable.

A related and crucial *Elements* insight should be mandatory reading for every self-satisfied television-news executive: "The infotainment strategy is faulty as a business plan because when you turn your news into entertainment, you are playing to the strengths of other media rather than your own. How can the news ever compete with entertainment on entertainment's terms? Why would it want to?"[19]

Indeed, if viewers really want a horse race, they have ESPN. If they want drama, they have cleverly scripted movies and shows with compelling characters and deliberate pacing. If they want sexual content that is actually sexy, a multibillion-dollar, cross-platform industry is on the task. News content simply cannot compete over the long term with those other venues if its offering of watered-down mimicry displaces its own strengths.

And what comparative advantage does news have over other forms of communication? It matters to our lives. Quoting again from the *Elements* critique:

> The value and allure of news is that it is different. It is based on relevance. The strategy of infotainment, though it may attract an audience in the short run and may be cheap to produce, will build a shallow audience because it is built on form, not substance. Such an audience will switch to the next "most exciting" thing because that audience was built on the spongy ground of excitement.[20]

Those "next most exciting things" cycle through the public consciousness frenetically and ephemerally in all facets of pop culture, especially on the Internet. For example, early in the second decade of this century one couldn't swing a pixelated cat without hitting "clickbait" articles with titles such as "When You Find Out Why This Orphan Told Off a Walmart Clerk, Your Jaw Will Drop." But Web surfers could only be tricked by links that did not actually blow minds or drop jaws so many times before they learned not to click on them.[21]

Thanks to a unique confluence of circumstances, a presidential election became the "next most exciting thing" on television in 2016. But the Clinton-Trump matchup will never be replicated, and citizens newly drawn to the spectator sport of horse-race politics will chase something else as soon as the novelty wears off if news organizations forgo their comparative advantage over other forms of communication.

Meanwhile, the outlets typically recognized as having content most consistent with the ideals of good journalism also reaped growth in 2016. Importantly, many outlets saw more customers willing to reward them with subscriptions, despite widely known workarounds to their digital paywalls (newspapers) or a purely voluntary subscription model (public radio). According to *New York Times* columnist Jim Rutenberg, "in the weeks since the election, magazines like The New Yorker, The Atlantic and Vanity Fair; newspapers including The New York Times, The Wall Street Journal, The Los Angeles Times and The Washington Post; and nonprofits like NPR and ProPublica have been reporting big boosts in subscription rates or donations."[22] The *Post* in particular—whose reporter David Fahrenthold received widespread plaudits and a Pulitzer Prize for his investigative election reporting—saw such a revenue boost that they committed to hiring more than sixty new staff members.[23]

Those who believe that American democracy cannot afford to wait for the rest of the news media to figure this out—including the ever-influential broadcast and cable networks and their websites—must use their leverage to alter the media's incentives.

Citizens: Force the Conversation

As badly as their arguments miss the point, partisan-bias cops still hover prominently over the mainstream news outlets. In her postmortem of general-election coverage titled "One Thing Voters Agree On: Better Campaign Coverage Was Needed," *New York Times* public editor Liz Spayd spent about half (516 of 1,164 words) of the column addressing charges of either a general liberal tilt, or a specifically anti-Trump tilt, to the coverage.[24] Missing from the column were reflections on the lack of substance—save for one fleeting reference to the "horse race"—the rampant liberal complaints that minor Clinton scandals received heavier coverage than more serious Trump scandals, and Trump's ability to leverage news biases into unprecedented dominance of the narrative.

It would be easy—not to mention consistent with this book's primary themes—to criticize her for worrying about the wrong biases. In fairness, however, it is likely that the tenor of the column was indexed to the range of complaints in her various mailboxes, inboxes, and feeds. If this is the case—or even if partisan-bias cops were overrepresented due to inertia generated from their years of successful dissemination of the charge—the challenge to citizens who care about the quality of news is clear: make your voices heard in ways that have a chance of reaching news producers.

Above all, "real bias" chargers must be as loud and as organized as partisan-bias cops. If the same techniques that have been used to push the liberal-bias myth deep into the consciousness of every working journalist—letters to the editor, e-mails, phone calls, tweets, etc.—are employed to raise awareness of the desire for high-quality news and the ways in which news content falls short, the critiques will eventually be too voluminous to ignore. This effort could also be aided by centralized organization. If an advocacy group were to combine the good-journalism orientation of Pew, Poynter, or Shorenstein with the social-media savvy and popular reach of MRC, then it could effectively focus and amplify the clamoring for democracy-aiding informational content.

News consumers also need to reward the most useful outlets with readership and paid subscriptions, particularly the nonprofit outlets that depend on audience patronage. By the same token, the only foolproof way to reorient the incentives of cable arguetainment is to turn it off. Every newspaper editor and owner is familiar with the "I'm canceling my subscription because of your liberal bias" letter. Producers of subpar news, in any platform, need to become acquainted with the "after thirty years of daily viewership, I can't take any more of your sensationalism and shouted talking points" letter.

Partisan-bias charges are a constant. The variable—with critical consequences for the future of journalism and democracy—is the degree to which more substantial critiques can join the conversation.

Notes

1. Thomas E. Patterson, "News Coverage of the 2016 General Election: How the Press Failed the Voters," Harvard Kennedy School: Shorenstein Center on Media, Politics, and Public Policy, December 7, 2016, accessed December 10, 2016, https://shorensteincenter.org/news-coverage-2016-general-election.
2. Franken, *Lies and the Lying Liars*, 1.
3. Rich Noyes, "If Hillary Wins, Liberal Journalists Paved Her Path to the Presidency," MRC NewsBusters, November 1, 2016, accessed November 29, 2016, http://www.newsbusters.org/blogs/nb/rich-noyes/2016/11/01/if-hillary-wins-liberal-journalists-paved-her-path-presidency.
4. Rich Noyes, "MRC Study: Documenting TV's Twelve Weeks of Trump Bashing," MRC NewsBusters, October 25, 2016, accessed November 29, 2016, http://www.newsbusters.org/blogs/nb/rich-noyes/2016/10/25/mrc-study-documenting-tvs-twelve-weeks-trump-bashing.
5. Scott Whitlock, "Study: Nets Squash Hillary's Terror Woes to Scold Trump's Gun Remark," MRC NewsBusters, August 10, 2016, accessed November 29, 2016, http://www.newsbusters.org/blogs/nb/scott-whitlock/2016/08/10/study-nets-squash-hillarys-terror-woes-scold-trumps-gun-remark.
6. Albeit not in a presidency, thanks to Bill Clinton's sworn testimony in 1998 about the sex acts he performed with White House intern Monica Lewinsky.
7. Amy Chozick, Nicholas Confessore, and Michael Barbaro, "Leaked Speech Excerpts Show a Hillary Clinton at Ease with Wall Street," *New York Times*, October 7, 2016, accessed December 1, 2016, http://www.nytimes.com/2016/10/08/us/politics/hillary-clinton-speeches-wikileaks.html.
8. Michael A. Cohen, "Media Should Stop Treating Clinton and Trump as Equals," *Boston Globe*, September 14, 2016, accessed December 1, 2016, https://www.bostonglobe.com/opinion/2016/09/14/media-should-stop-treating-clinton-and-trump-equals/e4qMIleYb-56VY69T4VYAKL/story.html.
9. The paid surrogates were Kayleigh McEnany, Scottie Nell Hughes, Jeffrey Lord, and Corey Lewandowski. On their hiring, see Hadas Gold, "Jeff Zucker Praises Corey Lewandowski, Slams Vice and BuzzFeed," Politico, August 2, 2016, accessed December 8, 2016, http://www.politico.com/blogs/on-media/2016/08/jeff-zucker-praises-corey-lewandowski-slams-vice-and-buzzfeed-226574.
10. Carlos Maza and Coleman Lowndes, "Video: CNN Has a Trump Surrogate Problem," Media Matters for America, October 14, 2016, accessed December 8, 2016, http://mediamatters.org/blog/2016/10/14/video-cnn-has-trump-surrogate-problem/213824.
11. For a particularly hard-hitting and comprehensive examination of the post-2016 media landscape, see Jay Rosen, "Winter Is Coming: Prospects for the American Press under Trump," PressThink, December 28, 2016, accessed December 28, 2016, http://pressthink.org/2016/12/winter-coming-prospects-american-press-trump.
12. "Word of the Year 2016 Is . . . ," English: Oxford Living Dictionaries, accessed December 20, 2016, https://en.oxforddictionaries.com/word-of-the-year/word-of-the-year-2016.
13. Kovach and Rosenstiel, *Elements*, 53.
14. Bryan Bender, Rachana Pradhan, Danny Vinik, Katy O'Donnell, and Taylor Gee, "13 Times Trump Was Dead Wrong at the Debate, and 2 Times Clinton Was," Politico, October 10, 2016, accessed December 19, 2016, http://www.politico.com/story/2016/10/debate-fact-check-hillary-clinton-donald-trump-229527.
15. Oliver Darcy, "Trump Catapults Cable News Outlets to Their Best Ratings Year Ever," *Business Insider*, December 21, 2016, accessed December 24, 2016, http://www.businessinsider.com/trump-cable-news-ratings-2016-12.

[16] Gold, "Jeff Zucker"; Ken Meyer, "CNN's Zucker Hits Back on Trump Coverage Criticism: People Want to Blame Someone for His Rise," Mediaite, April 25, 2016, accessed December 24, 2016, http://www.mediaite.com/online/cnns-zucker-hits-back-on-trump-coverage-criticism-people-want-to-blame-someone-for-his-rise.

[17] "2016 Is CNN's Most-Watched Year Ever," CNN Press Room, December 20, 2016, accessed December 24, 2016, http://cnnpressroom.blogs.cnn.com/2016/12/20/2016-is-cnns-most-watched-year-ever.

[18] Kovach and Rosenstiel, *Elements*, 248.

[19] Kovach and Rosenstiel, *Elements*, 222.

[20] Kovach and Rosenstiel, *Elements*, 222.

[21] Such headlines still exist, of course, in ads, link farms, and other unsavory corners of the Internet. But mainstream outlets like CNN and the *Huffington Post* have moved away from experimentation with these tactics, and they are easy fodder for parody sites such as ClickHole.

[22] Jim Rutenberg, "By Attacking the Press, Donald Trump May Be Doing It a Favor," *New York Times*, December 18, 2016, accessed December 24, 2016, http://www.nytimes.com/2016/12/18/business/media/by-attacking-the-press-donald-trump-may-be-doing-it-a-favor.html.

[23] Ken Doctor, "'Profitable' Washington Post Adding More than Five Dozen Journalists," Politico, December 27, 2016, accessed December 28, 2016, http://www.politico.com/media/story/2016/12/the-profitable-washington-post-adding-more-than-five-dozen-journalists-004900.

[24] Liz Spayd, "One Thing Voters Agree On: Better Campaign Coverage Was Needed," *New York Times*, November 19, 2016, accessed December 24, 2016, http://www.nytimes.com/2016/11/20/public-editor/one-thing-voters-agree-on-better-campaign-coverage-was-needed.html.

Bibliography

"2016 Is CNN's Most-Watched Year Ever." CNN Press Room, December 20, 2016. Accessed December 24, 2016. http://cnnpressroom.blogs.cnn.com/2016/12/20/2016-is-cnns-most-watched-year-ever.

Adair, Bill, and Angie Drobnic Holan. "PolitiFact's Lie of the Year: 'A Government Takeover of Health Care.'" PolitiFact, December 16, 2010. Accessed June 15, 2016. http://www.politifact.com/truth-o-meter/article/2010/dec/16/lie-year-government-takeover-health-care.

Allahpundit. "Study: Nightly Network News Covered Bush's Crumbling Job Approval 124 Times to This Point in Year Six—versus Nine Times for Obama." Hot Air, September 16, 2014. Accessed July 13, 2015. http://hotair.com/archives/2014/09/16/study-nighty-network-news-covered-bushs-crumbling-job-approval-124-times-to-this-point-in-year-six-versus-nine-times-for-obama.

Alterman, Eric. "Think Again: 'Working the Refs.'" Center for American Progress. Accessed December 18, 2015. https://www.americanprogress.org/issues/general/news/2005/05/26/1476/think-again-working-the-refs.

Annenberg Public Policy Center. "Call-In Political Talk Radio: Background, Content, Audiences, Portrayal in Mainstream Media." August 7, 1996. Accessed January 7, 2016. http://www.annenbergpublicpolicycenter.org/Downloads/Political_Communication/Political_Talk_Radio/1996_03_political_talk_radio_rpt.PDF.

Aronoff, Roger. "Media Are Big Losers in Election 2008." Accuracy in Media, November 3, 2008. Accessed April 25, 2016. http://www.aim.org/aim-column/media-are-big-losers-in-election-2008.

Arterton, F. Christopher. *Media Politics: The News Strategies of Presidential Campaigns.* Lexington, MA: Lexington Books, 1984.

Avirgan, Jody, and Clare Malone. "Why the Dean Scream Sounded So Different on TV." FiveThirtyEight, February 4, 2016. Accessed May 26, 2016. http://fivethirtyeight.com/features/why-the-dean-scream-sounded-so-different-on-tv.

Barbour, Christine, and Gerald C. Wright. *Keeping the Republic.* 7th ed. Los Angeles: SAGE CQ Press, 2015.

Barker, David, and Kathleen Knight. "Political Talk Radio and Public Opinion." *Public Opinion Quarterly* 64 (2000): 149–70.

Bartels, Larry M. *Presidential Primaries and the Dynamics of Public Choice.* Princeton, NJ: Princeton University Press, 1998.

Beale, Sara Sun. "The News Media's Influence on Criminal Justice Policy: How Market-Driven News Promotes Punitiveness." *William & Mary Law Review* 48 (2006): 397–481.

Bender, Bryan, Rachana Pradhan, Danny Vinik, Katy O'Donnell, and Taylor Gee. "13 Times Trump Was Dead Wrong at the Debate, and 2 Times Clinton Was." Politico, October 10, 2016. Accessed December 19, 2016. http://www.politico.com/story/2016/10/debate-fact-check-hillary-clinton-donald-trump-229527.

Bennett, W. Lance. *News: The Politics of Illusion.* 9th ed. Boston: Longman, 2012.

———. "Toward a Theory of Press-State Relations in the United States." *Journal of Communication* 40 (1990): 103–27.

Bennett, W. Lance, Regina G. Lawrence, and Steven Livingston. *When the Press Fails: Political Power and the*

News Media from Iraq to Katrina. Chicago: University of Chicago Press, 2007.

Boehlert, Eric. "The Press' Latest Double Standard for Democrats." Media Matters for America, July 20, 2015. Accessed July 25, 2015. http://mediamatters.org/blog/2015/07/20/the-press-latest-double-standard-for-democrats/204487.

Boorstin, Daniel J. *The Image; or, What Happened to the American Dream?* New York: Atheneum, 1962.

Borkoski, Kali. "Live Blog of the Health Care Decision (Sponsored by Bloomberg Law)." SCOTUSblog, June 28, 2012. Accessed May 4, 2016. http://www.scotusblog.com/2012/06/live-blog-of-the-health-care-decision-sponsored-by-bloomberg-law.

Boykoff, Maxwell T. "From Convergence to Contention: United States Mass Media Representations of Anthropogenic Climate Change Science." *Transactions of the Institute of British Geographers* 32 (2007): 477–89.

——. *Who Speaks for Climate? Making Sense of Media Reporting on Climate Change.* Cambridge: Cambridge University Press, 2011.

Butler, Daniel M., and Emily Schofield. "Were Newspapers More Interested in Pro-Obama Letters to the Editor in 2008? Evidence from a Field Experiment." *American Politics Research* 38 (2010): 356–71.

Center for Media and Public Affairs. "Campaign 2004 Final: How TV News Covered the General Election Campaign." *Media Monitor* 18 (2004). Accessed April 24, 2016. http://cmpa.gmu.edu/wp-content/uploads/2014/02/2004-1.pdf.

——. "Election Watch: Campaign 2008 Final: How TV News Covered the General Election Campaign." *Media Monitor* 23 (2009). Accessed April 24, 2016. http://cmpa.gmu.edu/wp-content/uploads/2013/10/media_monitor_jan_2009.pdf.

Chozick, Amy, Nicholas Confessore, and Michael Barbaro. "Leaked Speech Excerpts Show a Hillary Clinton at Ease with Wall Street." *New York Times*, October 7, 2016. Accessed December 1, 2016. http://www.nytimes.com/2016/10/08/us/politics/hillary-clinton-speeches-wikileaks.html.

Ciandella, Mike. "CNN Spends 78 Percent of Prime Time GOP Campaign Coverage on Trump." MRC NewsBusters, September 16, 2015. Accessed May 12, 2016. http://newsbusters.org/blogs/nb/mike-ciandella/2015/09/16/cnn-spends-78-percent-prime-time-gop-campaign-coverage-trump.

Cohen, Marty, David Karol, Hans Noel, and John Zaller. *The Party Decides: Presidential Nominations before and after Reform.* Chicago: University of Chicago Press, 2008.

Cohen, Michael A. "Media Should Stop Treating Clinton and Trump as Equals." *Boston Globe*, September 14, 2016. Accessed December 1, 2016. https://www.bostonglobe.com/opinion/2016/09/14/media-should-stop-treating-clinton-and-trump-equals/e4qMIleYb56VY69T4VYAKL/story.html.

Columbia Journalism Review. "Resources." Accessed February 1, 2016. http://www.cjr.org/resources.

Confessore, Nicholas, and Karen Yourish. "$2 Billion Worth of Free Media for Donald Trump." *New York Times*, March 15, 2016. Accessed May 12, 2016. http://www.nytimes.com/2016/03/16/upshot/measuring-donald-trumps-mammoth-advantage-in-free-media.html.

Cook, Timothy E. *Governing with the News: The News Media as a Political Institution.* Chicago: University of Chicago Press, 1998.

Cunningham, Brent. "Re-thinking Objectivity." *Columbia Journalism Review*, July–August 2003. Accessed March

14, 2016. http://www.cjr.org/feature/rethinking_objectivity.php.

D'Alessio, Dave. *Media Bias in Presidential Election Coverage, 1948–2008.* Lanham, MD: Lexington Books, 2012.

D'Alessio, Dave, and Mike Allen. "Media Bias in Presidential Elections: A Meta-Analysis." *Journal of Communication* 50 (2000): 133–56.

Darcy, Oliver. "Trump Catapults Cable News Outlets to Their Best Ratings Year Ever." *Business Insider*, December 21, 2016. Accessed December 24, 2016. http://www.businessinsider.com/trump-cable-news-ratings-2016-12.

Diamond, Jeremy. "Trump Launches All-Out Attack on the Press." CNN (website), June 1, 2016. Accessed June 1, 2016. http://www.cnn.com/2016/05/31/politics/donald-trump-veterans-announcement.

Dickens, Geoffrey. "Selling Socialism: The Media's Campaign for ObamaCare." Media Research Center, March 20, 2012. Accessed May 6, 2016. http://www.mrc.org/media-reality-check/selling-socialism-medias-campaign-obamacare.

Dimiero, Ben. "CNN Still Welcomes George Zimmerman's Racist Defender." Media Matters for America, November 22, 2013. Accessed July 10, 2015. http://mediamatters.org/blog/2013/11/22/cnn-still-welcomes-george-zimmermans-racist-def/197022.

Doctor, Ken. "'Profitable' Washington Post Adding More than Five Dozen Journalists." Politico, December 27, 2016. Accessed December 28, 2016. http://www.politico.com/media/story/2016/12/the-profitable-washington-post-adding-more-than-five-dozen-journalists-004900.

Dorman, Sam. "Hannity: CNBC Debate Was 'Single Worst Example of Media Bias' in 'Intergalactic History.'" CNSNews, October 30, 2015. Accessed October 30, 2015. http://www.cnsnews.com/blog/sam-dorman/hannity-cnbc-debate-was-single-worst-example-media-bias-intergalactic-history.

Dowdle, Andrew J., Randall E. Adkins, and Wayne P. Steger. "The Viability Primary: Modeling Candidate Support before the Primaries." *Political Research Quarterly* 62 (2009): 77–91.

Drennen, Kyle. "Networks Ignore Hillary Clinton's Favorability Plummeting to 39%." MRC NewsBusters, July 16, 2015. Accessed July 25, 2015. http://newsbusters.org/blogs/kyle-drennen/2015/07/16/networks-ignore-hillary-clintons-favorability-plummeting-39.

Dufresne, Chris. "In the Interest of Fairness, Duke Needs to Take a Foul." *Los Angeles Times*, April 9, 2001. Accessed January 5, 2016. http://articles.latimes.com/2001/apr/09/sports/sp-48870.

Entman, Robert M. "Media Framing Biases and Political Power: Explaining Slant in News of Campaign 2008." *Journalism* 11 (2010): 389–408.

FAIR. "Right and Early: Sunday Morning Shows Are GOP TV." Accessed December 19, 2015. http://fair.org/extra-online-articles/right-and-early.

Fogarty, Brian J. "Determining Economic News Coverage." *International Journal of Public Opinion Research* 17 (2005): 149–72.

Fox News (website). "RNC's Priebus Speaks Out on Debate Reforms; Christie, Huckabee Weigh In on Issue." November 2, 2015. Accessed November 15, 2015. http://www.foxnews.com/transcript/2015/11/02/rnc-priebus-speaks-out-on-debate-reforms-christie-huckabee-weigh-in-on-issue.

Fox News Insider. "This Line Got the Most Favorable Reaction Ever from a Luntz Focus Group." October 29, 2015. Accessed October 29, 2015. http://

insider.foxnews.com/2015/10/29/ frank-luntz-focus-group-reacts-ted-cruzs-criticism-cnbc-gop-debate-moderators.

Franken, Al. *Lies and the Lying Liars Who Tell Them: A Fair and Balanced Look at the Right.* New York: Dutton, 2003.

"From the Editors; The Times and Iraq." *New York Times,* May 26, 2004. Accessed March 14, 2016. http://www.nytimes.com/2004/05/26/world/from-the-editors-the-times-and-iraq.html.

Gabler, Neal. "We Wouldn't Have Donald Trump if the Media Hadn't Helped Destroy the Democratic Process First." AlterNet, March 4, 2016. Accessed July 5, 2016. http://www.alternet.org/election-2016/we-wouldnt-have-donald-trump-if-media-hadnt-helped-destroy-demo cratic-process-first.

Gallup. "Presidential Approval Ratings—George W. Bush." Accessed April 29, 2016. http://www.gallup.com/poll/116500/presidential-ap proval-ratings-george-bush.aspx.

Gasper, John T. "Shifting Ideologies? Reexamining Media Bias." *Quarterly Journal of Political Science* 6 (2011): 85–102.

GDELT Project. "2016 Campaign Television Tracker." Accessed May 14, 2016. http://television.gdeltproject.org/cgi-bin/iatv_campaign2016/iatv_campaign2016.

Gelman, Andrew, and Gary King. "Why Are American Presidential Election Campaign Polls So Variable When Votes Are So Predictable?" *British Journal of Political Science* 23 (1993): 409–51.

Gentzkow, Matthew, and Jesse M. Shapiro. "What Drives Media Slant? Evidence from U.S. Daily Newspapers." *Econometrica* 78 (2010): 35–71.

Gold, Hadas. "Jeff Zucker Praises Corey Lewandowski, Slams Vice and Buzz-Feed." Politico, August 2, 2016. Accessed December 8, 2016. http://www.polit ico.com/blogs/on-media/2016/08/jeff-zucker-praises-corey-lewandowski-slams-vice-and-buzzfeed-226574.

Goldberg, Bernard. *Bias: A CBS Insider Exposes How the Media Distort the News.* New York: Perennial, 2002.

Graber, Doris A., and Johanna Dunaway. *Mass Media and American Politics.* 9th ed. Los Angeles: SAGE CQ Press, 2015.

Groeling, Tim. "Media Bias by the Numbers: Challenges and Opportunities in the Empirical Study of Partisan News." *Annual Review of Political Science* 16 (2013): 129–51.

———. "Who's the Fairest of Them All? An Empirical Test for Partisan Bias on ABC, CBS, NBC, and Fox News." *Presidential Studies Quarterly* 38 (2008): 631–57.

Groseclose, Tim. *Left Turn: How Liberal Media Bias Distorts the American Mind.* New York: St. Martin's, 2011.

Groseclose, Tim, and Jeffrey Milyo. "A Measure of Media Bias." *Quarterly Journal of Economics* 120 (2005): 1191–237.

Gunther, Albert C., and Kathleen Schmitt. "Mapping Boundaries of the Hostile Media Effect." *Journal of Communication* 54 (2004): 55–70.

Hallin, Daniel C. "The Media, the War in Vietnam, and Political Support: A Critique of the Thesis of an Oppositional Media." *Journal of Politics* 46 (1984): 2–24.

———. *The "Uncensored War": The Media and Vietnam.* New York: Oxford University Press, 1986.

Harrington, David E. "Economic News on Television: The Determinants of Coverage." *Public Opinion Quarterly* 53 (1989): 17–40.

Haynes, Audrey A., Paul-Henri Gurian, Michael H. Crespin, and Christopher Zorn. "The Calculus of Concession: Media Coverage and the Dynamics of Winnowing in Presidential

Nominations." *American Politics Research* 32 (2004): 310–37.

Haynes, Audrey A., and Sarah G. Murray. "Why Do the News Media Cover Certain Candidates More than Others? The Antecedents of State and National News Coverage in the 1992 Presidential Nomination Campaign." *American Politics Quarterly* 26 (1998): 420–38.

Hetherington, Marc J. "The Media's Role in Forming Voters' National Economic Evaluations in 1992." *American Journal of Political Science* 40 (1996): 372–95.

Hibbing, John R., Kevin B. Smith, and John R. Alford. "Differences in Negativity Bias Underlie Variations in Political Ideology." *Behavioral and Brain Sciences* 37 (2014): 297–350.

Hines, Matt. "Jon Stewart 'Crossfire' Feud Ignites Net Frenzy." CNET. Accessed March 2, 2016. http://www.cnet.com/news/jon-stewart-crossfire-feud-ignites-net-frenzy.

Ho, Daniel E., and Kevin M. Quinn. "Measuring Explicit Political Positions of Media." *Quarterly Journal of Political Science* 3 (2008): 353–77.

Hofstetter, C. Richard. *Bias in the News: Network Television News Coverage of the 1972 Election Campaign.* Columbus: Ohio State University Press, 1976.

Hoft, Jim. "Media Double Standard: Ben Carson Is a Liar but Barack Obama Isn't a Kenyan." Gateway Pundit, November 6, 2015. Accessed February 2, 2016. http://www.thegatewaypundit.com/2015/11/media-double-standard-ben-carson-is-a-liar-but-barack-obama-isnt-a-kenyan.

Holan, Angie Drobnic. "Sarah Palin Falsely Claims Barack Obama Runs a 'Death Panel.'" PolitiFact, August 10, 2009. Accessed June 14, 2016. http://www.politifact.com/truth-o-meter/statements/2009/aug/10/sarah-palin/sarah-palin-barack-obama-death-panel.

Holmes, Jack. "The Dean Scream: An Oral History." *Esquire*, January 29, 2016. Accessed May 26, 2016. http://www.esquire.com/news-politics/a41615/the-dean-scream-oral-history.

Houck, Curtis. "Networks Ignore Hillary Clinton's Claim that Businesses Don't Create Jobs." Media Research Center, October 28, 2014. Accessed November 12, 2015. http://www.mrc.org/biasalerts/networks-ignore-hillary-clintons-claim-businesses-dont-create-jobs.

Iyengar, Shanto. *Is Anyone Responsible? How Television Frames Political Issues.* Chicago: University of Chicago Press, 1991.

———. *Media Politics: A Citizen's Guide.* 3rd ed. New York: Norton, 2016.

Kahn, Kim Fridkin, and Patrick J. Kenney. "The Slant of the News: How Editorial Endorsements Influence Campaign Coverage and Citizens' Views of Candidates." *American Political Science Review* 96 (2002): 381–94.

———. *The Spectacle of U.S. Senate Campaigns.* Princeton, NJ: Princeton University Press, 1999.

Karet, Brendan, and Tyler Cherry. "Fox News' Sean Hannity Feeds Donald Trump Fake Syrian Refugee Claim from Hoax Website." Media Matters for America, October 27, 2015. Accessed November 12, 2015. http://mediamatters.org/research/2015/10/27/fox-news-sean-hannity-feeds-donald-trump-fake-s/206449.

Key, V .O., Jr. *Politics, Parties, & Pressure Groups.* New York: Crowell, 1964.

Koren, Gideon, and Naomi Klein. "Bias against Negative Studies in Newspaper Reports of Medical Research." *Journal of the American Medical Association* 266 (1991): 1824–26.

Kovach, Bill, and Tom Rosenstiel. *The Elements of Journalism: What Newspeople Should Know and the Public Should Expect.* 3rd ed. New York: Three Rivers Press, 2014.

Kristof, Nicholas. "My Shared Shame: The Media Helped Make Trump." *New York Times*, March 26, 2016. Accessed July 3, 2016. http://www.nytimes.com/2016/03/27/opinion/sunday/my-shared-shame-the-media-helped-make-trump.html?_r=0.

Ladd, Jonathan. *Why Americans Hate the Media and How It Matters*. Princeton, NJ: Princeton University Press, 2012.

Larcinese, Valentino, Riccardo Puglisi, and James M. Snyder Jr. "Partisan Bias in Economic News: Evidence on the Agenda-Setting Behavior of U.S. Newspapers." *Journal of Public Economics* 95 (2011): 1178–89.

Lerer, Lisa, and Emily Swanson. "AP-GfK Poll: Clinton's Standing Falls among Democrats." Associated Press, July 16, 2015. Accessed July 25, 2015. http://ap-gfkpoll.com/featured/findings-from-our-latest-poll-21.

Limbaugh, Rush. "CNBC's Shameless Kill Show Debate." The Rush Limbaugh Show (website), October 29, 2015. Accessed October 29, 2015. http://www.rushlimbaugh.com/daily/2015/10/29/cnbc_s_shameless_kill_show_debate.

Lippmann, Walter. *Public Opinion*. New York: Free Press Paperbacks, 1922.

Long, Sharon K., and Dana Goin. "Most Adults Are Not Aware of Health Reform's Coverage Provisions." Urban Institute Health Policy Center: Health Reform Monitoring Survey, February 6, 2014. Accessed July 25, 2016. http://hrms.urban.org/briefs/awareness-of-provision.html.

Lowry, Dennis T., and Jon A. Shidler. "The Sound Bites, the Biters, and the Bitten: An Analysis of Network TV News Bias in Campaign '92." *Journalism and Mass Communication Quarterly* 72 (1995): 33–44.

Mayer, William G. "Why Talk Radio Is Conservative." *The Public Interest* 154 (2004): 86–103.

Maza, Carlos, and Coleman Lowndes. "Video: CNN Has a Trump Surrogate Problem." Media Matters for America, October 14, 2016. Accessed December 8, 2016. http://mediamatters.org/blog/2016/10/14/video-cnn-has-trump-surrogate-problem/213824.

McChesney, Robert W., and John Nichols. *The Death and Life of American Journalism*. Philadelphia: Nation Books, 2010.

McGowen, Ernest B., and Daniel J. Palazzolo. "Momentum and Media in the 2012 Republican Presidential Nomination." *Presidential Studies Quarterly* 44 (2014): 431–46.

Media Research Center. "Dan Rather's Liberal Bias." Accessed January 15, 2016. http://archive.mrc.org/projects/rather20th/welcome.asp.

———. "MRC Study Proves It: CNBC Agenda Was to Undermine GOP Candidates." October 30, 2015. Accessed October 31, 2015. http://www.mrc.org/press-releases/mrc-study-proves-it-cnbc-agenda-was-undermine-gop-candidates.

Meirick, Patrick C. "Motivated Misperception? Party, Education, Partisan News, and Belief in 'Death Panels.'" *Journalism & Mass Communication Quarterly* 90 (2012): 39–57.

Meyer, Ken. "CNN's Zucker Hits Back on Trump Coverage Criticism: People Want to Blame Someone for His Rise." Mediaite, April 25, 2016. Accessed December 24, 2016. http://www.mediaite.com/online/cnns-zucker-hits-back-on-trump-coverage-criticism-people-want-to-blame-someone-for-his-rise.

MRC Business. "Uncritical Condition." November 4, 2010. Accessed May 6, 2016. http://www.mrc.org/special-reports/uncritical-condition.

Niven, David. "Objective Evidence on Media Bias: Newspaper Coverage of Congressional Party Switchers." *Journalism and Mass Communication Quarterly* 80 (2003): 311–26.

———. *Tilt? The Search for Media Bias.* Westport, CT: Praeger, 2002.

Noyes, Rich. "If Hillary Wins, Liberal Journalists Paved Her Path to the Presidency." MRC NewsBusters, November 1, 2016. Accessed November 29, 2016. http://www.newsbusters.org/blogs/nb/rich-noyes/2016/11/01/if-hillary-wins-liberal-journalists-paved-her-path-presidency.

———. "MRC Study: Documenting TV's Twelve Weeks of Trump Bashing." MRC NewsBusters, October 25, 2016. Accessed November 29, 2016. http://www.newsbusters.org/blogs/nb/rich-noyes/2016/10/25/mrc-study-documenting-tvs-twelve-weeks-trump-bashing.

———. "MRC Study: TV Buries the Bad News on Obama's Collapsing Polls." MRC NewsBusters, September 8, 2014. Accessed July 13, 2015. http://newsbusters.org/blogs/rich-noyes/2014/09/08/mrc-study-tv-buries-bad-news-obamas-collapsing-polls.

———. "MRC Study: TV News Is Trying to Winnow the Field of GOP Candidates." Media Research Center, November 9, 2015. Accessed May 12, 2016. http://www.mrc.org/media-reality-check/mrc-study-tv-news-trying-winnow-field-gop-candidates.

———. "TV's Campaign '16 News: An Avalanche of Trump Coverage, Not Much for Others." Media Research Center, August 4, 2015. Accessed May 12, 2016. http://www.mrc.org/media-reality-check/tvs-campaign-16-news-avalanche-trump-coverage-not-much-others.

Nyhan, Brendan. "Does the US Media Have a Liberal Bias? A Discussion of Tim Groseclose's *Left Turn: How Liberal Media Bias Distorts the American Mind.*" *Perspectives on Politics* 10 (2012): 767–71.

Oreskes, Naomi, and Erik Conway. *Merchants of Doubt.* New York: Bloomsbury Press, 2010.

Patterson, Thomas E. "News Coverage of the 2016 General Election: How the Press Failed the Voters." Harvard Kennedy School: Shorenstein Center on Media, Politics, and Public Policy, December 7, 2016. Accessed December 10, 2016. https://shorensteincenter.org/news-coverage-2016-general-election.

———. *Out of Order.* New York: Vintage, 1994.

Peake, Jeffrey S. "Presidents and Front-Page News: How America's Newspapers Cover the Bush Administration." *Harvard International Journal of Press/Politics* 12 (2007): 52–70.

Pew Research Center. "Press Widely Criticized, but Trusted More than Other Information Sources." Accessed December 18, 2015. http://www.people-press.org/2011/09/22/press-widely-criticized-but-trusted-more-than-other-institutions.

Pew Research Center: Journalism & Media Staff. "Six Things to Know about Health Care Coverage." June 21, 2010. Accessed June 12, 2016. http://www.journalism.org/2010/06/21/six-things-know-about-health-care-coverage.

———. "What Americans Learned from the Media about the Health Care Debate." June 19, 2012. Accessed June 12, 2016. http://www.journalism.org/2012/06/19/how-media-has-covered-health-care-debate.

———. "Winning the Media Campaign: How the Press Reported the 2008 General Election." October 22, 2008. Accessed December 18, 2016. http://www.journalism.org/2008/10/22/winning-media-campaign.

PollyVote. "Time for Change Model." Accessed April 29, 2016. http://pollyvote.com/en/components/econometric-models/time-for-change-model.

Puglisi, Riccardo, and James M. Snyder Jr. "The Balanced US Press." *Journal of the European Economic Association* 13 (2015): 240–64.

——. "Newspaper Coverage of Political Scandals." *Journal of Politics* 73 (2011): 931–50.

RealClearPolitics. "Polls: President Bush Job Approval." Accessed October 2, 2014. http://www.realclearpolitics.com/epolls/other/president_bush_job_approval-904.html.

——. "Polls: President Obama Job Approval." Accessed October 2, 2014. http://www.realclearpolitics.com/epolls/other/president_obama_job_approval-1044.html.

"Remembrances." *Newsweek*, May 2, 1994. LexisNexis Academic.

Robinson, Eugene. "No, the Media Didn't Create Trump." *Washington Post*, March 28, 2016. Accessed July 1, 2016. https://www.washingtonpost.com/opinions/no-the-media-didnt-create-trump-covering-him-is-their-job/2016/03/28/11ffc554-f516-11e5-9804-537defcc3cf6_story.html.

Robinson, Michael J., and Margaret A. Sheehan. *Over the Wire and on TV: CBS and UPI in Campaign '80*. New York: Russell Sage Foundation, 1983.

Romer, Daniel, Kathleen Hall Jamieson, and Sean Aday. "Television News and the Cultivation of Fear of Crime." *Journal of Communication* 53 (2003): 88–104.

Rosen, Jay. "He Said, She Said Journalism: Lame Formula in the Land of the Active User." PressThink, April 12, 2009. Accessed March 14, 2016. http://archive.pressthink.org/2009/04/12/hesaid_shesaid.html.

——. "Winter Is Coming: Prospects for the American Press under Trump." PressThink, December 28, 2016. Accessed December 28, 2016. http://pressthink.org/2016/12/winter-coming-prospects-american-press-trump.

Rosenstiel, Tom, Marion Just, Todd Belt, Atiba Pertilla, Walter Dean, and Dante Chinni. *We Interrupt This Newscast: How to Improve Local News and Win Ratings, Too.* Cambridge: Cambridge University Press, 2007.

Ruane, Kathleen Ann. "Fairness Doctrine: History and Constitutional Issues." Congressional Research Service: CRS Report for Congress, July 13, 2011. Accessed January 7, 2016. http://www.fas.org/sgp/crs/misc/R40009.pdf.

Rutenberg, Jim. "By Attacking the Press, Donald Trump May Be Doing It a Favor." *New York Times*, December 18, 2016. Accessed December 24, 2016. http://www.nytimes.com/2016/12/18/business/media/by-attacking-the-press-donald-trump-may-be-doing-it-a-favor.html.

Ryan, Tim. "Media Coverage Distorts Iraq Reality." *FrontPage Magazine*, September 21, 2005. Accessed March 4, 2016. http://archive.frontpagemag.com/readArticle.aspx?ARTID=7222.

Saad, Lydia. "Most Americans Believe Crime in U.S. Is Worsening." Gallup, October 31, 2011. Accessed March 10, 2016. http://www.gallup.com/poll/150464/americans-believe-crime-worsening.aspx.

Savillo, Rob. "Report: Once Again, Sunday Morning Talk Shows Are White, Male, and Conservative." Media Matters for America. Accessed December 19, 2015. http://mediamatters.org/research/2013/10/11/report-once-again-sunday-morning-talk-shows-are/196404.

Schiffer, Adam J. "Assessing Partisan Bias in Political News: The Case(s) of Local Senate Election Coverage." *Political Communication* 23 (2006): 23–39.

——. *Conditional Press Influence in Politics.* Lanham, MD: Lexington Books, 2008.

Shafer, Jack. "Donald Trump Talks Like a Third-Grader." Politico, August 13, 2015. Accessed May 28, 2016. http://www.politico.com/magazine/story/2015/08/donald-trump-talks-like-a-third-grader-121340.

Shea, Daniel M., Joanne Connor Green, and Christopher E. Smith. *Living Democracy*. 4th ed. Boston: Pearson, 2014.

Sides, John, and Lynn Vavreck. *The Gamble: Choice and Chance in the 2012 Presidential Election*. Princeton, NJ: Princeton University Press, 2013.

Sigal, Leon V. *Reporters and Officials: The Organization and Politics of Newsmaking*. Lexington, MA: D.C. Heath, 1973.

Smith, Glen R. "Politicians and the News Media: How Elite Attacks Influence Perceptions of Media Bias." *International Journal of Press/Politics* 15 (2010): 319–43.

Sorauf, Frank J. "Political Parties and Political Analysis." In *The American Party Systems*, ed. William Nisbet Chambers and Walter Dean Burnham. New York: Oxford University Press, 1967.

Soroka, Stuart N. "The Gatekeeping Function: Distributions of Information in Media and the Real World." *Journal of Politics* 74 (2012): 514–28.

Spayd, Liz. "One Thing Voters Agree On: Better Campaign Coverage Was Needed." *New York Times*, November 19, 2016. Accessed December 24, 2016. http://www.nytimes.com/2016/11/20/public-editor/one-thing-voters-agree-on-better-campaign-coverage-was-needed.html.

Steger, Wayne P. *A Citizen's Guide to Presidential Nominations: The Competition for Leadership*. New York: Routledge, 2015.

Steinberg, Dan. "Even Christian Laettner Thinks Refs Are Sometimes Biased in Favor of Duke." *Washington Post*, March 10, 2015. Accessed January 5, 2016. https://www.washingtonpost.com/news/dc-sports-bog/wp/2015/03/10/even-christian-laettner-thinks-refs-are-sometimes-biased-in-favor-of-duke.

Stempel, Guido H., III. "The Prestige Press Covers the 1960 Presidential Campaign." *Journalism Quarterly* 38 (1961): 157–63.

Stevenson, Robert L., Richard A. Eisinger, Barry M. Feinberg, and Alan B. Kotok. "Untwisting *The News Twisters*: A Replication of Efron's Study." *Journalism Quarterly* 50 (1973): 211–19.

Stokols, Eli, Hadas Gold, and Nick Gass. "Trump Turns Blame on Reporter in Battery Case." Politico, March 29, 2016. Accessed June 1, 2016. http://www.politico.com/story/2016/03/trump-campaign-manager-charged-with-misdemeanor-battery-221336.

Trackalytics. "Donald J. Trump." Accessed May 24, 2016. http://www.trackalytics.com/twitter/profile/realdonaldtrump.

"Transcript: Read the Full Text of the CNBC Republican Debate in Boulder." *Time* (website), October 28, 2015. Accessed October 29, 2015. http://time.com/4091301/republican-debate-transcript-cnbc-boulder.

Vallone, Robert P., Lee Ross, and Mark R. Lepper. "The Hostile Media Phenomenon: Biased Perception and Perceptions of Media Bias in Coverage of the Beirut Massacre." *Journal of Personality and Social Psychology* 49 (1985): 577–85.

Vavreck, Lynn. *The Message Matters: The Economy and Presidential Campaigns*. Princeton, NJ: Princeton University Press, 2009.

Viser, Matt. "For Presidential Hopefuls, Simpler Language Resonates." *Boston Globe*, October 20, 2015. Accessed May 28, 2016. http://www.bostonglobe.com/news/politics/2015/10/20/donald-trump-and-ben-carson-speak-grade-school-level-that-today-voters-can-quickly-grasp/LUCBY6uwQAxiLvvXbVTSUN/story.html.

Watts, Mark D., David Domke, Dhavan V. Shah, and David P. Fan. "Elite Cues and Media Bias in Presidential

Campaigns: Explaining Public Perceptions of a Liberal Press." *Communication Research* 26 (1999): 144–75.

West, Darrell M. *The Rise and Fall of the Media Establishment*. Boston: Bedford/St. Martin's, 2001.

Western Carolina University Office of Public Relations. "Western Grad Slams, Attracts National Media Attention in Iraq." Accessed March 4, 2016. http://www.wcu.edu/pubinfo/news/Ryan05.htm.

Whitlock, Scott. "Study: Nets Squash Hillary's Terror Woes to Scold Trump's Gun Remark." MRC NewsBusters, August 10, 2016. Accessed November 29, 2016. http://www.newsbusters.org/blogs/nb/scott-whitlock/2016/08/10/study-nets-squash-hillarys-terror-woes-scold-trumps-gun-remark.

———. "Wash Post, NYT Devote over 3800 Words to Hyping Scalise Scandal." Media Research Center, December 31, 2014. Accessed January 5, 2015. http://mrc.org/biasalerts/wash-post-nyt-devote-over-3800-words-hyping-scalise-scandal.

Willies, Egberto. "ABC News Segment a Classic Illustration of Media Republican Bias." Daily Kos, November 2, 2014. Accessed November 10, 2014. http://www.dailykos.com/story/2014/11/02/1341153/-ABC-News-segment-a-classic-illustration-of-media-Republican-bias.

———. "Ted Cruz Got One Thing Right at the Republican Debate." Daily Kos, October 29, 2015. Accessed October 30, 2015. http://www.dailykos.com/story/2015/10/29/1442033/-Ted-Cruz-got-one-thing-right-at-the-Republican-Debate.

"Word of the Year 2016 Is . . ." English: Oxford Living Dictionaries. Accessed December 20, 2016. https://en.oxforddictionaries.com/word-of-the-year/word-of-the-year-2016.

Yoder, Katie. "AP, Dallas News, WashPo, etc., Lie about Ted Cruz' Abortion Statement." MRC NewsBusters, March 13, 2014. Accessed February 2, 2016. http://www.newsbusters.org/blogs/katie-yoder/2014/03/13/ap-dallas-news-washpo-etc-lie-about-ted-cruz-abortion-statement.

Zaller, John. "A New Standard of News Quality: Burglar Alarms for the Monitorial Citizen." *Political Communication* 20 (2003): 109–30.

Index

Note: Page locators in italics indicate figures and tables.

145

Lightning Source UK Ltd.
Milton Keynes UK
UKHW02f1403031217
313774UK00016B/549/P